AF505840

Regional Growth Dynamics in India in the Post-Economic Reform Period

Regional Growth Dynamics in India in the Post-Economic Reform Period

Biswa Swarup Misra

First published 2007 by
PALGRAVE MACMILLAN
Houndmills, Basingstoke, Hampshire RG21 6XS and
175 Fifth Avenue, New York, N.Y. 10010
Companies and representatives throughout the world

PALGRAVE MACMILLAN is the global academic imprint of the Palgrave Macmillan division of St. Martin's Press, LLC and of Palgrave Macmillan Ltd. Macmillan® is a registered trademark in the United States, United Kingdom and other countries. Palgrave is a registered trademark in the European Union and other countries.

ISBN-13: 978–0–230–00491–7
ISBN-10: 0–230–00491–1

This book is printed on paper suitable for recycling and made from fully managed and sustained forest sources. Logging, pulping and manufacturing processes are expected to conform to the environmental regulations of the country of origin.

A catalogue record for this book is available from the British Library.

Library of Congress Cataloging-in-Publication Data
Misra, Biswa Swarup, 1975–
    Regional growth dynamics in India in the post-economic reform
    period/Biswa Swarup Misra.
        p.   cm.
    Includes bibliographical references and index.
    ISBN 0–230–00491–1 (cloth)
    1. India—Economic policy—1991–   2. Regional planning—India.
    3. India—Economic conditions—Regional disparities.   I. Title.
    HC435.3.M54 2007
    338.954—dc22   2006050874

10   9   8   7   6   5   4   3   2   1
16   15   14   13   12   11   10   09   08   07

Printed and bound in Great Britain by
Antony Rowe Ltd, Chippenham and Eastbourne

*Dedicated to the fond
memory of my grandparents
Bhubaneswar Misra and Rajmani Devi*

Contents

4 State Finances 101

**5 Analytics of Credit–Output Behaviour for
Indian States** 133

List of Tables

List of Figures

Preface

Growth matters because it paves the way for a better standard of life. India has a population nearing 1,100 million which accounts for almost 17 per cent of the world's population. India has pursued a strategy of state-led planned economic development for almost four decades in order to secure a better life for its growing population since it became a democracy. Notwithstanding the commitment at the policy level to improve the lot of the masses, 36 per cent of the population was still poverty stricken as of 1993–4. Following the economic crisis of 1991, India has pursued sweeping economic reforms.

There is now a broad consensus that India's economic prospects have improved in the post-1990 period. This has been hailed a success due to the reform measures. However, this reform process should only be considered a true success if it has improved the standard of living for its huge population. In this context, how the post-reform growth process has touched the lives of the people is a matter for investigation. The scenario found at the aggregate level often conceals the varied growth experience at the disaggregated level. A manageable level of disaggregation in the case of India is to be found at the state level. This book is an attempt to understand the dimensions of growth at the regional level in the post-economic reforms period.

The views expressed in this book are my own and not of the Reserve Bank of India. I hope the themes addressed will add to a better understanding of the dynamics of the Indian economy in recent times.

Biswa Swarup Misra

Acknowledgements

I am indebted to the Reserve Bank of India, for the excellent research atmosphere and academic infrastructure which has motivated me to pursue my research interests. I am grateful to Professor Nawal Kishore Chaudhary for his guidance, support and encouragement. While working on this project, I have benefited immensely from my interactions with Shri Ramesh Kolli, Additional Director General of the Central Statistical Organization and Shri Bijay Pratap Singh, Director, Directorate of Statistics, Government of Bihar.

I am grateful to Professor K.L. Krishna, Dr Suman Mohapatra and Shri Akshya Kumar Panda for having patiently read the manuscript and to suggest improvements.

Encouragement from Dr Narendra Jadhav, Shri S.S. Mishra, Dr Ranjit Kumar Pattnaik and Shri S. Ganesh (all from the Reserve Bank of India) and Shri S. Govindan (of the Union Bank of India) have been a constant source of strength. In the work environment, Shri Rajendra Rajak and Shri Ajay Kumar Sinha provided active co-operation while working on this project.

On the personal front, my father has been a constant motivator throughout this project. I adore the affections of my family members and Shri Anantaram Mishra. Of my peer group and circle of friends, discussions with Sarat Chandra Dhal, Satyananda Sahoo, Sanjiv, Satyabrata and Samir have always been stimulating.

I am indebted to Shri Jit Narain Prasad Singh for his invigorating presence and unqualified support which has contributed immensely to the timely completion of the project. My elder brother has been instrumental in completion of the project.

Keith Povey and associates undertook painstaking editorial refinements that have rendered the content into its present form. I owe my gratitude to them.

And finally, special thanks are due to Ms Amanda Hamilton, economics editor at Palgrave Macmillan, and her team for the encouragement and excellent support in all stages of production. The usual disclaimers apply.

BISWA SWARUP MISRA

List of Abbreviations

A&N Islands	Andaman and Nicobar Islands
ACP	Annual Credit Plan
ADF	Augmented Dickey–Fuller
AIDIS	All India Debt and Investment Survey
ASI	Annual Survey of Industries
BHEP	Bharat Hydro Electric Corp
BPL	Below Poverty Line
CAGR	Compound annual growth rates
CD	Credit to Deposit ratio
CIEM	Composite Index of Expenditure Management
CIFH	Composite Index of Fiscal Health
CMDs	Chairman-cum-Managing Directors
CPI-UNME	Consumer Price Index for Urban Non-Manual Employees
CPIAL	Consumer Price Index for Agricultural Labourers
CPIIW	Consumer Price Index for Industrial Workers
CRAFICARD	Committee to Review Arrangements for Institutional Credit for Agricultural and Rural Development
CRMI	Composite Resource Mobilization Index
CSO	Central Statistical Organization
DoH	Directorate of Horticulture
DoS	Directorate of Statistics
DVC	The Damodar Valley Corporation
EC	Error-Correction
ECM	Error Correction Model
FISM	Financial Intermediation Services Indirectly Measured
FMOLS	Fully Modified Ordinary Least Squares
FPC	Fifth Pay Commission
FRBM	Fiscal Responsibility and Budget Management
FRL	Fiscal Responsibility Legislation

GB	Gramin Bank
GCS	General Category States
GDP	Gross Domestic Product
GFD	Gross Fiscal Deficit
GMM	Generalized Method of Moments
GSDP	Gross State Domestic Product
GVA	Gross Value Added
GVO	Gross Value of Output
HDI	Human Development Index
HYV	High-yielding variety
IIP	Index of Industrial Production
IMF	International Monetary Fund
IRDP	Integrated Rural Development Programme
IT	Information Technology
KGB	Kshetriya Gramin Bank
LDCs	Less Developed Countries
LLC	Levin, Lin and Chu
LSDV	Least Square Dummy Variable
MFI	Measure of Fiscal Impulse
MFTRP	Medium Term Fiscal Reform Programme
MoA	Ministry of Agriculture
NABARD	National Bank for Agricultural and Rural Development
NDTL	Net demand and time liabilities
NHB	National Horticulture Board
NHDR	*National Human Development Report*
NPAs	Non-performing assets
NSDP	Net State Domestic Product
NSS	National Sample Survey
NSSO	National Sample Survey Organization
NTPC	National Thermal Power Corporation
OECD	Organization for Economic Cooperation and Development
OLS	Ordinary Least Squares
PCI	Per capita income
PGC	Power Grid Corporation
PNSDP	Per capita net state domestic product
RBI	Reserve Bank of India
RCI	Rank Concordance Index
RRB	Regional Rural Bank
SARFESAI	Securitization and Reconstruction of Financial Assets and Enforcement of Security Interest

SASA	State Agricultural Statistics Authority
SBI	State Bank of India
SCBs	Scheduled Commercial Banks
SCS	Special Category States
SDI	Social development index
SDP	State Domestic Product
SDPG	SDP growth
SEB	State Electricity Boards
SIDC	Small Industries Development Corporation
SLBC	State Level Bankers' Committee
SLR	Statutory Liquidity Ratio
SNA	System of National Accounts
SURE	Seemingly Unrelated Regression Estimation
TFC	Twelfth Finance Commission
UN	United Nations
UPSCB	Uttar Pradesh State Cooperative Bank
UTs	Union Terittories
VA	Value added
VAR	Vector Auto Regression
VAT	Value Added Tax

1
Introduction

The Indian economy has come a long way since the days of economic crisis in the early 1990s. The reform measures pursued after the economic crisis helped India to tap into its latent potential to emerge as a global player. The GDP growth of 5.4 per cent recorded in the decade prior to the crisis accelerated to 6.3 per cent over the period from 1992–3 to 2005–6. The present euphoria of high growth is a sharp contrast to the uncertainty about India's economic destiny just 15 years back. Though there has been a setback to growth over the period from 1996–7 to 1999–2000, the resurgence of growth to 8 per cent during the three-year period 2003–4 to 2005–6 speaks of the resilience of the Indian economy. Further, the draft approach paper for the Eleventh Five-Year Plan (2006) envisages an 8.5 per cent growth horizon for the Indian economy. According to the Indian Finance Minister, it took 14 years for India to transform from a 'poor and perhaps a forgotten country' (Chidambaram, 2006) to a thriving and increasingly prominent emerging economy. This welcome transformation is an outcome of the reform measures pursued over the last 15 years. Going beyond the actual reform measures, what is important to note is the change in the economic paradigm guiding India's approach to economic policy-making.

The rethinking on India's economic policies and the need for reform measures have been in the air since the mid-1980s when a new government, with Rajiv Gandhi as Prime Minister, was installed. The vision of the then Prime Minister about the Information and Technology (IT) sector has put India 20 years down the line on the world map as a key player. The IT sector continues to play a significant role in shaping India's image as an emerging economic super power even today.

It is as difficult to be wise in the *ex ante* sense as it is easy to be wise in the *ex post* sense. In retrospect, the faults in India's economic policy-making and missed opportunities are well documented in the Indian economic literature. Broadly, it is the story of how export pessimism and an inward-looking policy orientation in the early years of planning prevented India benefiting from the great opportunities that rising volumes of world trade had to offer. Export pessimism gave way to an import-substitution-based growth strategy, which insulated the economy from external competition. Moreover, the need to rationalize limited economic resources led to a licence or permit quota system which stalled competition within the economy. The bureaucratic permit quota system over time created vested interests and a perverted incentive structure, and eventually competition in the economy was the casualty. Economic gains from rent-seeking activities seemed to outweigh the merits of encouraging competition in the economy. A better idea would have been to create a level playing field that would have encouraged competition.

There is no denying the fact that there was a need for a state-led heavy industrialization strategy in the early years after Independence when India's attempt was to be self-reliant. Though easier said than done, perhaps the right time for a course correction in policy would have been in the mid-1960s when the first phase of state-led mega-investment projects was over. The Chinese aggression in 1962, the death of Jawaharlal Nehru (the architect of independent India) in 1964, aggression by Pakistan in 1965 and droughts in 1966–7 created difficult conditions for the Indian economy, polity and society. The political vacuum created by Nehru's death was filled more with political rhetoric than economic marksmanship. As politics shapes the contours of economic policy, prudent economic policy-making served political exigency. Having found a high incidence of poverty even after two decades of development planning, 'Garibi Hatao' ('Crush poverty!') was the political slogan given by the late, charismatic Indian Prime Minister, Indira Gandhi, who took over the reins of power in 1966. While poverty reduction has been an overarching objective, and rightly so, India simply was not pursuing the right kind of economic policies to address it effectively. The broad policy framework remained that of an inward-looking import-substitution-led growth strategy throughout the 1970s and early 1980s. Much stress, however, was placed on poverty reduction programmes during this period without giving due consideration to the pitfalls associated with them.

The various poverty alleviation programmes, such as Integrated Rural Development Programme (IRDP), were success stories when taken up as pilot projects; but the results were far below expectations when implemented on an all-India basis. What was ignored was that, for a country such as India, a subcontinent with vast diversity in topography, culture and initial conditions, a straitjacket approach, however well designed, was not going to serve the purpose. The policy-makers, though they have admitted this fact in the past, nonetheless repeated such attempts 'on an experimental basis'. This was tried for at least two decades. Perhaps the mindset was that things would automatically fall into place, even though there was a greater likelihood of it not materializing. The policy-makers bet a lot on a slim possibility, ignoring the lessons of past reality. Programmes aimed at direct poverty alleviation involved a lot of discretion which gave scope for corruption. The government reported the leakages from this kind of programme yet accepted them as fact of life, and still there was this innocuous belief that somehow these policies would work. The idea that growth could be an antidote to poverty did not find favour with Indian policy-makers till the 1990s. Another dimension of India's economic policy (largely up to the 1980s, but extending slightly even into the 1990s, which was disturbing) was the state patronage of inefficiency; not letting market forces get to work in matters which should have been guided more by business than by social considerations created vested interests. For instance, the decision to take sick private units into the government fold to protect employment in the late 1970s in hindsight turned out to be a blunder.

In spite of the various deficiencies in economic policy-making, the laudable aspect of India's development paradigm has been the emphasis on an inclusive pattern of development. How far the plans, programmes and policies designed to cater to the needs of the disadvantaged have actually succeeded is a matter of conjecture. Nonetheless, the commitment at the political and policy level for improving the economic status of the underprivileged, a concomitant of vibrant democracy, merits credit. This can be contrasted with the development paradigm pursued in China where growth focused more on urban areas, while rural China was left high and dry in the growth process. The Chinese government seems to have suddenly woken up to tackling the growing unrest in rural Chinese provinces in recent times. According to its Prime Minister, China is confronted with a 'major historic task' of addressing the concerns of its rural masses where unemployment is pervasive. While China was at one extreme, pursuing growth without the benefit of human considerations, India at the other extreme was saddled with socialist concerns at least until the 1980s.

The economic crisis in 1991, which had been brewing since the early 1980s, was triggered by a spate of external developments. Problems in the Gulf and the disintegration of the USSR[1] snowballed into a crisis. Again, in hindsight, the crisis of 1991 turned out to be a blessing in disguise. This crisis moment was used as an opportunity to clear the shadow of political exigency which lingered over sound economic logic. Managing the crisis required a number of stabilization measures. It was also important to drive home the point that structural reform measures were needed if similar situations were not to recur. India was fortunate to have a bold personality in P.V. Narasimha Rao as the Prime Minister, and Manmohan Singh, the present Prime Minister, as the Finance Minister; Singh had the uncanny ability to see the need for structural reforms to avoid a recurrence of economic crisis. The gamut of policy changes which otherwise would have been politically unacceptable appeared as an unavoidable solution to the growing impasse.

Reform measures undertaken in different segments of the economy are an area which falls beyond scope of this discussion. While not commenting in detail about the various reform initiatives, we will touch upon broad contours of major reform initiatives which have changed the character of the principal–agent relationship in the Indian economy. The Industrial Policy of 1991 brought an end to the licence quota regime and paved the way for improving the efficiency of industrial production by removing constraints on capacity creation and encouraging competition. The Narasimham Committee of 1991 unshackled the financial sector, especially the banking sector, from administrative controls. The Chelliah Committee addressed fundamental distortions in the tax system in 1993. Sweeping reforms at the macro level continued and culminated with the convertibility of the rupee on trade accounts in 1993–4. Many researchers into India's economic performance are of the view that, by 1993–4, major gains from the reform measures were already being felt.[2] The following three years, beginning with 1994–5, were all years of robust economic growth. This was attributed to the unleashing of productive potential from the policy quagmire of the past. Though there was evidence of growth fatigue seen in the later part of 1990s, there has been a resurgence in economic growth in the last couple of years. Overall, India is on a path of higher growth in the post-reform period.

Higher growth, however, can be better accepted and sustained if growth is broadly based and favourably affects a large number of people. The broad-based character of the growth process is more relevant in the democratic set-up of a country such as India where rising aspirations can only be met by growth that is evenly shared across regions. Under the broad rubric of growth, balanced regional development has been one of the explicit planks of economic policy in India since the early days of planning. For instance, the Indian government's 1956 Industrial Policy Resolution asserted that 'only by securing a balanced and coordinated development of the industrial and agricultural economy in each region, can the entire country attain higher standards of living'. In a similar vein, the National Integration Council in 1961 emphasized the importance of regional balance in economic development as a positive factor in promoting national integration.[3] The Third Plan explicitly mentioned that 'balanced development of different parts of the country, extension of the benefits of economic progress to the less developed regions and widespread diffusion of industry are among the major aims of planned development'. The subsequent plans have also reiterated the need for a more balanced regional development.

To bring about regional parity, the centre has adopted a gamut of policies from time to time to influence the rates of growth in poorer states so as to reduce their economic distance from their richer counterparts. A major government instrument in bringing about parity across the states is the transfer of financial resources to the poorer states. Important in this respect is the role of the Finance Commission (provided for in the Constitution) and the Planning Commission, an extended arm of central government. The Finance Commission decides the principles on which transfer of central taxes and other financial resources is made from the centre to the states. Acting as fiscal dentists, various Finance Commissions have tried to reduce interstate disparity by giving preferential treatment to the poorer states by allocating larger grants to them than their population would warrant and by transferring resources from the better-off states to them (see Ramesh (2002)). The Planning Commission, for its part, allocated greater Plan assistance to the backward states. This assistance was given in the form of both grants and loans on the basis of a formula whereby the degree of backwardness of a state is given due consideration. The Eleventh and the Twelfth Finance Commissions have started linking grants to the fiscal reform initiatives of the states, thus encouraging the states to follow a prudent fiscal path.

Apart from financial assistance, certain proactive measures – such as decisions regarding public investment, nationalization of banks and various schemes for poverty eradication – were designed to address the concerns of regional disparity. For instance, while planning for public investment in major industries such as steel, fertilizers, oil refining, petrochemicals, machine making, heavy chemicals, power and irrigation projects, roads, railways, post offices and other infrastructural facilities, the location of the enterprise has been a major consideration. Further, the government provided incentives to the private sector to invest in backward areas through subsidies, tax concessions and banking and institutional loans at subsidized rates. The system of licensing private industrial enterprises, which prevailed up until the onset of reforms, was also used by the government to encourage the location of industries in backward areas. In addition, various welfare schemes were launched by different ministries for development in the more backward regions. In particular, poverty eradication programmes (including the Food for Work Programme, the IRDP and others) have been adopted since the 1970s. Similarly, the nationalization of banks in 1969 and the subsequent spread of their branch network were assertive steps to extend banking services to the rural hinterland. Banks and other public sector financial institutions worked with a mandate to encourage banking habits amongst the populace of the relatively backward regions and also to promote investment in these areas.

Benefits from the concerted efforts on the part of the centre, however, have not been shared equally amongst regions. In spite of the various efforts, regional imbalance remains an issue of concern to this day. Policy intentions and outcomes do not seem to match, as has been pointed out in a number of studies. If one explores the causes of persisting inequality in the growth experience of the Indian states, a number of issues stand out. The genesis of some regions' underdevelopment can be traced to their socio-economic and political organization itself. The agrarian structure in some of the states is quite regressive and in many states land reform has been implemented in letter only and not in spirit. For instance, in Bihar and Orissa land consolidation has been tardy, whereas it played an important role in the agricultural development of Punjab and Haryana. The backward states seem to have been beset by a vicious circle of economic backwardness. Low levels of economic development and production means inadequate financial resources and limited expenditure on infrastructure, development planning and social services. And this low level of expenditure in turn leads to low levels of production. Political and administrative failures also aggravate backwardness.

Notwithstanding these pitfalls, there have also been positive developments on certain counts. For instance, there has been a decline in interstate industrial disparity, especially in the organized manufacturing segment. There is also less disparity in terms of social welfare as represented by life expectancy, infant mortality and literacy. The disparity in agriculture shrank as the green revolution technology spread during the 1970s to Andhra Pradesh, Tamil Nadu, Karnataka, Eastern Uttar Pradesh and parts of Rajasthan, and during the 1980s to the eastern states of Bihar, West Bengal, Orissa and Assam. On the whole, while there has been economic growth in all states, the rates of growth of different states have covered a wide range leading to huge interstate disparities. Leaving aside the centre's attempts to mitigate regional inequity, when it comes to assessing the poorer states' own efforts to catch up with their relatively better-off counterparts, it is interesting to find that the states pursued a relatively uniform set of policies until the 1990s. The role of the states up to that point was confined to implementing policies laid down by the central government.[4] Policies with regard to subjects which are on the state list, such as irrigation, in which one would expect significant variation across the states, were tackled in the same way across the whole country. The situation by the end of the 1990s was, however, quite different. Individual states took a lead in introducing reforms in different areas: for instance, Orissa privatized its power sector; Andhra Pradesh set up user groups across the state to manage the distribution of canal irrigation; and Madhya Pradesh introduced the Education Guarantee Scheme whereby any village of a particular size was entitled to a school.

Broadly, three sets of factors contributed to the diversity in economic policies followed across the states in the 1990s. First of all, with the paradigm shift in the approach to economic management and policy towards liberalization at the centre, state level reforms have become a necessity. With central government no longer being able to direct investment through licensing, the states themselves had to take the initiative in promoting an enabling environment for investment and growth. Second, the changing political character at the centre (with no single party having a majority) has given the states a greater say in matters concerning them. With the emergence of coalition government at the centre, the political authority of the central government weakened in the 1990s. The growth of regional parties has provided a greater political space for the states, and in a way has contributed to greater diversity in economic policies.

The mounting fiscal stress at the state level since the mid-1990s is the third factor which has forced the states to adopt a pragmatic approach to their public finances.[5] The emphasis on fiscal reforms at the state level, however, needs to be seen as part of the larger shift in the perception of the role of government in both economic and social development. There is recognition by the states of the need to control the growing burden of subsidies by ensuring that these are transparent, closely targeted and not open-ended. A consensus seems to be emerging that non-merit subsidies must be phased out, even if it is not possible to stop them in one go. There is also a growing realization that appropriate user charges, which are periodically revised, must be levied on power, irrigation and other major economic and social infrastructure services. According to Howes, Lahiri and Stern (2003), the state level fiscal crisis in the second half of the 1990s generated a sense of systemic crisis and a feeling that things could not continue along the lines of the past and hence gave enormous momentum to the reform process at the state level. With the gradual retreat of the centre's overall control over matters deciding their fortunes, it has become incumbent on the part of the states to chart a policy course that will further their growth prospects.

In sum, the 1990s onwards has been quite an eventful period for the Indian states, and they have adopted a reformist approach.

Their success in the post-reform period, however, is conditional upon their successfully redressing many of their structural weaknesses, which date back to the pre-reform period.[6] Sustainable development is known to be a complex phenomenon and will require concerted efforts in a number of directions. Historical conditions, resource endowments and political initiative (or lack of it) are only some of the factors that need to be appreciated in any development scheme. Nonetheless, the performance of different states can be compared and contrasted in some important areas which have been less traversed but which remain central to the development theme. First there is the issue of growth. The hurdle of the Hindu rate of growth could be crossed in the post-economic reform period. However, it is a matter of investigation whether the growth phenomenon has been shared equally amongst the different regions in this period. Which sectors have been the drivers of growth? Specifically, one would be interested to find out how the relatively poorer states have performed compared to their richer counterparts. Further, is there any evidence of poorer states catching up with their richer counterparts in the post-reform period? This is broadly the focus of discussion in Chapters 2 and 3.

Though economic reforms were wide ranging in character, the financial and fiscal sectors were the focus of reforms in the initial years in the states. A significant policy initiative is seen in the fiscal sector, beginning with the Chelliah Committee Report on reforming the taxation system and later the enactment of the 2003 Fiscal Responsibility and Budget Management (FRBM) Act. Though reform initiatives in the fiscal dimension were initially confined to the central government, the deteriorating fiscal health of the state governments has also been a matter of concern. A number of initiatives were spearheaded with the central government taking the lead to restore order to state finances, the latest being the Fiscal Responsibility Legislation (FRL) enacted by 19 states. The Twelfth Finance Commission (2004) has also encouraged the remaining states to adopt FRLs. In the light of the initiatives to restore fiscal health, Chapter 4 will discuss the evolution of state finances in the post-reform period and address some fiscal issues concerning the states.

The banking sector can play a crucial role in promoting regional equity by mobilizing resources and channelling these resources to finance production activity across the states. Financial sector reforms were initiated in India in 1992–93 to promote a diversified, efficient and competitive financial system. Banks were supposed to evolve as truly commercial entities in the post-reform scenario. In the new scenario, how the credit–growth relationship has evolved at the state level is an interesting matter for enquiry. In the broader canvas of the credit–growth relationship, one issue which is still controversial today is the causal relationship between credit and output. Employing the recent developments in panel data econometrics, we attempt to throw fresh light on this much-debated issue. A comparative sectoral perspective on the growth of credit and output and also the causal relation between the two will be the subject of discussion in Chapter 5.

India has adopted a multi-agency approach towards meeting credit needs in rural areas. Apart from commercial banks and co-operatives, the institution of regional rural banks (RRBs), established in 1975, has played a vital role in expanding the reach of banking to the rural hinterlands. With joint shareholding[7] by central government, the state government concerned and the sponsoring commercial bank, the inception of RRBs was a unique effort to integrate commercial banking into the broad policy thrust towards social banking, whilst remaining aware of local peculiarities.

RRBs were supposed to evolve as specialized rural financial institutions for developing the rural economy by providing credit to small and marginal farmers, agricultural labourers, artisans and small entrepreneurs. Notwithstanding their contribution to the development of the rural economy, the financial viability of RRBs has been a key policy concern. In an attempt to restore viability, an amalgamation of RRBs has been carried out since September 2005. A merger of RRBs is not only a merger of their balance sheets but also, more significantly, a synthesis of the different work cultures, management practices and business strategies of the merged entities. In the present milieu of restructuring and amalgamation, the broader question remains unanswered as to what will be the role of sponsoring banks *vis à vis* the merged entities. In the limited sense of balance sheet strengthening, one can appreciate the merger of the RRBs that are making profits. The merger of profit- and loss-making RRBs even in this limited sense raises certain apprehensions. Chapter 6 is devoted to unravelling the factors that affect the performance of the RRBs, the role the sponsor bank has to play in the post-amalgamation phase and some thoughts on future restructuring strategies for RRBs.

Agriculture is the mainstay in most of the states as far as employment is concerned. Again, given the effects of agriculture on the other sectors of the economy, it is necessary for agricultural growth to attain higher planes. How the agriculture sector has fared in the post-reform period will have implications for sustaining overall growth at higher levels. Agricultural production depends on a confluence of factors beginning with the behaviour of the monsoon and also involving, the use of agricultural inputs and infrastructural facilities. More specifically, apart from the quantum of rainfall, its spatial and temporal distribution will influence agricultural production. Public investment in infrastructure, such as irrigation, electricity, the transport network and warehousing, and the application of inputs such as high-yielding variety (HYV) seeds and fertilizer are crucial in shaping decisions regarding agricultural operations. Against this backdrop, it would be instructive to study and disentangle the impact of different factors on agricultural production and productivity. As a case study, the factors influencing agricultural production in Orissa, one of the agriculturally backward states of India, is considered in Chapter 7. Policy simulations have been carried out to determine areas where focused attention is needed to augment agricultural production.

2
Growth Performance

At the time of Independence, the initial conditions for economic development across India varied significantly. This was mostly due to historical reasons. Prior to Independence, only about 30 per cent of the territories of the present-day India were directly governed by the British Crown. The rest of India comprised independent princely or native states, which were ruled by princes and chiefs.[1] In all, there were 652 such big and small princely and native states. With such a large number of heterogeneous entities in its fold, the political unity of India was a concern at the time of Independence. Disparity leads to dissension and as such, for India to hold together as a nation and develop as a mature democracy, it was a political necessity to work for balanced regional development. Seen from another angle, the provinces under direct British rule had better exposure and access to modern practices in trade, industry, communication, technology and above all education compared to the large number of independent princely states. If India with such a large number of heterogeneous entities aspired to develop as a 'nation', it had to embark on a policy of balanced regional development. Moreover, balanced regional development is a necessary step towards securing economic justice which is one of the fundamental tenets of the Indian Constitution. Further, the 42nd Amendment Act, 1976, of the Constitution, made an explicit orientation towards a socialist state in India which bolstered the need for balanced regional development. Thus one finds balanced regional development to be a recurring theme in the designing of India's economic policy. Consequently, resource allocation for planned development was used as an instrument to promote it.

The economic crisis of 1991, however, has altered India's approach to economic policy. In the post-crisis period, structural reform measures were pursued which laid greater emphasis on market forces in the allocation of resources in the economy. With resource allocation left to the market, apprehensions were raised that the growth pattern in the post-reform phase would be skewed in favour of the already better-off states. To what extent these concerns are justified can be judged through a thorough analysis of growth behaviour in the post-reform period. Against this backdrop, the present chapter analyses the growth performance of Indian states in the post-reform period. The rest of the chapter is schematized as follows. Section 2.1 chronicles the alternative approaches to studying the performance of the states and the reasons for concentrating on the growth analysis. Some of the data issues pertaining to regional growth analysis are discussed in section 2.2. Section 2.3 discusses the behaviour of the absolute and per capita state domestic product (SDP) growth across the states in the pre-reform and the post-reform periods. The changing structural composition of SDP at the state level is covered in section 2.4. Section 2.5 deals with the variability of the SDP and its components in the spatial and temporal dimensions. The contribution of different sectors of the economy to growth and changes and output, in the post-reform period, are discussed in sections 2.6 and 2.7 respectively, while section 2.8 contains some concluding observations.

2.1 Alternative approaches to the states' economic performance

As far as the methodology to study the performance of the states is concerned, a number of approaches have been suggested in the literature. Broadly speaking, they are the composite development index approach, rank analysis, and growth analysis. International bodies such as the United Nations (UN) construct an annual human development index (HDI) to classify nation states into three broad categories of 'high', 'medium' and 'low' human development. An analysis of the index value over the years would give an idea of the progress made by nations over time in critical development indicators. Following this approach, the government of India in 2002 published the *National Human Development Report* (NHDR) which classified Indian states in terms of their achievement in human development over the period 1981–2001. The HDI as per the NHDR is based on quality of life ('life expectancy at age 1' and 'Infant Mortality Rate'), education ('literacy rate for children above 7 years of age' and 'intensity of formal education') and standard of living (the per capita real consumption expenditure adjusted for inequality).

Taking this line of approach further, the Council for Social Development has come out with a social development index (SDI), which has a broader canvas than the HDI. The SDI is based on six broad dimensions of well being: demography, healthcare, basic amenities, unemployment and poverty, education, and social deprivation. The SDI has been derived separately for the larger and relatively smaller states for two data points, 1991 and 2001 (see Table 2.1). Further, it has been derived for the rural and urban areas separately.[2] Using the population proportions in rural and urban areas, we have computed the overall index for the different states. The SDI in 2001, when looked at beside that of 1991, suggests improvement for all states except Kerala amongst the larger states. However, the smaller states – Manipur, Meghalaya, Mizoram and Nagaland – have suffered deterioration in the SDI in 2001 as compared to 1991.

If we probe further into the relative rankings of the different states looking for differences between the larger and smaller states, the following points emerge: first, though there has been a slight fall in the index value in 2001 compared to 1991 for Kerala, it has retained the top position in SDI in 2001. Punjab, Himachal Pradesh and Jammu & Kashmir have also maintained their relative position, being amongst the top four performers in the SDI reckoning. Second, Andhra Pradesh, Karnataka and Haryana have significantly improved on the SDI and the consequent rankings. Third, the world seems not to have changed for Bihar, Uttar Pradesh, Madhya Pradesh and Orissa, the bottom four states in the SDI scale between 1991 and 2001. Fourth, Gujarat and Maharashtra are the two states which have seen only marginal improvement in their SDI and have actually suffered a decline in their rankings. Fifth, Goa, Sikkim, Tripura and Arunachal Pradesh in the smaller states category have improved their SDI ranking in 2001.

Overall, the dispersion measured by coefficient of variation in the SDI both for the larger and the smaller states has come down in the post-reform period. This is suggestive of the positive development

Table 2.1   Social Development Index

States/UTs	1991 Index	1991 Ranking	2001 Index	2001 Ranking
Andhra Pradesh	31.3	13	43.5	9
Assam	37.6	8	40.7	12
Bihar	16.8	17	17.3	20
Gujarat	40.9	5	44.1	11
Haryana	37.5	9	46.0	5
Himachal Pradesh	53.0	2	64.2	2
Jammu & Kashmir	47.8	4	52.3	4
Karnataka	34.9	10	45.9	8
Kerala	69.0	1	67.2	1
Madhya Pradesh	21.6	15	30.6	17
Maharashtra	40.5	6	42.8	10
Orissa	24.9	14	28.8	16
Punjab	50.2	3	59.9	3
Rajasthan	32.1	12	37.5	13
Tamil Nadu	38.2	7	45.7	6
Uttar Pradesh	19.0	16	25.8	18
West Bengal	32.8	11	39.0	14
Chhattisgarh			30.4	15
Jharkhand			20.2	19
Uttaranchal			42.5	7
Smaller states				
Arunachal Pradesh	25.0	9	35.9	8
Delhi	50.9	3	52.7	3
Goa	56.3	2	65.6	1
Manipur	45.3	5	44.3	5
Meghalaya	25.0	8	24.1	9
Mizoram	62.4	1	58.7	2
Nagaland	47.2	4	39.2	7
Sikkim	41.0	6	48.7	4
Tripura	31.0	7	42.9	6

UTs = Union Territories.
Source: *India: Social Development Report* by the Council for Social Development, New Delhi, Council for Social Development (2006).

that has taken place across both the smaller and the larger states on a broad set of indicators in the post-reform period. Though the SDI kind of composite index is a good pointer in evaluating the performance of the states, such indices, however, are difficult to compute on a year-by-year basis, given the stringent data requirements.

While commenting on the growth performance of the Indian states, some researchers have adopted a score-based analysis. Debroy and Bhandari (2003),[3] for instance, assign scores to states under eight broad heads: prosperity and budget (7 indicators), law and order (4 indicators), health (7), education (5), consumer market (4), agriculture (5), infrastructure (7) and investment (6 indicators). They use principal component analysis to assign weights to the different indicators to obtain scores under each head. The states are then ranked on the basis of scores. As per their ranking, Punjab, Kerala, Himachal Pradesh, Tamil Nadu and Haryana occupy the top five positions and Chhattisgarh, Uttar Pradesh, Orissa, Jharkhand and Bihar occupy the bottom five positions amongst the big states in 2004. Amongst the smaller states, Pondicherry, Delhi and Mizoram occupy the top three, and Manipur, Meghalaya and Tripura the bottom three positions in 2004. The study broadly concludes that the states from north and south top the chart in the 2004 rankings.

The authors themselves, however, advise caution concerning the robustness of the rankings. It is possible that a state is ranked above another state without substantial differences in the scores. Hence, it is the scores and not the ranks which actually matter. Based on a large set of indicators, the ranks assigned gain credibility. Though derived from a much richer information set, the problem with composite indices or score-based analysis is the availability of reliable data. Many of the variables used to construct the indices or to obtain scores (ranks) are based on national level surveys that are undertaken quinquennially or at 10-yearly intervals, and at times without any specified frequency on an 'as and when' basis. Such analysis, given the huge resource requirement, is undertaken at discrete time points and it is difficult to evaluate the performance of the states on a continuous basis. As such, we concentrate on growth analysis for which the level of economic activity proxied by the SDP is the basic unit for analysis and is available on an annual frequency. Next, we take up certain issues that need to be appreciated while using the SDP data.

2.2 Data issues

One of the primary issues involved in assessing the growth performance in the post-reform period is to draw a line of demarcation between the pre- and the post-reform periods. Montek S. Ahluwalia was the first to devote focused attention to the state-level perform-ance under economic reforms. The study was done in the year 2000 and covered the period from 1980–1 to 1998–9. His study considered 1991–2 to be the dividing line when assessing the post-reform economic performance. Being the first such attempt, the study had, amongst other things, data limitations.[4] But by choosing 1991–2 as the dividing year, the study assumes that reform measures had an impact from the moment of their announcement. This assump-tion in all probability may not hold true given the time lag between announcement of policy and its implementation at the state level. In view of this, we consider the period 1981–93 as indicative of the pre-reform period and 1994–2004 to represent the post-reform period, thereby settling for 1993–4 as the dividing year for our analysis.

This is done primarily on two accounts. First, even though reform measures such as industrial de-licensing and others were initiated in 1991, most of them would have taken some time to play out. In other words, the possible lag effect of the reform measures is accounted for in choosing the dividing line to assess the post-reform economic performance of the states. Second, the SDP figures, which are the basic input for any study on the growth performance at the regional level, are available from a new base in 1993–4. We have SDP figures available from the old base of 1980–1 and the new base of 1993–4.

There are two broad ways in which SDP data available from the 1980–1 and the 1993–4 bases could have been rendered comparable. One way is to shift forward the SDP from the 1980–1 base so as to make it comparable to the 1993–4 base, and the alternative is to take back the SDP figure available from the 1993–4 to the 1980–1 base. Splicing done in the above manner is rather mechanical but nonetheless gives some element of uniformity to the variable under analysis. Some authors try to apply a modified method where correc-tions for both price and quantity are accounted for while splicing (Bhattacharya and Sakthivel 2004). This method is rather involved and would be a wholesome exercise in itself. As such, we have applied the standard splicing. As we are interested in analysing the perform-ance of the states in the post-reform period, it is better to work with the new base figures available from 1993–4 onwards rather than use the SDP figures also available from the 1980–1 base. Hence, we have converted the SDP from the 1980–1 base to the 1993–4 base.

Applying splicing to the SDP series, however, involves a number of issues as discussed below. The foremost is the issue of 'at what level' to apply splicing. Splicing can be done for the subcomponents of SDP and the spliced subcomponents can be added up to get the spliced SDP series. For instance, the spliced primary sector output is obtained by first splicing the subcomponents such as 'agriculture', 'forestry and logging', 'fishing' and 'mining and quarrying', and the spliced subcomponents are then added up to get the spliced primary sector output. In a similar manner, spliced secondary and tertiary sector output can be obtained from their subcomponents. Spliced primary, secondary and tertiary sector outputs can be summed up to get the spliced SDP series. The other option is to first splice the SDP series and then distribute that spliced SDP among the primary, secondary and tertiary subcomponents based on the proportion that each subcomponent accounted for in the total output on the old base. The spliced SDP series obtained by the above two methods, however, will not match and one has to work with some rough approximations in either case.

However, obtaining the SDP figure and the three broad subsectors of primary, secondary and tertiary by adding the individually spliced components could be quite erroneous in certain cases. A glaring example of how erroneous things can be if we obtain the SDP figure by summing the individually spliced subsector outputs is the tertiary sector output in Kerala. For Kerala, the 1993–4 figure for 'Real Estate, Ownership of Dwellings and Business Services' from the 1980–1 and the 1993–4 bases are Rs131,203 and Rs439 lakh (lakh being 100,000), giving a splicing factor of 298. If this splicing factor is used as a component to derive the tertiary sector output, the tertiary sector output is overestimated by as much as 10 percentage points compared to the tertiary sector output obtained by directly splicing the tertiary sector output. Which method to adopt will depend on the purpose at hand. The spliced SDP series obtained from the spliced subcomponents of SDP ensures additive decomposition and as such is preferable, if one is interested in analysing the share of different sectors in the SDP. Alternatively, direct splicing of the SDP series or any of its components is preferable if one wishes to comment on the growth of SDP or any of its subcomponents. To comment on growth, we have applied splicing directly to the series concerned in this study; but, while analysing sectoral shares, we have ensured further decomposition at the appropriate level.

India has in all 35 regions comprising 28 States, six Union Territories (UTs) and the National Capital Territory, New Delhi. The mountainous states of the north and north-eastern part of India are considered as a 'special category' by the Planning Commission. Following this classification, 11 out of the 28 states are identified as Special Category States (SCS) and the rest as General Category States (GCS). The SCS are so termed, because they receive special treatment in allocation of funds released for planned development from the Planning Commission. While for the GCS the proportion of loans is 70 per cent and that of grants is 30 per cent, for the SCS the proportions are 10 and 90 per cent respectively. Most of the studies on India's regional economic performance (such as Shand and Bhide, 2000; Ahluwalia, 2002a; 2005) consider the performance of 14 major states, mostly belonging to the GCS. Because of their special features, Ahluwalia has excluded the north-eastern and other SCS from his study. While deliberating on growth at the state level, it is common to find discussions centring on the GCS, and at times Assam and Himachal Pradesh are also included.

Like Ahluwalia, many other researchers on India's regional growth performance have justified the exclusion of the SCS on the ground that the 14 states account for bulk of the population and output.[5] The reason for concentrating on the 14 major states is mainly twofold: lack of availability of consistent data and the difference in the structure of their economies in contrast to the SCS. A third reason that is cited in favour of concentrating on 14 states only is that these states account for a major share of both output and population, and thus are representative. While by the yardstick of the structure of economy the SCS and the Union Territories are placed on a different footing, it would be interesting to see how the SCS as a group have performed, given the 'special' attention paid to them, compared with the GCS, on various growth parameters. It is true that the Special Category States are not on a comparable footing with the General Category States and, as such, they should not be lumped together. But then by the same principle that the SCS share some commonality, they can be treated as a homogeneous group and it would be interesting to study how the SCS have performed *vis-à-vis* the GCS in the post-reform period.

Though the SDP data are available from the Central Statistical Organization (CSO), there are a number of data issues which deserve due consideration while using these data (see Appendix 2.1). Availability of consistent data is another issue which guides the studies on regional economy. Further, in case SDP data or their subcomponents are not available for one or two years, we have projected the data to get a consistent SDP series for 1981–2004. Appendix 2.2 lists the periods for which SDP data are available for different states in the study period and also the methodology adopted to project the SDP figures. This chapter analyses the growth performance of the states in the post-reform period in some detail. To draw a comparative perspective, the growth performance in the period prior to the reforms is also considered.

2.3 Behaviour of growth: spatial and temporal dimensions

Before we embark upon an analysis of the growth performance at the state level, we begin with a brief review of the growth performance at the all-India level. Between 1950–1 and 2003–4, GDP has increased by 10.2 times, population by a factor of three and, consequently, per capita GDP by 3.4 times. While the GDP grew by the famous Hindu rate of growth of 3.6 per cent per annum in the first 30 years of planning, the growth rate had picked up to 5.7 per cent per annum in the post-1980 period.[6] Segregating the post-1980 period further into the subperiods 1981–93 and 1994–2004, one finds that GDP growth has gone up from 5.4 per cent per annum in 1981–93 to 6.0 per cent in 1994–2004. The GDP growth rate has been at its best in the post-1993–94 period compared to all the previous subperiods. A similar scenario emerges when we investigate the growth performance in per capita terms (Table 2.2). The per capita GDP growth mimics the growth pattern of absolute GDP across the various subperiods. As the 1993–4 to 2003–4 period is also characterized by the lowest population growth when compared to any other, per capita GDP growth has also been the highest in this period. Given this overall picture, we now turn our attention to the situation in the states.

At the state level, the SDP represents output. Table 2.3 depicts the SDP growth of the GCS, SCS and also some UTs for the periods 1981–93 and 1994–2004. Specifically, we have considered the growth

Table 2.2 Growth of the Indian economy (%)

Period	GDP	Per capita GDP	Population
1950–1–1979–80	3.5	1.3	2.2
1980–1–1992–3	5.3	3.2	2.1
1993–4–2003–4	*6.0*	*4.1*	*1.9*
1980–1–2003–4	5.7	3.6	2.0
1950–1–2003–4	4.3	2.2	2.1

Note: GDP figures are at factor cost and at constant prices.
Growth rates are compound annual growth rates, computed using a semi log specification
of output over time.

profile of 14 states in the GCS, 6 states in the SCS and four UTs. The GCS account for the bulk in all-India population and output. Compared to the period 1981–93, when their share was 86.3 per cent in GDP and 93.3 in all-India population, it has declined to 84.1 and 92.8 respectively in the period 1994–2004. The SCS account for 4.1 per cent of all-India population and 2.9 per cent of GDP during 1994–2004. While their share in GDP has gone down from 3.4 to 2.9, population share has remained the same across the two subperiods. The four UTs account for only 3.4 per cent of all-India GDP. It is interesting to observe that the share of UTs as a group in the all-India services sector GDP at 5 per cent was higher than their share in all-India GDP. Their share in all-India population was just 1.5 per cent during 1994–2004, increasing from 1.4 per cent during 1981–93. Ideally, the Gross State Domestic Product (GSDP) and per capita GSDP figures over a particular time period should differ by population growth in that period. Here, because of rounding errors, the relationship between GSDP, per capita GSDP and population growth may not hold in some cases.

Certain interesting features emerge from Table 2.3. First, the overall growth performance of the GCS and SCS as a group was only marginally better in the post-reform phase compared to the period preceding it. The difference in the GSDP growth for the GCS and SCS as a group has not changed across the two subperiods. Second, in absolute terms, the GCS have grown faster than the SCS in both the subperiods. Third, in per capita terms, the gap between the GCS and SCS as a group, however, has narrowed in the post-reform period. This is because of the lower population growth in the SCS in the 1994–2004

Table 2.3   Growth of GSDP and per capita GSDP (%)

State	1981–93 GSDP	1994–2004 GSDP	1981–93 Per capita GSDP	1994–2004 Per capita GSDP	1981–93 Population	1994–2004 Population
Andhra Pradesh	5.7	5.6	3.5	4.5	2.2	1.1
Undivided Bihar	3.9	5.0	1.7	2.5	2.1	2.5
Gujarat	5.1	6.2	3.1	4.1	1.9	2.0
Haryana	6.2	6.0	3.7	3.5	2.4	2.4
Karnataka	5.5	7.3	3.6	5.8	1.9	1.4
Kerala	4.0	5.4	2.6	4.5	1.4	0.9
Undivided Madhya Pradesh	4.5	4.0	2.1	2.0	2.4	2.0
Maharashtra	6.3	5.0	3.9	3.1	2.3	1.9
Orissa	3.9	3.9	2.0	2.5	1.8	1.4
Punjab	5.2	4.1	3.2	2.4	1.9	1.7
Rajasthan	7.0	5.6	4.4	3.1	2.5	2.5
Tamil Nadu	5.4	5.0	4.0	4.0	1.4	1.0
Undivided Uttar Pradesh	4.8	3.6	2.4	1.7	2.3	1.9
West Bengal	4.8	7.0	2.6	5.5	2.2	1.5
Combined GCS	*5.2*	*5.3*	*3.0*	*3.5*	*2.1*	*1.8*
Arunachal Pradesh	8.7	3.3	5.3	1.3	3.2	2.0
Assam	3.6	2.7	1.4	1.2	2.2	1.5
Himachal Pradesh	5.1	6.5	3.1	4.7	1.9	1.7
Manipur	5.2	6.4	2.5	4.1	2.6	2.2
Meghalaya	5.7	6.9	2.7	4.3	2.9	2.5
Tripura	6.0	8.9	2.9	7.8	3.0	1.1
Combined SCS	*4.4*	*4.5*	*2.0*	*2.9*	*2.3*	*1.6*
A&N Islands	5.2	2.1	1.0	0.3	4.2	1.8
Delhi	7.9	8.5	3.5	4.7	4.2	3.7
Goa	6.0	7.9	4.4	6.2	1.5	1.6
Pondicherry	3.4	13.8	0.4	11.7	3.0	1.9
Combined UTs	*7.6*	*7.3*	*3.6*	*4.4*	*3.8*	*2.8*
Combined All India	5.4	6.0	3.2	4.0	2.2	1.9

Note: A&N Islands: Andaman and Nicobar Islands.

period. Fourth, growth recorded by the GCS states fell rather short compared to all-India growth in the post-reform period. In fact, the gap between the two has widened in the post-reform phase compared to the pre-reform one.

Fifth,though all-India GDP growth increased significantly from 5.4 to 6 per cent, GSDP growth for the GCS as a group increased marginally from 5.2 to 5.3 per cent, and for the SCS as group it increased from 4.4 to 4.5. So the notching-up of all-India GDP growth in the post-reform phase is explained by the higher growth of that segment of the economy, which is exclusively under the central government domain. One finds that the GCS and the SCS comprising 20 states accounted for 87 per cent of all-India GDP during 1994–2004, but only 73 per cent of the all-India service sector output during that period. Thus the growth differential between the GDP and GSDP is perhaps explained by the higher growth of certain segments of the service sector, which is under central government jurisdiction.[7]

Sixth, though the GSDP growth of UTs as a group has marginally slackened in the post-reform period, they have grown at a faster pace than the GCS and the SCS in both the pre-reform and the post-reform period. Seventh, to begin with, the UTs had a very high population growth of 3.8 per cent per annum in the pre-reform period, which significantly decreased to 2.8 in the post-reform period. Consequently, the per capita GSDP growth for UTs has jumped up from 3.6 to 4.4 per cent per annum. The better growth record of the UTs as a group, however, needs to be viewed in the context that the four UTs account for a very small proportion of the all-India population and the GDP. Overall, there has been a noticeable improvement in per capita GSDP for all three categories of states in the post-reform period because of the sobering effect of a slowdown in population growth during this period.

Table 2.4 presents the growth rate of GSDP and per capita GSDP across the states. The growth figures being shown by state enables us to draw the following inferences. Seen in terms of GSDP, Bihar, Gujarat, Karnataka, Kerala and West Bengal experienced higher growth in the post-reform period compared to the pre-reform stage. Except for Bihar, the post-reform growth in the other four states was also higher than the growth recorded for GCS as a group. Bihar, though, did better compared to its own past, but this was not sufficient to equal or exceed the overall GCS group performance. Thus if we judge the states' performance by the criterion that they have not only done better than their own past but also have surpassed the growth recorded by GCS as a group, only four states (Gujarat, Karnataka, Kerala and West Bengal) meet this criterion.

It is interesting to observe that Andhra Pradesh, Haryana and Rajasthan have also performed better than GCS average in the post-reform period despite having witnessed a deceleration in growth in these years. For Madhya Pradesh, Maharashtra, Punjab, Tamil Nadu and Uttar Pradesh, GSDP growth has declined in the 1994–2004 period and is also below the combined GCS growth in the same period. Of these five states, Tamil Nadu and Maharashtra share the same feature of having a growth record better than the combined GCS in the 1980s, which has decelerated to such an extent that they are now below the GCS average. Madhya Pradesh, Punjab and Uttar Pradesh were to begin with poor performers compared to the combined GCS, and this has further worsened in the post-reform period. In the SCS category, except for Arunachal Pradesh and Assam, the other four states have witnessed marked acceleration in the growth of their GSDP in the post-reform period. Further, out of the four UTs considered, all except the Andaman and Nicobar (A&N Islands) have seen an acceleration of GSDP growth in the post-reform period. While two-thirds of the states in the SCS category did better than GSDP growth for the group in the post-reform period, in the GCS category it was only half.

Amongst the GCS, per capita growth has gained momentum in seven states: Andhra Pradesh, Bihar, Gujarat, Karnataka, Kerala, Orissa and West Bengal. Of these seven, Bihar and Orissa, in spite of their better per capita GSDP growth during 1994–2004, could not reach the level of combined GCS per capita GSDP growth. In Tamil Nadu per capita GSDP growth has been of the order of 4 per cent per annum in both the pre- and the post-reform period. While the per capita growth rate has slackened a bit for Haryana and Madhya Pradesh, there has been a marked decline for Maharashtra, Punjab, Rajasthan and Uttar Pradesh in the post-reform period. If one considers the performance of the newly created states,[8] their per capita GSDP performance has been better than their parent states in the post-reform phase. Slowdown in growth of population is seen both for the GCS and SCS; however, it is more marked for the SCS. Amongst the GCS, Bihar, Gujarat, Haryana, Madhya Pradesh, Maharashtra, Rajasthan and

Table 2.4 Growth of GSDP and per capita GSDP in the newly created states (%)

State	1994–2004 GSDP constant	1994–2004 Per capita GSDP constant	1994–2004 Population
Undivided Bihar	5.0	2.5	2.5
Undivided Madhya Pradesh	4.0	2.0	2.0
Undivided Uttar Pradesh	3.6	1.7	1.9
Jharkhand	5.1	2.8	2.3
Uttaranchal	4.1	2.2	1.8
Bihar	4.9	2.3	2.5
Madhya Pradesh	4.1	2.0	2.1
Uttar Pradesh	3.5	1.2	2.3
Chhattisgarh	3.9	2.3	1.5

Uttar Pradesh had a population growth in the post-reform period which was higher than the population growth for the combined GCS. Again, out of these seven states, only Bihar and Gujarat experienced an acceleration in population growth during 1994–2004. While the growth in population was marginal for Gujarat, it was substantial for Bihar. Further, while Andhra Pradesh and West Bengal could contain population growth to a great extent in the post-reform period, Karnataka, Orissa and Tamil Nadu also made good progress in this regard. Having discussed the broad growth trajectory of the GCS, SCS and UTs, it becomes pertinent to enquire whether any pattern emerges when sectoral growth rates are considered. This will be discussed in the next section.

2.4   Sectoral growth in the post-reform period

The sectoral growth pattern has been one of a deceleration in growth in the primary and secondary sector and an acceleration of growth in the tertiary segment in the post-reform period. This pattern holds for the three broad categories of states, (GCS, SCS and UTs) and also at the all-India level (see Table 2.5). Deceleration in growth was also seen for the secondary sector except for the SCS. Further, deceleration was sharper for agriculture and manufacturing than for the primary

Table 2.5 Absolute growth rates (%)

States	1981–93	1994–2004	1981–93	1994–2004	1981–93	1994–2004	1981–93	1994–2004	1981–93	1994–2004	1981–93	1994–2004
	Agriculture		Primary		Manufacturing		Secondary		Tertiary		SDP	
Andhra Pradesh	2.3	2.3	2.4	3.3	8.9	4.9	7.8	5.6	7.8	7.3	5.7	5.6
Bihar	1.3	3.2	2.1	3.5	4.7	4.1	5.2	5.8	5.3	6.3	3.9	5.0
Gujarat	0.3	1.2	0.8	1.1	7.7	7.6	7.5	7.3	6.8	8.0	5.1	6.2
Haryana	4.4	1.8	4.4	1.8	9.4	6.9	8.4	6.5	7.4	9.8	6.2	6.0
Karnataka	3.1	1.9	3.0	2.0	8.0	7.3	7.0	8.2	7.4	10.3	5.5	7.3
Kerala	3.4	−2.4	2.9	−1.6	4.1	1.9	3.5	5.2	5.2	8.7	4.0	5.4
Madhya Pradesh	3.3	−0.5	2.5	1.0	6.2	5.0	6.5	5.7	6.4	5.9	4.5	4.0
Maharashtra	3.7	1.3	3.7	1.5	6.8	2.6	6.4	3.1	7.6	7.4	6.3	5.0
Orissa	0.5	−0.5	1.2	1.8	7.1	2.6	6.7	2.7	6.1	6.7	3.9	3.9
Punjab	4.8	2.1	4.7	2.2	8.6	4.6	7.1	5.1	4.2	5.9	5.2	4.1
Rajasthan	5.5	1.6	5.8	2.5	6.3	6.3	7.8	6.3	8.5	7.9	7.0	5.6
Tamil Nadu	4.0	−1.0	4.2	−0.6	3.9	2.7	4.9	3.9	6.6	8.1	5.4	5.0
Uttar Pradesh	2.9	1.7	2.8	2.3	8.6	2.8	7.2	3.9	6.1	4.6	4.8	3.6
West Bengal	5.4	3.4	5.2	3.5	3.4	5.6	4.2	6.0	5.0	9.7	4.8	7.0
GCS	*3.1*	*1.5*	*3.1*	*2.0*	*6.5*	*4.5*	*6.4*	*5.1*	*6.5*	*7.5*	*5.2*	*5.3*

Table 2.5 (Continued)

States	1981–93	1994–2004	1981–93	1994–2004	1981–93	1994–2004	1981–93	1994–2004	1981–93	1994–2004	1981–93	1994–2004
	Agriculture		Primary		Manufacturing		Secondary		Tertiary		SDP	
Arunachal Pradesh	8.9	1.3	8.5	−0.7	8.2	1.8	7.9	2.0	9.6	8.3	8.7	3.3
Assam	2.5	0.6	2.3	0.6	2.6	3.2	3.7	2.0	5.0	5.1	3.6	2.7
Himachal Pradesh	3.1	2.3	2.3	2.0	13.6	12.5	7.7	8.5	6.6	8.0	5.1	6.5
Manipur	1.4	3.5	2.4	3.4	7.0	8.3	7.6	9.0	6.9	7.1	5.2	6.4
Meghalaya	0.8	6.3	2.6	6.6	8.3	5.4	4.5	9.2	8.1	6.4	5.7	6.9
Tripura	3.5	4.5	3.0	4.2	4.9	6.8	4.7	19.7	9.2	8.5	6.0	8.9
SCS	*2.7*	*1.6*	*2.5*	*1.5*	*4.5*	*6.4*	*5.1*	*6.2*	*6.0*	*6.3*	*4.4*	*4.5*
A&N Islands	3.6	1.8	5.9	−1.4	3.0	−10.8	0.4	2.0	5.4	5.1	5.2	2.1
Delhi	4.2	0.0	4.4	−0.3	8.3	4.4	8.3	6.9	7.9	9.3	7.9	8.5
Goa	2.3	3.4	1.7	1.1	7.3	13.5	7.5	13.4	6.7	6.6	6.0	7.9
Pondicherry	−0.5	−1.3	1.6	−0.4	7.7	22.8	2.7	20.8	5.4	10.3	3.4	13.8
UTs	*3.4*	*−1.6*	*3.9*	*−4.0*	*8.2*	*4.8*	*7.8*	*6.6*	*7.8*	*8.1*	*7.6*	*7.3*
All India	3.2	2.1	3.1	2.2	6.7	6.0	7.1	5.8	6.5	8.0	5.4	6.0

Note: Growth rates for GSDP constant.
Bihar, Uttar Pradesh and Madhya Pradesh figures correspond to the undivided entity.

and secondary sectors respectively. Tertiary sector growth increased by a full percentage point for the GCS group in the post-reform period compared to the preceding period (1981–93). Notwithstanding the better tertiary sector performance for the GCS as a group, in five states – Andhra Pradesh, Madhya Pradesh, Maharashtra, Rajasthan and Uttar Pradesh – tertiary sector growth has plummeted in the post-reform period. Growth deceleration was the norm when one considers the secondary sector performance with Bihar, Karnataka, Kerala and West Bengal as exceptions. If we look at the manufacturing component within the secondary sector, the deceleration phenomenon is more pronounced for all states except West Bengal. Rajasthan has been barely able to sustain the growth momentum of its manufacturing in the post-reform phase. As with the secondary sector, deceleration in primary sector growth is observed in the majority of the states in the post-reform phase except for Andhra Pradesh, Bihar, Gujarat and Orissa.

Agriculture growth across the states had a pattern similar to that of the primary sector with Orissa now sharing the majority attribute of a deceleration in the post-reform phase. Growth deceleration for all the sectors as well as the overall SDP is found for four states (Madhya Pradesh, Maharastra, Rajasthan and Uttar Pradesh). While Madhya Pradesh, Rajasthan and Uttar Pradesh are the traditionally identified poor performers, the addition of Maharashtra to this set is something that belies general perception. Though all sectors in Maharashtra have witnessed deceleration, it is sharpest in the case of the secondary sector, followed by the primary sector and then the tertiary sector. Maharashtra, traditionally seen as the industrial capital of the country and as one of India's best performing states, has not been able to sustain the growth momentum in the post-reform period.

In the SCS category, in all states except Arunachal Pradesh and Assam, there has been acceleration in the secondary sector SDP growth. This is in contrast to the GCS, where deceleration in secondary sector growth was the norm. Primary sector and agricultural growth gathered momentum in Manipur, Meghalaya and Tripura in the post-reform period. Arunachal Pradesh stands out as the only SCS which experienced deceleration in growth in all the sectors in the post-reform period. It is observed that the general category states which experienced deceleration in tertiary growth also had deceleration in SDP growth, but Meghalaya and Tripura in the SCS category had a better SDP growth performance in the post-reform period, notwithstanding the deceleration in their tertiary sector growth. As far as the UTs are concerned, all four studied here have experienced a deceleration in primary sector growth in the post-reform period. Except for Delhi, growth of the secondary segment gathered momentum in the post-reform period. In their growth of the tertiary segment, while Delhi and Pondicherry could attain robust growth, A&N Islands and Goa suffered a deceleration.

2.5 Variability of state domestic product

While growth per se is important, stability is equally a matter of concern. We now discuss the stability of growth across the states during the post-reform period. Like the GDP figure at the all-India level, the variability of GSDP for the GCS and the SCS as a group has come down (see Table 2.6). Only for the UTs as a group has variability of SDP increased. When we analyse the intersectoral variability of GCS, the following points emerge. First, for the GCS as a group, while variability of output originating from the primary and the tertiary sectors has declined, that from the secondary sector has increased in the post-reform period. Second, except for Bihar and Madhya Pradesh, variability of SDP has declined in all the states. Third, variability of SDP from the primary sector has become more pronounced in the post-reform period for Andhra Pradesh, Bihar, Kerala, Madhya Pradesh and Uttar Pradesh. Fourth, though variability of the secondary sector output for the GCS as a group has increased, ten out of the fourteen states experienced a decline in variability. Only Bihar, Karnataka, Maharashtra and Rajasthan exhibited a more volatile growth pattern. Fifth, except for Bihar, Maharashtra, Punjab and West Bengal, tertiary sector output showed less volatility for all states in the post-reform period. Bihar is the only state where variability of output in all the sectors, as well as of the overall SDP, has increased during this period. Seventh, Gujarat, Haryana, Orissa and Tamil Nadu are characterized by a decline in variability in all the sectors and in SDP.

If we look at the SCS as a group, except for the tertiary sector, growth has been more stable in the primary and secondary segments in the post-reform period. SDP variability for the SCS as a group has also declined in the post-reform period. Across the states within

Table 2.6 Variability of SDP across states and sectors

State	SDP		Primary		Secondary		Tertiary	
	1981–93	1994–2004	1981–93	1994–2004	1981–93	1994–2004	1981–93	1994–2004
Andhra Pradesh	6.18	3.76	9.61	10.80	5.64	4.01	5.07	1.27
Bihar	5.75	7.41	11.32	13.86	8.21	19.44	2.79	4.75
Gujarat	13.72	6.87	44.66	27.57	13.01	7.85	3.88	2.38
Haryana	7.13	2.81	12.51	5.56	7.99	1.22	5.09	3.26
Karnataka	4.02	2.74	8.46	8.24	4.86	5.88	2.36	1.28
Kerala	3.70	2.83	7.05	7.16	5.62	5.54	3.36	2.68
Madhya Pradesh	6.08	7.05	9.03	15.95	8.21	5.73	3.61	3.29
Maharashtra	4.91	4.43	16.52	7.87	5.02	8.11	3.39	4.22
Orissa	10.39	5.64	16.03	11.31	11.76	8.95	5.49	3.11
Punjab	2.47	1.84	4.68	4.01	3.91	3.82	1.71	2.68
Rajasthan	13.56	9.28	28.26	24.79	8.28	9.30	7.80	3.71
Tamil Nadu	4.49	3.83	12.39	9.99	8.50	7.15	4.69	2.79
Uttar Pradesh	3.06	2.95	3.45	4.20	5.96	5.39	3.09	2.11
West Bengal	3.11	0.53	8.53	4.60	2.66	2.38	1.79	2.32
GCS	*3.13*	*1.82*	*6.22*	*5.50*	*3.55*	*3.82*	*1.40*	*1.07*
Arunachal Pradesh	4.60	6.13	10.37	6.86	13.39	20.24	6.66	6.59
Assam	3.20	1.58	4.48	2.56	7.11	6.23	3.26	3.62
Himachal Pradesh	5.81	1.58	11.70	3.50	11.43	6.96	3.48	3.79
Manipur	2.25	4.91	3.60	4.64	3.83	12.85	2.02	5.30
Meghalaya	4.83	2.20	12.10	4.35	5.95	6.67	3.08	2.12
Tripura	4.83	4.79	7.28	5.09	12.44	26.17	5.58	3.65
SCS	*2.54*	*1.11*	*4.10*	*1.68*	*4.95*	*4.94*	*1.76*	*2.13*
A&N Islands	8.88	5.97	5.91	3.62	76.76	18.56	9.89	12.82
Delhi	4.77	6.84	8.96	22.07	6.46	14.02	5.58	8.22
Goa	7.34	6.18	7.27	5.20	16.45	14.15	6.53	7.07
Pondicherry	5.18	9.25	8.68	8.63	9.83	27.51	1.79	7.52
UTs	*4.05*	*6.81*	*6.45*	*12.32*	*5.45*	*12.79*	*5.05*	*7.39*
All India	*2.35*	*1.45*	*5.11*	*5.24*	*3.23*	*3.24*	*1.24*	*1.55*

Note: Variability as defined by standard deviation. The Coefficient of Variation (CV) is the most preferred measure of dispersion; a disadvantage of the CV is that it fails to be useful when the average is close to zero. As such, we have tried to see the variability of growth through the standard deviation.

SCS, growth of SDP has become more stable for all states except Arunachal Pradesh and Manipur. Primary sector output has been more stable for all states except for Manipur. Arunachal Pradesh, Manipur, Meghalaya and Tripura experienced higher volatility of secondary sector output in the post-reform period. Volatility of the tertiary sector output became more pronounced in Assam, Himachal Pradesh and Manipur. While Manipur at one extreme witnessed higher volatility in output, Meghalaya, on the other extreme, experienced lower volatility across all sectors (except for the secondary sector) in the post-reform period. For the UTs as a group, overall SDP (as well as SDP originating from all the three major subsectors) was more volatile. Amongst the UTs, SDP growth was more stable in the post-reform period for Delhi and Pondicherry. The variability of primary sector SDP came down for all the UTs under study except for Delhi. Volatility of secondary sector SDP increased for both Delhi and Pondicherry. However, increased variability was seen in all the four UTs in the tertiary segment in the post-reform period.

2.6 Sectoral shares in output

That India has graduated from a predominantly primary producing economy to a services-led economy and the industrial revolution has bypassed it has been a matter for continuing debate. Papola (2005) provides a brief overview of the state of the debate and also his own perspective on the sustainability of services-led growth. Before we delve into the relative merits of such growth, we chronicle the structural transformation in the post-reform period across states. While at the all-India level the tertiary sector has contributed more than half of the GDP in the post-reform period, the magnitude of its contribution has varied significantly across the three different categories of states: for instance, while the tertiary sector's contribution to SDP is around 72 per cent for the UTs, it is of the order of only 44 per cent for the GCS and SCS as groups (see Table 2.7). The same is the case for the primary sector's contribution to SDP: while for GCS, the primary sector's contribution is around 29 per cent, the same figures for SCS and UTs are 20 and 3.5 per cent respectively in the post-reform period. The contribution of the secondary sector to the total output is minimal and varies from 20 to 27 per cent across the different groups of states. As we do not find a uniform pattern of sectoral contribution across the GCS, SCS and UTs, it would be instructive to go further down (to state level) under these three broad categories.

The following points emerge in this context. First, while a decline in the primary sector share is a universal phenomenon, share of

Table 2.7 Share of different sectors in GSDP(%)

State	Agriculture		Manufacturing		Primary		Secondary		Tertiary	
	1981–93	1994–2004	1981–93	1994–2004	1981–93	1994–2004	1981–93	1994–2004	1981–93	1994–2004
Andhra Pradesh	35.8	25.4	11.7	15	42	31.2	18.9	23.2	39.1	45.6
Bihar	42.6	32.1	12.9	13.2	51.3	42.3	17.6	19.8	31.1	37.9
Gujarat	29.1	18.7	23.5	30.9	35.7	22.8	29.6	37.7	34.7	39.5
Haryana	45	34.9	17.3	20.5	45.6	35.5	24.9	27.8	29.5	36.7
Karnataka	36.1	26.1	16.6	18.5	40.2	29.1	24.5	27.1	35.2	43.9
Kerala	27.2	19.8	11.5	11.3	34.1	24.4	19.1	20.7	46.8	54.8
Madhya Pradesh	35.6	28.3	13.4	16.6	45.4	36.3	21.2	26.8	33.4	36.9
Maharashtra	19.9	15.1	25.5	24.3	23.3	17.2	34.5	31.7	42.3	51.1
Orissa	41.3	27.3	10.6	11.1	50.3	40	18.8	19.4	30.9	40.6
Punjab	46.8	41	12	15.8	47.2	41.5	18.6	23.4	34.2	35.1
Rajasthan	40.1	29.4	13.2	14.1	43.1	33.4	21.9	26.6	35	40
Tamil Nadu	23.3	17.2	29.3	24.9	25.7	19.2	35.1	33.4	39.3	47.4
Uttar Pradesh	41.4	34.3	12.1	14.9	43.8	36.8	20	23.5	36.2	39.7
West Bengal	27.6	24.6	19	16.3	34	29.8	23.9	22.3	42.1	47.9
GCS	*33.6*	*25.1*	*17.3*	*19*	*38.4*	*29.2*	*24.5*	*27.1*	*37.1*	*43.7*
Arunachal Pradesh	33.3	27.6	3.6	4	48.2	36.5	21.3	24.3	30.5	39.2
Assam	37.2	31.8	9.5	9.2	51.1	42.9	15.1	15.2	33.9	41.9
Himachal Pradesh	31	19.5	5.9	14	39.9	25.6	22.1	34	38	40.3
Manipur	34.7	25.2	12.2	8	39.9	30.9	19.7	21.1	40.3	48
Meghalaya	32.6	22.7	2.1	2.5	40.8	32.3	12.6	14.8	46.6	52.8
Tripura	36.9	24	3.3	2.9	45.8	29.5	11.1	16.9	43.1	53.6
SCS	*35.6*	*27.4*	*8.1*	*9*	*47.6*	*20.1*	*16.3*	*20.1*	*36.1*	*43.4*
A&N Islands	32.4	22.3	7.6	6.4	47	33.4	12.9	23.3	40.1	43.3
Delhi	5.6	1.5	13.7	13.5	6	1.6	20.2	22	73.8	76.4
Goa	13.9	8	20.1	26.2	26.2	15.5	25.3	33.6	48.5	50.9
Pondicherry	14.4	5.4	23	43.5	20.4	9.5	44.6	47.3	35	43.2
UTs	*7.2*	*2.6*	*14.7*	*16*	*9.2*	*3.5*	*21.8*	*24.6*	*69*	*71.9*
All India	*32.2*	*24.3*	*15.4*	*17.2*	*35.3*	*26.5*	*19.9*	*22.1*	*44.7*	*51.4*

Note: The figures for the newly created states have been included in the parent states. Shares as of GSDP at constant prices.

secondary sector has declined in Maharashtra, Tamil Nadu and West Bengal in the post-reform period. The changing share of different sectors in SDP brings out the structural transformation at the state level in the post-reform period. If we see the shares for the newly created states (see Table 2.8), we find that the maximum contribution

Table 2.8 Share of different sectors in GSDP for the newly-created states, 1994–2004 (%)

State	Agriculture	Manufacturing	Primary	Secondary	Tertiary
Jharkhand	19.2	25.3	38.4	33.5	28.1
Uttaranchal	31.9	12.2	36.4	23.5	40.1
Bihar	41.4	4.3	45.1	9.9	45.1
Madhya Pradesh	30.8	15.5	36.5	25.6	37.9
Uttar Pradesh	34.4	15.0	36.9	23.5	39.6
Chhattisgarh	21.0	19.7	35.3	30.1	34.6
Jammu & Kashmir	28.4	6.0	33.3	17.8	48.9
Nagaland	24.9	3.0	28.8	15.1	56.0
Sikkim	26.5	7.2	28.5	22.7	48.8
Mizoram	21.8	12.6	23.7	21.7	54.6

to SDP is from the primary sector in Jharkhand and Chhattisgarh. Nonetheless, Jharkhand is industrially more developed compared to the parent state of Bihar if we consider the contribution made by manufacturing share to SDP. In Uttaranchal, the tertiary sector contributes the largest maximum to SDP, followed by the primary and the secondary sectors in that order.

The range of variation amongst the GCS in the tertiary sector's contribution to SDP has increased in the post-reform period. For example, the range (which varied between 46.8 per cent for Kerala to 29.5 for Haryana in the 1981–93 period) has increased in the 1994–2004 period to, between 54.8 per cent for Kerala and 35.1 per cent for Punjab. The range for the secondary sector's contribution to SDP has also increased in the post-reform period from 17.5 to 18.3 per cent. The range of the secondary sector's contribution to SDP, which varied between 17.6 for Bihar to 35.1 for Tamil Nadu in the pre-reform period, increased to 19.4 for Orissa to 37.7 for Gujarat in the post-reform period. Only in case of the primary sector's contribution to SDP has the range of variation decreased in the post-reform period. The primary sector's share in SDP had a range of variation of 28 per cent, with 23.3 per cent for Maharashtra and 51.3 per cent for Bihar in the pre-reform period. This range has narrowed to 25.1 per cent with 17.2 per cent for Maharashtra and 42.3 per cent for Bihar in the post-reform period. Like the secondary sector, the range of contribution of the manufacturing sector in SDP has also increased in the post-reform period. Orissa had the lowest share of manufacturing at 10.6 per cent and Tamil Nadu the highest at 29.3 per cent, with a range of 18.7 during 1981–1993. In the 1994–2004 period, the range has increased to 19.8 per cent with the share for manufacturing in SDP for Orissa at 11.1 per cent and 30.9 per cent for Gujarat. As far as agriculture is concerned, its highest share was in Punjab at 46.8 per cent and the lowest was for Maharashtra at 19.9 per cent, with a range of 26.9 during the pre-reform phase. This range has marginally come down to 25.9 with the share for Maharashtra at 15.1 and that for Punjab at 41 per cent of the SDP in the post-reform period.

For the SCS, the range of variation of the contribution of primary and secondary sectors to state SDP has increased, and that for the tertiary sector has declined in the post-reform period. For instance, contribution of the tertiary sector was lowest for Arunachal Pradesh at 30.5 per cent and highest for Meghalaya at 46.6 per cent in the pre-reform period, giving a range of 16.1 per cent. This has come down to 14.4 per cent in the post-reform period, with 39.2 per cent for Arunachal Pradesh and 53.6 per cent for Tripura. While the range of contribution of the primary sector has increased from 11.2 to 17.3 per cent in the post-reform period, the states which accounted for the lowest (Himachal Pradesh) and the highest (Assam) contribution of the primary sector in their output has, however, remained the same. As far as UTs are concerned, the range of variation of contribution to different sectors to SDP has declined for all the three broad sub-sectors. However, in the case of manufacturing's contribution to SDP, the range of variation has more than doubled from 15.4 to 37.1 per cent. This is because of a substantial rise in manufacturing sector's contribution from 23 per cent to 43.5 per cent of SDP for Pondicherry in the post-reform period.

In the preceding sections we have discussed the growth of different sectors across the states and the changing shares of different sectors in the SDP in the pre-reform and post-reform period. The discussion of the growth profile in the 'share' and 'growth' dimension leads us to comment on the relative importance of different sectors in their contribution to the growth for the states and how the same has changed over time. This we take up in the next section.

2.7   Sectoral contribution to growth

For GCS as a group, the contribution of the primary and secondary sectors to growth has come down and that of tertiary sector has gone up in the post-reform period (see Table 2.9). This is also observed

Table 2.9   Contribution of different sectors to growth (%)

State	Primary		Secondary		Tertiary	
	1981–93	1994–2004	1981–93	1994–2004	1981–93	1994–2004
Andhra Pradesh	17.6	18.3	26.4	23.2	56.0	58.5
Bihar	28.4	29.9	23.7	23.0	47.9	47.1
Gujarat	5.2	4.1	43.5	44.8	51.3	51.1
Haryana	31.8	10.9	35.9	30.3	32.2	58.9
Karnataka	21.3	8.0	31.1	30.1	47.6	61.9
Kerala	24.8	−7.4	16.1	19.8	59.2	87.6
Madhya Pradesh	25.1	8.7	31.3	38.1	43.6	53.2
Maharashtra	13.3	5.3	34.5	19.3	52.2	75.5
Orissa	16.3	18.3	31.1	13.1	52.6	68.6
Punjab	42.9	21.6	26.0	28.9	31.1	49.5
Rajasthan	35.2	14.5	24.2	29.9	40.6	55.6
Tamil Nadu	19.6	−2.2	32.2	25.8	48.2	76.4
Uttar Pradesh	25.4	23.2	30.6	25.7	43.9	51.1
West Bengal	36.8	14.9	20.9	18.9	42.4	66.2
GCS	22.9	11.2	30.0	26.5	47.1	62.4
Arunachal Pradesh	48.2	−7.3	18.8	14.8	33.0	92.4
Assam	33.0	9.9	15.7	11.0	51.3	79.1
Himachal Pradesh	17.8	7.7	34.5	44.4	47.7	47.8
Manipur	15.0	16.6	49.3	29.8	35.7	53.7
Meghalaya	18.1	30.9	10.0	19.9	72.0	49.3
Tripura	22.6	13.9	8.3	37.1	69.1	49.0
SCS	27.3	12.1	20.6	27.7	52.1	60.3
A&N Islands	44.4	−17.5	18.4	22.2	37.2	95.3
Delhi	2.2	−0.1	13.7	17.9	84.1	82.2
Goa	7.2	2.2	34.6	57.8	58.1	39.9
Pondicherry	10.5	−0.3	31.8	71.3	57.7	29.0
UT	3.3	−2.1	15.5	22.1	81.2	79.9
All India	20.2	9.7	26.2	21.5	53.6	68.8

at the all-India level. There has also been a decline in the primary sector's contribution to SDP for the SCS and the UTs. Though the tertiary sector's contribution to SDP has increased for the SCS, it has undergone a slight decline, albeit from already very high levels in the case of the UTs as a group. However, in contrast to the GCS, the contribution of the secondary sector to the SDP growth has increased for the SCS and UTs in the post-reform period. Within the GCS, the contribution of primary sector to growth has increased only for Andhra Pradesh, Bihar and Orissa in the post-reform period. Kerala and Tamil Nadu showed a negative contribution of the primary sector to growth in the post-reform period. Bihar in the post-reform period has replaced Punjab in the pre-reform era in having the highest contribution to growth originating from the primary sector. While the contribution of the primary sector to growth has increased from 28 per cent to 30 per cent for Bihar, it has declined from 43 per cent to 22 per cent for Punjab in the post-reform period. The contribution of the primary sector to growth shows wide variation in the post-reform period: from a negative 7.4 per cent for Kerala to a positive 30 per cent for Bihar. Overall as a group, the contribution of primary sector to growth has almost halved from 22.9 per cent to 11 per cent for the GCS in the post-reform period.

Though the decline in the contribution of the secondary sector to SDP growth in the post-reform period is more common, Gujarat, Kerala, Madhya Pradesh, Punjab and Rajasthan are the exceptions. While the rise was modest for Gujarat (1 per cent), Kerala (4 per cent) and Punjab (3 per cent), it was much higher for Madhya Pradesh (7 per cent) and Rajasthan (6 per cent). Amongst all states, the contribution of the secondary sector to growth has been the highest for Gujarat both in the pre- and in the post-reform period. The small rise in the contribution from the secondary sector to SDP growth in Gujarat needs to be viewed in the context that the secondary sector's contribution has increased from an already high level of 43.5 per cent in the pre-reform period to 45 per cent in the post-reform period. Further, the contribution of secondary sector to growth, while it increased from a decent 31 per cent in the pre-reform period to 38 per cent for Madhya Pradesh, in Maharashtra it has decreased from 35 per cent to 19 per cent, and for Orissa from 31 per cent to 13 per cent in the post-reform period.

The contribution of the services sector to growth ranged from 47 per cent for Bihar to 88 per cent for Kerala. In the majority of the GCS, the fall in the primary and secondary sector's contribution to growth has been replaced by a rise in the tertiary sector's contribution to growth. Amongst the SCS, Manipur and Meghalaya witnessed a rise in the contribution of the primary sector to growth in the post-reform period. While the rise was marginal for Manipur, it was substantive for Meghalaya, (i.e., from 18 per cent in the pre-reform period to 31 per cent in the post-reform period). Arunachal Pradesh, which had 48 per cent of its growth contributed by the primary sector, has transformed itself into a purely service-based economy with 93 per cent of growth contributed by the tertiary sector in the post-reform period. The contribution of the secondary sector to SDP growth declined for Arunachal Pradesh, Assam and Manipur in the post-reform period and increased for Himachal Pradesh, Meghalaya and Tripura. While the decline was substantial for Manipur (from 49 per cent to 30 per cent in the secondary sector), the rise was appreciable for Tripura from 8 per cent to 37 per cent in the post-reform period. Most of the states in both the GCS and the SCS category have experienced an increase in the contribution of their tertiary sector to SDP growth. Only Bihar and Gujarat in the GCS category have undergone a marginal decline and Meghalaya and Tripura amongst the SCS witnessed a sharp decline in the contribution of their tertiary sector to SDP growth. As far as the UTs are concerned, the primary sector's contribution to growth declined for all the four UTs in the post-reform period. In fact, it was negative for all UTs under study except for Goa in the post-reform period. The secondary sector's contribution to SDP growth has increased for all the four UTs with a substantive rise in the cases of Goa and Pondicherry. Interestingly, while the contribution of the service sector to SDP for UTs as a group has been stable at around 80 per cent in both the pre- and post-reform periods, it has increased tremendously from 37.2 per cent to 95.3 per cent for A&N Islands. Goa and Pondicherry in the post-reform period have shared a growth pattern which is led by the secondary sector.

2.8   Concluding observations

Aspiring to join the league of developed economies by 2020 from a crisis-ridden economy in 1991 has been a great transformation for

India in the last 15 years. This transformation is attributed to the changes in economic policies pursued in the aftermath of the macroeconomic crisis in 1991. How the states have fared under the new economic policy has been the subject of discussion in this chapter. Growth behaviour was analysed for states in the GCS, SCS and UTs categories in two time periods, 1981–93 and 1994–2004. All-India GDP growth rate was at its peak in the 1993–4 period compared to all the other previous subperiods. GDP growth has gone up from 5.4 per cent per annum in 1981–93 to 6.0 per cent in 1994–2004. First, the overall growth performance of the GCS and SCS as a group was only marginally better in the post-reform phase compared to the period preceding it. The difference in the GSDP growth for the GCS and SCS as a group has not changed across the two subperiods. Second, in absolute terms, the GCS have grown faster than the SCS in both the subperiods. Third, in per capita terms, the gap between the GCS and SCS as a group, however, has narrowed in the post-reform period. This is due to lower population growth in the SCS in the 1994–2004 period. Fourth, growth recorded by the GCS states fell rather short of the all-India growth rate in the post-reform period. In fact, the gap between the two has widened in the post-reform phase compared to the pre-reform phase. Fifth, even though all-India GDP growth increased significantly from 5.4 to 6 per cent, GSDP growth for the GCS as a group increased marginally from 5.2 to 5.3 per cent, and for the SCS as a group it increased from 4.4 to 4.5. So the rise in all-India GDP growth in the post-reform phase is explained by the higher growth of the service segment of the economy which is exclusively under the domain of the central government.

The GSDP growth of UTs as a group has marginally slackened in the post-reform period. The UTs have grown at a faster pace than the GCS and the SCS in both the pre-reform and the post-reform periods. To begin with, the UTs had a very high population growth of 3.8 per cent per annum in the pre-reform period which significantly came down to 2.8 in the post-reform period. Consequently, the per capita GSDP growth for UTs has jumped up from 3.6 to 4.4 per cent per annum. The better growth record of the UTs as a group, however, needs to be viewed in the context that they account for a very small proportion of the all-India population and the GDP. Overall, there has been noticeable improvement in per capita GSDP for all the three categories of states in the post-reform period because of the sobering effect that a slowdown in population growth had during this period.

The sectoral growth pattern has been one of deceleration in growth in the primary and secondary sectors and an acceleration of growth in the tertiary segment in the post-reform period. This pattern holds for all the three broad categories of the states, and also at the all-India level. Like the GDP figure at the all-India level, the variability of SDP for GCS and SCS as a group has come down in the post-reform period. Only for the UTs as a group, however, has the variability of SDP increased in the post-reform period. For the GCS as a group, the variability of the output originating from the primary and the tertiary sector has declined, while that for the secondary sector has increased in the post-reform period. If we look at the SCS as a group, except for the tertiary sector growth has been more stable in the primary and secondary segments in the post-reform period. SDP variability for the SCS as a group has also declined in the post-reform period. For the UTs as a group, overall SDP as well as SDP originating from all the three major subsectors was more volatile in the post-reform period. Not only has the share of the tertiary sector increased in the post-reform period, but it has seen higher growth rates and is characterized by lower volatility in the post-reform period. Overall, these results give an element of stability to the high growth momentum noticed in the first eleven years after the reforms.

Appendix 2.1   Data issues

The SDP data published by the CSO spreads over 14 subsectors. The classification of the primary, secondary and tertiary sectors is based on the following scheme.

Primary Sector: Agriculture
Forestry and Logging
Fishing
Mining and Quarrying
Secondary Sector: Manufacturing (Registered and Unregistered)
Construction
Electricity, Gas and Water Supply
Tertiary Sector: Transport (by Railways and other means)
Storage
Communication
Trade, Hotel and Restaurants
Banking and Insurance
Real Estate, Ownership of Dwellings and Business Services
Public Administration Other Services

The primary source of information on SDP is the Bureau/Directorate of Statistics (DoS) of the different state governments. The DoS, however, uses information provided by the CSO in estimating the value added in a number of sectors. Component-wise SDP and the contribution of different sectors to it as reported by the statistical bureaus of the different states are compiled and published by the Central Statistical Organization.[9] A bird's eye view of the interdependence of the central agency, CSO and the state-level DoS in estimating the SDP is given in Table 2A.1. The SDP data are not strictly comparable across states, although the DoS broadly follows a uniform methodology prescribed by the CSO. It is important to keep in mind while dealing with the SDP figures that the CSO does not refine the SDP series of different states to make them consistent with each other, though discussions take place between teams from the states and CSO to reconcile computational differences.

It is worth noting that the concept of SDP indicates the income originating in different states and not the total income accruing to them. At present, there are no estimates of net factor income accruing to a state from outside its boundaries, and therefore it is not possible to take them into account. Highlighting these lacunae in the Indian statistical system, Singh and Srinivasan (2002) contend, 'While SDP is far from ideal as proxy, it is the only feasible measure for empirical work.' The State Bureaus report SDP in both gross and net terms and also at the current market prices and constant prices. At present, the post-1980 SDP figures are available from CSO at two different bases, 1980–1 and 1993–4. For the SDP figures available in the 1980–1 base the reported classification is silent on components of SDP that constitute the primary, secondary and the tertiary subsectors. The SDP figures in the 1993–4 base, however, clearly indicate which subsectors comprise the three broad subsectors.

The scheme of classification of the primary, secondary and tertiary sectors is important in the light of the debate that India has entered into a service sector-led growth trajectory without industrial prominence preceding it. The controversy relates to the classification of construction. While some agencies, such as the Reserve Bank of India, include it under the tertiary sector, the CSO puts it in the secondary sector. Without going into the merit of such a classification, in our analysis we will adopt the CSO classification in defining the constituents of the different subsectors. The SDP figures are available in gross terms and also in net terms after accounting for depreciation; but, given the controversy regarding the computation of depreciation by the states, we have made use of the gross SDP in the estimation of growth rates.

Appendix 2.2   A note on projection of output and population

In any exercise involving the states of India, given the data constraint, discretion is needed in choosing the number of states, the period of study and above all the variables for consideration. Though much depends on the objectives of the study, one is obliged to do some balancing. If we choose to include all the states for study, data availability (especially for some of the hilly states and Union Territories) is a constraint. The State Bureaus are the primary source for the information on output. Many a time, the lag with which SDP data are made available differs considerably across the State Bureaus. This poses a challenge in deciding the terminal year for any empirical study. For instance, as of 21 November 2005, SDP data for 2004–5 were available for Andhra Pradesh, Assam, Bihar, Jharkhand, Kerala, Madhya Pradesh, Meghalaya, Orissa, Pondicherry, Rajasthan and Tamil Nadu, whereas for Jammu and Kashmir, Nagaland and Uttaranchal, SDP data were available only till the year 2001–2, a lag of three years! For the majority of the states, however, SDP data are available up to the year 2003–4. Choosing 2004–5 as the terminal year for the study would have required projection of SDP data for a large number of states which, after all, would be an approximation only. If one would like to keep artificial constructs to a minimum, then possibly one has to contend with the year 2002–3 as the terminal year for the study, which to many would appear rather dated. To strike a balance between making the study period not so dated and at the same time taking due care to keep projected figures in the period of analysis to the minimum, 2003–4 has been taken as the terminal year in the study.

Table 2A.1 lists states for which output figures have been projected to make the data consistent for all states under study. Output, though important, needs to be normalized by the population to make it more acceptable. In India, the prime source for population is the decadal census figures. To get yearly population figures, one way is to spread out the decadal growth evenly over the years. This kind of extrapolation, though mathematically correct, imposes a behaviourial pattern on the data. Fortunately, the CSO, while publishing SDP figures by state, also reports the population figures drawn from a more scientific Sample Registration System. Years for which these population figures are not available have also been projected up to the terminal year of the study, 2003–4.

Table 2A.1 Years for which output and population figures have been projected

State	NSDP constant	GSDP constant	Population
Andaman & Nicobar Islands	2004	2004	2004
Goa	2004	2004	2004
Jammu & Kashmir	2003 and 2004	2003 and 2004	2003 and 2004
Nagaland	2003 and 2004	2003 and 2004	2003 and 2004
Tripura	2004	2004	2004
Uttaranchal	2003 and 2004	2003 and 2004	2003 and 2004
Pondicherry			2003 and 2004
Mizoram			2004
West Bengal			2004

NSDP = Net state domestic product.
Source: CSO.

The SDP and its subcomponents have been projected based on the Compound annual growth rates (CAGR) for the available period since 1993–4. For instance, for Uttaranchal, components of SDP have been projected for the year 2002–3 and 2003–4 on the basis of the CAGR for the period 1993–4 up to 2001–2. For Sikkim (GSDP constant) in 2001–2, Electricity, Gas and Water Supply had a negative output so CAGR could not be computed. The outputs from this segment for the projected years have been assumed to be nil. Similar methodology is followed for projecting the output of the Electricity subcomponent for Jammu & Kashmir (GSDP constant). Hence, the projected figures for secondary sector and thus SDP for these two states are an under-estimation to the extent that the Electricity subsector in these two states had a positive output in 2002–3 and 2003–4.

The population figures have been projected on the basis of average population growth recorded in the previous three years for which actual population figures were available. For instance, the population figure for West Bengal for 2003–4 is projected by applying the average population growth recorded between 2000–1, 2001–2 and 2002–3 to the population figures of 2002–3 and so on. However, for A&N Islands for 2003–4, the average population growth recorded between 2001–2 and 2002–3 is applied as a negative population growth was recorded there during 2000–1. As we are also dealing with the sectoral output, its growth and share in the SDP, it would be only right to flag the issue of non-availability of information at the sectoral level. Tables 2A.2 and 2A.3 list the sectors and periods for which data on different sectors

Table 2A.2   Non-availability of sectoral GSDP

Sector	Period	State
Registered manufacturing	1981–2004	Arunachal Pradesh
Mining	1981–2004	Manipur
Forestry	1981–93	Pondicherry
Mining	1981–2004	Pondicherry
Mining	1981–93	Manipur and Tripura
Storage	1981–93	Kerala, Rajasthan and Arunachal Pradesh
Storage	1981–2004	Andhra Pradesh, Bihar, Madhya Pradesh, Maharashtra, Punjab, Uttar Pradesh, West Bengal, A&N Islands and Pondicherry
Communication	1981–2004	Punjab

Table 2A.3   Non-availability of sectoral NSDP

Sector	Period	State
Registered manufacturing	1981–2004	Arunachal Pradesh
Mining	1981–93	Manipur
Mining	1981–89	Nagaland and Tripura
Mining	1999–2004	Manipur
Forestry	1981–93	Pondicherry
Rail	1981–2004	Punjab, A&N Islands, Jammu & Kashmir, Manipur and Meghalaya
Rail	1981–93	Arunachal Pradesh
Mining	1981–93	Manipur and Tripura
Storage	1981–93	Rajasthan, Uttar Pradesh, Arunachal Pradesh and Nagaland
Storage	1981–2004	Bihar, Kerala, Madhya Pradesh, Maharashtra, Punjab, West Bengal, Jammu & Kashmir and Pondicherry
Communication	1981–2004	Punjab and Jammu & Kashmir
Transport by other means	1981–93	Punjab

are not available for the series on GSDP at constant prices and NSDP at constant prices respectively. However, in some cases, such as storage in Nagaland, data on 'Storage' have been included under 'transport by other means'. Absence of compact sectoral information for different states acts as a limiting factor as regards the degree and level of decomposition that can be carried out while studying sectoral output.

Appendix 2.3 SDP estimation methodology: co-ordination between CSO and DoS

The estimation of SDP is an intricate affair. For a particular state, the DoS concerned liaises with the CSO to estimate the SDP figures. The DoS of each state broadly follows a uniform methodology prescribed by the CSO to estimate the SDP. In practice, both the CSO and the DoS estimate the SDP for a state independently, and subsequently the discrepancies (if any) in the two sets of estimates are sorted out through a process of discussion and possible reconciliation. It may be noted that the scope of the reconciliation extends to differences in computational errors and not the methodology adopted by the CSO and DoS to generate the SDP figures. The consultation process generally is a week-long affair where statisticians from the state and the CSO sort out data discrepancies sitting across the table. Ultimately, what are made available in the public domain are the SDP estimates of the concerned DoS and not that of the CSO.

Broadly, GSDP is the gross value added (GVA) from different sectors of the state economy net of the 'financial intermediation services indirectly measured (FISM)'. Following the recommendations of the 1993 UN System of National Accounts (1993 SNA), FISM is allocated to agriculture, livestock, mining and quarrying, manufacturing (registered and unregistered), electricity and gas, transport, construction, storage, trade, hotels and restaurants, business services, and other services (CSO 1999). CSO provides the estimate of FISM for a state based on the respective estimates of GSDP from the banking and insurance industry. The estimated FISM for a state are allocated to different economic activities on the basis of the GVA estimates of different sectors within that state.

Now, we take up the methodology pursued in practice by the DoS to estimate the GVA for different sectors. Our discussions will be more general in nature and the details will vary across the states. However, particulars, wherever given, correspond to the state of Bihar and the Bihar DoS.

Primary sector

Agriculture

GVA in agriculture is obtained as the difference between the value of agricultural output and value of agricultural input. Agricultural output figures are derived at the state level by the DoS through a combination of estimates from 'crop cutting surveys' and 'eye estimates'. Crop cutting surveys are undertaken for 19 crops, nine vegetables and five fruits, which together account for more than 90 per cent of agricultural output. Eye estimate is done on the basis of 5 per cent of the villages of a state for a production estimate of 'other minor crops'. Agricultural input figures are provided to the DoS by the CSO based on the all-India agricultural input data available with the Ministry of Agriculture (MoA). CSO provides each state's agricultural input figures to the DoS. Agricultural input figures are obtained from the cost of cultivation surveys undertaken in the states by the Ministry of Agriculture. The MoA assigns the cost of cultivation (input) survey task to agricultural universities situated in the states. The agricultural universities conduct the input survey for four to five major crops in the state concerned. The result of the survey is not made public and is directly sent to the MoA. Based on information available with MoA, CSO provides the input figure to the DoS. In Bihar, the Rajendra Agricultural University does the survey on behalf of MoA.

Differences in CSO and DoS estimates for GVA in the agriculture sector. One general source of discrepancy in the GVA figures of CSO and DoS for the agriculture sector relates to horticulture (fruits and vegetables). The cause of the difference arises because CSO's estimate of the production figure for horticulture is based on the information furnished by the National Horticulture Board (NHB). However, the production estimates of some forecast crops (potato, onion, chilli and banana for Bihar) are done by SASA (State Agricultural Statistics Authority). For Bihar, DoS is the concerned SASA. NHB also gets production estimates of the forecast crops and other crops through its state-level arm, the Directorate of Horticulture (DoH). DoH reports information on area and production to NHB. CSO makes use of horticulture production and area figures provided by NHB for all crops except for the forecast crops under horticulture. As CSO's estimate of a part of horticulture value added is obtained from agencies other than the DoS, there is a difference in the estimates of DoS and CSO.

Animal husbandry

Agriculture also includes animal husbandry. GVA in Animal Husbandry is obtained as follows: production data of Animal

Husbandry items are provided by the State Animal Husbandry Department. Production estimates are made not only for 'direct produce' but also for 'increments in stock'. Increments in stock are estimated on the basis of the growth rate of the animal population obtained from the latest Livestock Census. There is also the issue of valuing byproducts including the skin, flesh and bone of dead animals. Byproducts are estimated at rates as old as 1955–6. In this category, not much discrepancy is found between the CSO and the DoS figures.

Fishing

GVA from both and accounted and unaccounted segments is considered. For the accounted fishing segment, the State Pisciculture Board provides data on prices and GVA. GVA for the unaccounted fishing segment is imputed at the rate of 12.5 per cent on the accounted fish production figure. The cost of accounted fishing is taken at the rate of 10 per cent of accounted fishing output, whereas the cost of unaccounted fishing is taken at 1 per cent of unaccounted fishing. We can explain this through a small example. If the accounted fishing output is Rs100, then the GVA from fishing can be obtained as Rs100 + (12.5 per cent of Rs100) − (10 per cent of Rs100) + (1 per cent of Rs12.5) = Rs102.625. For fishing there is no major discrepancy in the figures reported by CSO and DoS.

Mining

GVA for the mining sector is computed based on the information on production, price and input rates supplied to the DoS and CSO by the Indian Bureau of Mines located in Nagpur. Mining also includes major and minor minerals (stone, chip, sands and soil). Minor minerals information is provided by the Mining Department of the state governments concerned. Generally there is no difference in the GVA estimates of DoS and CSO for this sector.

Forestry

The Principal Chief Conservator of Forests provides information on major and minor forest produce. The main contributor in this segment is fuel wood. Production information on fuel wood is obtained from the consumer expenditure survey which gives per capita monthly expenditure on fuel wood in rural and urban areas. Growth in the consumption of fuel wood is based on responses from successive consumer expenditure surveys. Byproducts used as fuel in the agriculture sector are taken as the input and are deducted from the output; 6 per cent of total fuel wood consumed in manufacturing and cremation is added to the input. Here also there is no major difference between CSO and DoS figures.

Secondary sector

Manufacturing

Manufacturing consists of a registered segment and an unregistered one. The information provided by Small Industries Development Corporation (SIDC), a central government entity, is used by the DoS to obtain the unregistered component of manufacturing output. The registered manufacturing data is obtained from the Annual Survey of Industries (ASI). ASI is carried out under the aegis of the National Sample Survey Organization (NSSO). ASI covers a number of units registered under the Factories Act of 1948 in a state based on the employment criterion. ASI covers all industrial units with more than 200 employees and the survey is carried out for 50 per cent of the establishments that employ more than 100 and less than 200 employees.

Electricity

Electricity sector output is derived by the expenditure method. The accounts of State Electricity Boards (SEBs) give the excess of revenue over expenditure, which constitutes the value added from electricity sector. For the central government, electricity companies including DVC, NTPC, BHEPC and PGC, CSO gives the value added for the state to the DoS.

Gas

Refers to bio gas. Information on value added from this sector is provided by CSO to DoS. CSO obtains the figures from the Khadi & Village Industries Commission and the Ministry of Non-Conventional Energy Sources. Estimation of output depends on the number of plants in the state. The value added per plant is based on a benchmark from previous detailed studies on the functioning of certain bio gas plants.

Water Supply

Provision of water supply is done by four agencies: the state government, private enterprise, local bodies and central government. Value added is proxied by the expenditure. For the state sector, expenditure on water supply provided for in the state budget is taken as the output. For local bodies, the output figure is taken to be the salary expenses incurred for provisioning of water in areas of their respective jurisdiction. The compensation or earnings of people engaged in water provisioning in the private sector is obtained from the National Sample Survey (NSS) data which is inflated by the Consumer Price Index for Agricultural Labourers (CPIAL) for the rural areas and by CPI-UNME (Consumer Price Index for urban non-manual employees) for the urban areas.

Construction

Construction activity falls under three broad categories: construction by the government (whether central or state), corporations and the private sector. Estimates of GVA for this sector are based on the expenditure approach. Central and state government budgets give out expenditure under construction for the public sector. For private sector expenditure, reports are obtained from the All India Debt and Investment Survey (AIDIS) and the compound growth rate of residential houses based on two consecutive census results. For the non-residential portion, construction GVA is estimated on the basis of AIDIS and output growth of agriculture and the manufacturing sector. For final estimates of construction, the percentage of GVA to Gross Value of Output (GVO) is used. The value added in the central construction activities in the central government fold is provided by the CSO.

AIDIS also gives the expenditure on building materials. It is assumed that a certain percentage of agricultural output is used for construction activity in rural areas and in urban areas; a specific percentage of manufacturing output goes on construction activity in urban areas.

Services sector

Trade, hotels and restaurants

For trade, the value added from the trade sector broadly consists of both the public and the private sectors. Private sector trading further consists of the organized and the unorganized segments. The value added (VA) in the public trade and organized private trade is provided by the CSO. The DoS computes the value added for unorganized trading. The VA per worker in unorganized trading activities is based on the 'enterprise survey' conducted by the NSS. NSS provides VA per worker both for rural and urban areas. The workforce engaged in the urban and rural trading segment is obtained from CSO. The decennial growth rate of population is used to project the population engaged in trading in a particular year. A rise in the CPI is taken to represent the increase in VA. As such, the VA per worker obtained for a benchmark survey year is inflated by the rise in CPIAL and CPI-UNME to get the VA per worker index for the rural and urban areas respectively for a particular year. The VA per worker is multiplied by the projected population to get the VA from the trading segment for reporting in the SDP estimation.

For hotels, VA is obtained from enterprise survey. The methodology of computing GVA from trade sector is applied to compute the value added from the hotel segment.

Banking and insurance

The VA in the banking and insurance sector is directly provided by the CSO to the DoS.

Real estate, ownership of dwellings, business and legal sector

For real estate, the VA is computed both for rural and urban areas. The enterprise survey gives the VA per worker in real estate for a particular year. Using the approach followed for computing VA, CPIAL and CPI-UNME is used for inflating the VA per worker index to derive the VA from the real estate segment in the rural and urban areas respectively, and the compound growth rate of the workforce is based on enterprise surveys.

The ownership of dwellings is computed for rural and urban areas. The rental value of dwellings is obtained from the enterprise survey. The census gives the number of residential buildings, so:

$$VA = \text{rental value} - \text{cost of maintenance of dwelling units}$$

Rental value is known for a particular year by NSS results. The index approach is followed to arrive at the rental value in the year of estimation. However, the index of rental value is inflated using the price index for urban housing provided by the Labour Bureau, Shimla. The DoS takes half of the growth in urban housing index as the index for rural housing in respective year. AIDIS provides data on repair and maintenance in the base year. The cost of construction index is supplied by the CSO for both rural and urban areas. The cost of maintenance is inflated by the cost of construction index to obtain the cost of maintenance in a particular year.

Public administration

Budget documents belonging to the state governments give salaries, wages and pensions for total government employees (say, RsX), the salaries, wages and pensions of government employees engaged in construction, education, health and sanitation (say, RsY), the direction and administration salary part of construction, education, health and sanitation departments (including the salary of the secretary of the health department or the secretary of education department: say RsZ), and the salary of those officials who are not directly involved with the basic activity of that sector. A teacher is entrusted with the responsibility of teaching but a secretary in the state's education department is involved with the state's education policy. The salary of the secretary falls under public administration value added for the contribution of his services, whereas the salaries of employees in construction, education, health and sanitation departments are included under 'other services':

$$\text{Value added from public administration} = \text{Rs}X + \text{Rs}Z - \text{Rs}Y$$

The value added from public administration also includes expenditure on public administration by the urban and rural local bodies. Estimates regarding central government and quasi-government are provided by the CSO and are added together to obtain an estimate for the public sector.

3
Income Inequality

In the post-reform period, India has witnessed relatively better economic growth compared to the pre-reform period. Higher growth is vouched for, as it enlarges the scope for improving the welfare of the people. Higher growth, however, would be meaningful if the benefits of growth contributed to the well-being of larger sections of people spread across the length and the breadth of the country rather than being confined to a narrower cross-section of the populace or a few specific regions. In other words, the growth process has to be inclusive as the welfare of the people is the prime consideration. The benefits of growth need to be broadly based not only for humanistic concerns but also for the necessary popular support for the sustenance of the growth process. Skewed benefits of growth confined to a particular cross-section of people or to specific regions for a relatively longer period create tensions in the social fabric and would be potential threats to the very growth process. The distributional dimensions of growth thus assume equal, if not greater, importance than growth itself. Hence it becomes imperative that the inequality implications of the growth process be analysed in some detail. A detailed analysis of inequality in the context of present-day India becomes more relevant as the economy has witnessed a new set of economic policies which places greater reliance on market forces. This chapter is devoted to the study of inequality across regions in the post-reform period. To draw a comparative perspective, the scenario with regard to inequality for the pre-reform period is also considered.

Before starting our analysis of income differential across the states, we briefly discuss the movements with regard to an indicator of abject inequality, namely poverty. Poverty levels in India used to be as high as 36 per cent in the year 1993–4, the starting point of the post-reform period. In view of the high incidence of poverty the efficacy of economic growth in overcoming poverty will be a pointer to help assess whether the growth process has been inclusive in nature. Thus one is interested to know how India has fared in reducing poverty in the post-reform period. Estimates of poverty, which are obtained through quinquennial surveys, are indicative of consumption-based inequality. In addition, one can discuss income inequality for which information on a higher (annual) frequency is available. It is entirely possible that the poorer regions may be growing at a higher rate but nonetheless inequality across the regions is either maintained or even increasing. Further, whether the relatively poorer states have been able to catch up with the richer counterparts will provide additional perspectives on the evolution of regional inequality during the post-reform period.

By 1999–2000, poverty levels in India had been reduced to 26 per cent, a decrease of 1.66 per cent per annum between 1993–4 and 1999–2000. Given the methodological differences in the estimation of poverty between 1993–4 and 1999–2000, much credence could not be given to the accuracy of the 1999–2000 estimates of poverty.[1] The methodological confusion created in the 55th round of NSSO (1999–2000) was tackled in the 61st round of NSSO surveys conducted during July 2004 to June 2005. The findings from the 61st round of NSS estimates, however, are quite humbling as far as the record with regard to poverty reduction during the period 1999–2000 to 2004–5 is concerned. The Below Poverty Line (BPL) population has come down by only 0.74 per cent per year between 1999–2000 and 2004–5 which, in net terms, is around eight crore (crore = 10 00 000) people every year. This latest finding belies the earlier optimism about reducing poverty in the post-reform period. Notwithstanding the methodological difference for the 1999–2000 estimates of poverty, the percentage of people living below the poverty line has decreased from 36 per cent in 1993–4 to 26 per cent in 1999–2000, and further to 22 per cent in 2004–5.

Although the percentage of population living below the poverty line has come down during the post-reform period, the growing population has neutralized this decline when one considers the absolute number of the BPL population. The BPL population in India at 22 per cent of poverty turns out to mean 230 million people in 2004–5. This is suggestive of the relatively unchanged position in India as far as the BPL population is concerned during the reform period. More details, when available from the NSSO estimates, would throw light on the achievement of different states in the matter of poverty reduction. In the absence of details on state specific incidence of poverty from the 2004–5 NSSO estimates, we couch our discussion in terms of income inequality.

The rest of the chapter is organized along the following lines: section 3.1 discusses inequality in terms of per capita income differential across the states. Analysis of inequality across states through the rank analysis has been done in section 3.2. Section 3.3 studies the movement in inequality indices over time. This section also discusses the decomposition of inequality across the sectors and the impact of a marginal change in income from a particular source on inequality. Section 3.4 provides a detailed discussion on convergence behaviour of Indian states in the post-reform period. Concluding observations on inequality of income are covered in Section 3.5.

3.1   Income differential across states

A crude indicator of inequality across the regions is the difference in the highest and the lowest per capita income (PCI). How the PCI differential has evolved over time gives a broad idea of whether growth has become more or less equalized (see Table 3.1). We will couch our discussion separately for the General Category States (GCS) and the Special Category States (SCS).

For the former group, the GCS, the difference between the highest PCI (Punjab) and lowest PCI (Bihar), which was Rs5,102 in 1981, had grown to Rs7,683 by 1990 with no change in the states occupying the top and bottom position. The scenario of Bihar having the lowest PCI and Punjab having the highest had not changed by 1993, the final year of the pre-reform period in our classification. Have the relative positions changed in the post-reform years? Not until 2000. Notwithstanding Bihar's unchanged PCI position relative to the other states up to 2004, there have been new contenders for the topmost PCI position. Punjab and Bihar shared the top and bottom positions respectively until as late as 1999. In the year 2000, Maharashtra replaced Punjab in having the highest PCI. Punjab then regained the

Table 3.1 Per capita state income over the years (Rs)

State	1981	1984	1987	1990	1993	1994	1997	2000	2002	2004
GCS										
Andhra Pradesh	4,586	5,295	4,976	6,691	6,777	7,416	8,514	9,445	10,609	11,333
Bihar	3,363	3,680	4,162	4,092	3,731	3,750	3,903	4,233	4,127	4,701
Gujarat	6,480	7,826	7,604	8,832	10,325	9,796	13,206	13,298	13,232	16,779
Haryana	7,549	7,894	8,999	10,363	10,895	11,079	12,591	13,308	14,181	15,721
Karnataka	4,980	5,446	5,777	6,732	7,460	7,838	8,990	10,912	12,029	13,141
Kerala	5,666	5,284	5,460	6,408	7,259	7,983	9,145	10,430	10,762	12,328
Madhya Pradesh	5,113	5,374	4,952	5,735	6,093	6,572	6,975	7,846	7,622	8,310
Maharashtra	7,145	7,566	7,820	10,016	11,257	12,183	13,464	15,262	14,642	16,479
Orissa	4,149	4,443	4,534	5,365	4,663	4,896	4,773	5,735	5,802	6,487
Punjab	8,465	9,176	10,425	11,775	12,426	12,710	13,705	14,809	15,195	15,800
Rajasthan	4,284	5,349	5,009	6,016	6,927	6,182	7,862	8,555	8,763	9,685
Tamil Nadu	5,305	5,602	6,215	7,415	8,368	8,955	10,451	12,167	12,484	12,976
Uttar Pradesh	4,095	4,373	4,494	5,106	5,177	5,151	5,789	5,749	5,716	6,116
West Bengal	4,984	5,293	5,514	5,862	6,449	6,756	7,880	9,320	10,380	11,621
SCS										
Arunachal Pradesh	4,113	4,768	5,749	6,187	7,895	8,733	8,590	8,890	9,401	9,678
Assam	4,611	5,277	5,157	5,446	5,588	5,715	5,793	5,785	6,066	6,520
Himachal Pradesh	5,760	5,837	6,347	7,608	7,665	7,870	9,140	11,051	11,326	12,302
Jammu & Kashmir	6,004	6,067	6,117	5,849	6,140	6,543	6,978	7,384	7,541	8,751
Manipur	4,416	4,761	4,941	5,249	5,867	5,841	6,016	7,090	7,445	10,795
Meghalaya	5,547	5,519	5,695	6,506	6,590	6,893	7,602	8,996	9,905	10,797
Nagaland	5,920	7,434	7,675	8,432	9,525	9,129	9,880	8,726	11,674	7,858
Tripura	3,998	3,859	3,897	4,820	5,097	5,534	6,239	7,967	9,664	12,218

Source: CSO.

highest PCI position in the years 2001 and 2002, only to be replaced by Maharashtra again in the year 2003. The new face in the highest position in 2004 is Gujarat. The differential between the highest and lowest PCI increased to Rs12,078 in the year 2004.

For the SCS, Jammu & Kashmir and Tripura occupied the highest and lowest PCI positions with an income differential of Rs2,006 in the year 1981. From 1982 to 2004, Nagaland had the best PCI among the SCS with Tripura lingering as the lowest PCI. There has been some mobility in the extreme points in the post-reform period for the SCS. In 1997 Assam replaced Tripura at the bottom, while

Nagaland continued to have the highest PCI. For the years 1999 and 2000, Himachal Pradesh replaced Nagaland in occupying the top PCI position and Assam continued to be the lowest. Again for three years during 2001–3, Nagaland had the highest PCI. In 2004, Himachal Pradesh again occupied the highest PCI position. Assam continued to bring up the rear for eight years, from 1997 to 2004. The income differential between the top and bottom PCI has consistently increased, from Rs3,595 in 1994 to Rs5,782 in 2004.

Analysis of income position, however, becomes cumbersome beyond a certain point and is of limited use when commenting on the mobility of states in the middle of the ladder. To get a holistic perspective on the income mobility of the states, we undertake a rank analysis of the GCS and SCS.

3.2 Rank analysis

The evolution of state rankings among the GCS and SCS in the post-reform period is depicted in Table 3.2. The states have been ranked in descending order of PCI (the state with the highest PCI is ranked 1 and the state with the second highest PCI is ranked 2, and so on). While Punjab, Haryana, Maharashtra, Gujarat and Tamil Nadu occupy the top five places in that order, Bihar, Orissa and Uttar Pradesh, Rajasthan and Madhya Pradesh are the lowest five states in the pre-reform period. Among the SCS category, Nagaland turns out to be the best, and Tripura the worst, performer.

In the post-reform period, among the GCS, both Punjab and Maharashtra have the same average rank with the latter having a slightly smaller dispersion. Gujarat, Haryana and Tamil Nadu are the three other best performers in terms of PCI ranks. Bihar, Orissa, Uttar Pradesh, Madhya Pradesh and Rajasthan occupy the bottom five ranks. So we find the world does not seem to have changed for the top five or the bottom five performers in between the pre- and post-reform periods. To give credence to the ranks, the average rank obtained by the states in the study period and the degree of dispersion of ranks over the years are also provided. To ascertain the stability or concordance between the rankings of the states in different years the coefficient of concordance has been computed. The coefficient of concordance signifies the agreement of ranks over the entire period and for the subperiods for the general and special category states. The steps involved in computing the coefficient of concordance are

Table 3.2 Ranking of states (1994–2004)

States	1994	1995	1996	1997	1998	1999	2000	2001	2002	2003	2004	Average rank	Standard deviation of ranks	Worse years cases
GCS														
Andhra Pradesh	8	8	8	8	10	8	8	8	8	9	9	8.4	0.7	3
Bihar	14	14	14	14	14	14	14	14	14	14	14	14.0	0.0	0
Gujarat	4	4	3	3	3	3	4	5	4	4	1	3.4	1.0	6
Haryana	3	3	4	4	4	4	3	3	3	3	4	3.5	0.5	5
Karnataka	7	7	7	7	6	6	6	6	6	6	5	6.2	0.6	4
Kerala	6	6	6	6	7	7	7	7	7	7	7	6.7	0.5	7
Madhya Pradesh	10	11	11	11	11	11	11	11	11	11	11	11.0	0.3	0
Maharashtra	2	2	1	2	1	2	1	2	2	1	2	1.6	0.5	7
Orissa	13	13	13	13	13	13	13	13	12	13	12	12.8	0.4	9
Punjab	1	1	2	1	2	1	2	1	1	2	3	1.6	0.7	5
Rajasthan	11	9	10	10	8	10	10	10	10	10	10	9.7	0.8	9
Tamil Nadu	5	5	5	5	5	5	5	4	5	5	6	5.0	0.4	1

Uttar Pradesh	12	12	12	12	12	12	12	12	13	12	13	12.2	0.4	2
West Bengal	9	10	9	9	9	9	9	9	9	8	8	8.9	0.5	9
SCS														
Arunachal Pradesh	2	3	2	3	3	3	3	5	5	5	5	3.7	1.2	4
Assam	7	6	6	8	8	8	8	8	8	8	8	7.6	0.8	8
Himachal Pradesh	3	2	3	2	2	1	1	2	2	2	1	1.9	0.7	8
Manipur	6	7	8	7	7	7	7	7	7	6	6	6.9	0.6	8
Meghalaya	4	4	4	4	4	4	2	3	3	3	4	3.5	0.7	7
Tripura	8	8	7	6	6	5	5	4	4	4	3	5.2	1.7	5
Jammu & Kashmir	5	5	5	5	5	6	6	6	6	7	7	5.8	0.8	6
Nagaland	1	1	1	1	1	2	4	1	1	1	2	1.5	0.9	3

Table 3.3   Coefficient of concordance

Period	GCS	SCS
1981–93	0.94	0.85
	(297.00)	(125.00)
1994–2004	0.98	0.83
	(159.00)	(77.00)
1981–2004	0.95	0.75
	(140.00)	(64.00)

Note: The figures in parentheses indicate the computed Chi-square values.

discussed in Appendix 3.1. We find that the null hypothesis of rank disagreement is rejected for both the subperiods and for both GCS and SCS (see Table 3.3).

Following the methodology of Boyle and McCarthy (1997), one can construct an index of concordance to ascertain the mobility of the ranks over the years. Boyle and McCarthy (1997) proposed a simple measure for assessing the intertemporal mobility of states (or countries) in terms of the ranking of the states by income levels. Boyle and McCarthy (1997) proposed a multi-annual version (RCt) and a binary version (RCat) of the rank concordance index. The multi-annual measure, extending over the whole period, contains all possible pairs of years for which the binary measure could be computed. We have calculated the multi-annual measure for the intertemporal mobility in the ranks of the states. The details on the computation of the index of concordance are dealt with in Appendix 3.2. The measure seeks to capture the change in the rankings as reflected by Kendall's index of rank concordance. The value of the rank concordance measure lies between zero and unity. The closer the value of the measure to zero, the greater is the extent of mobility within the distribution. We have computed[2] the index of concordance for each category of states and also for the pre- and post-reform periods (see Table 3.4). The index of concordance indicates that among the GCS, the relative income position of the different states did not differ much over the entire 24-year period. In contrast to the GCS, there is fair amount of mobility in the rankings of the SCS when we consider the full 24-year period. Seen in terms of the pre- and post-reform subperiods, the concordance index indicates that the mobility of the GCS has been virtually nil in the

Table 3.4 Index of rank concordance

Year	GCS	SCS	GCS	SCS	GCS	SCS
1981	1.00	1.00	1.00	1.00		
1982	0.98	0.95	0.98	0.95		
1983	0.98	0.96	0.98	0.96		
1984	0.94	0.97	0.94	0.97		
1985	0.94	0.97	0.94	0.97		
1986	0.95	0.96	0.95	0.96		
1987	0.94	0.94	0.94	0.94		
1988	0.95	0.92	0.95	0.92		
1989	0.94	0.89	0.94	0.89		
1990	0.94	0.88	0.94	0.88		
1991	0.94	0.87	0.94	0.87		
1992	0.94	0.86	0.94	0.86		
1993	0.94	0.85	0.94	0.85		
1994	0.94	0.84			1.00	1.00
1995	0.94	0.85			0.99	0.98
1996	0.94	0.84			0.99	0.96
1997	0.95	0.84			0.99	0.94
1998	0.95	0.83			0.99	0.94
1999	0.95	0.82			0.99	0.92
2000	0.95	0.80			0.99	0.88
2001	0.95	0.78			0.99	0.86
2002	0.95	0.77			0.99	0.85
2003	0.95	0.76			0.99	0.84
2004	0.95	0.75			0.98	0.83

post-reform period. For the SCS, there has been some mobility across the states in both the pre-reform and the post-reform periods. Thus we find that there is nothing peculiar associated with the post-reform period as far as the mobility in income position of either category of states is concerned. If the GCS are exhibiting immobility in PCI ranks in the post-reform period, it is a characteristic that has been observed since the pre-reform days.

3.3 Inequality measures

To add robustness to our findings based on rank analysis, we use several other measures of inequality of per capita income across the states under the 'general' and 'special' category. This also helps us to understand better the dynamics of inequality in income over time. We report the Gini coefficient and a series of other summary inequality measures: the Theil Entropy Index, the Kakwani Index, the Theil Index and the Mehran Index. These measures were selected to reflect a variety of inequality attributes of the income distributions. The Gini coefficient is sensitive to changes across the distribution. It meets the criteria of mean independence (double everyone's income and the value of the index remains the same), symmetry (any two individuals can exchange their positions in the income scale but the index of inequality does not change), independence from sample size, and the Pigou–Dalton transfer sensitivity (inequality is increased when a transfer is made from a poor person to a rich one). Gini and Theil Indices are measures that rank the distribution of income with equal weights above and below the average. The Entropy Index is most sensitive to changes at the lower end of the distribution. The Theil Index is more balanced in giving weight across the distribution and so is closer to the Gini in that regard. The Mehran Index gives higher weights to low incomes. The Kakwani Index is similar to the Gini, which is 1 minus the area under the Lorenz Curve measuring the inequality in the distribution of income, except that the Kakwani Index squares the area under the Lorenz Curve so that larger values are given greater weights. The Gini coefficient is the most widely used indicator of inequality.

Before we give a detailed analysis of inequality based on the Gini coefficient, we discuss the status with regard to inequality in per capita income as suggested by a broad array of inequality indices (Table 3.5). The evolution in the index values brings out the following points. First, all the inequality measures reported indicate a worsening of inequality over the years for both the general and the special category states. Second, the extent of rise in inequality has been much lower for the SCS than the GCS. More of the rise in inequality indices occurred in the pre-reform period than in the post-reform period and this was even more marked for the general category states. Now we discuss the evolution of the Gini over time.

As far as the GCS are concerned, in the 1994–2004 period, amongst all sectors, the Gini coefficient was greatest for the secondary sector and smallest for the primary sector. Though the Gini for the primary sector did not show any sustained upward trend, by 1993 it had gone up to 0.19 from 0.16 in 1981. In subsequent years it hovered around the 1993 value; it increased to 0.20 in 2004. The tertiary

Table 3.5 Inequality measure over the years

Year	Entropy index (GE(a), a = −1)		Kakwani measure		Mehran measure		Theil index (GE(a), a = 1)	
	GCS	SCS	GCS	SCS	GCS	SCS	GCS	SCS
1981	0.033	0.013	0.019	0.007	0.202	0.132	0.033	0.012
1982	0.035	0.016	0.021	0.009	0.210	0.148	0.035	0.016
1983	0.037	0.017	0.022	0.010	0.214	0.145	0.037	0.017
1984	0.032	0.017	0.019	0.010	0.192	0.146	0.032	0.017
1985	0.035	0.016	0.021	0.009	0.209	0.139	0.036	0.015
1986	0.039	0.016	0.024	0.009	0.217	0.136	0.041	0.014
1987	0.037	0.018	0.023	0.010	0.211	0.149	0.040	0.017
1988	0.039	0.016	0.024	0.010	0.218	0.136	0.041	0.017
1989	0.039	0.015	0.023	0.010	0.217	0.137	0.040	0.016
1990	0.043	0.016	0.025	0.010	0.230	0.143	0.043	0.016
1991	0.046	0.017	0.026	0.010	0.238	0.150	0.045	0.017
1992	0.047	0.016	0.027	0.010	0.241	0.148	0.045	0.016
1993	0.060	0.019	0.032	0.012	0.267	0.157	0.054	0.020
1994	0.062	0.017	0.032	0.010	0.272	0.148	0.054	0.017
1995	0.062	0.020	0.032	0.012	0.273	0.164	0.053	0.020
1996	0.072	0.023	0.035	0.014	0.283	0.173	0.058	0.023
1997	0.075	0.018	0.036	0.011	0.290	0.156	0.061	0.018
1998	0.069	0.018	0.034	0.011	0.281	0.155	0.056	0.018
1999	0.071	0.017	0.034	0.009	0.283	0.150	0.057	0.016
2000	0.074	0.017	0.035	0.010	0.286	0.146	0.058	0.016
2001	0.075	0.024	0.036	0.014	0.290	0.178	0.058	0.022
2002	0.080	0.023	0.036	0.013	0.289	0.173	0.058	0.021
2003	0.080	0.022	0.038	0.012	0.298	0.171	0.062	0.020
2004	0.081	0.022	0.037	0.012	0.293	0.171	0.060	0.020

sector had a Gini coefficient close to that of the primary sector but much lower than that of the secondary sector. The Gini for the period 1981–6 remained at 0.18 and it came down to 0.17 during the period 1987–91. By 1994, the Gini for the tertiary sector had increased to 0.20 and it remained at that level until 1999; since then it has gradually increased to 0.22. Gini for the overall income or NSDP conveys a status quo picture in the post-reform period. Starting with 0.14 in 1981, it gradually deteriorated to 0.17 by 1990 and further to 0.19 by 1993. Except for a decline in 1995 to 0.18, it has remained more or less the same ever since (see Figure 3.1).

For the SCS, the interesting finding is that the Gini coefficient for the tertiary sector has declined substantially over the entire period of our study. The decline was more perceptible in the pre-reform period. It declined from 0.26 in 1981 to 0.16 in 1993 and further to 0.11 by the year 2004. Gini coefficients for overall income have gone up in both the pre- and post-reform period, with much of the increase noticed in the pre-reform period. For the primary sector, much of the deterioration had taken place by 1993. Between 1994 and 1999,

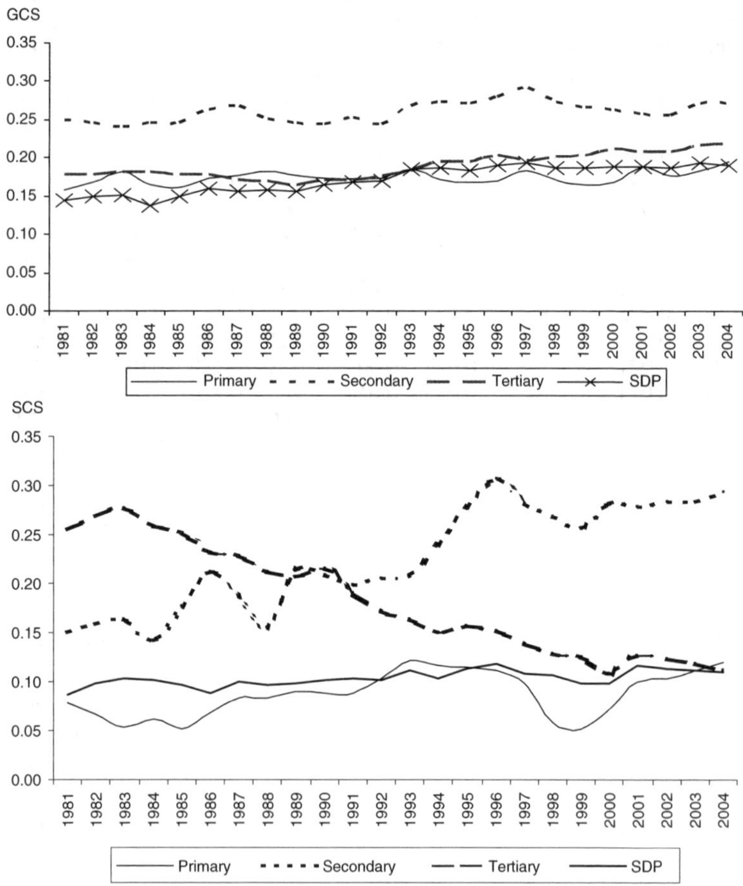

Figure 3.1   Sectoral Gini, GCS and SCS

Gini for the primary sector had declined but it started picking up again from 2000 and by 2004 had reached the peak level of 1993. In the secondary sector, the Gini coefficient increased from 0.15 to 0.21 between 1981 and 1993 and it deteriorated further in the post-reform period to 0.29 in 2004.

Having found that inequality of income has worsened over the years, it would be relevant from a policy perspective to enquire whether inequality is pervasive in all sectors of the economy or whether it is confined to a few specific sectors. In other words, deciphering the sectoral pattern of inequality can help in identifying the sources of inequality. Towards this end, we segregate the economy into three broad sectors: primary, secondary and tertiary. Shorrocks (1982), Lerman and Yitzhaki (1985) and Stark, Taylor and Yitzhaki (1986) have suggested methods to decompose the Gini coefficient by income source. The decomposition method also allows the calculation of the impact that a marginal change in a particular income source will have on inequality. Lopez-Feldman (2005) has operationalized this sort of decomposition. The results of Shorrocks (1982) and Lerman and Yitzhaki (1985) show that the Gini coefficient for total income inequality, G, when decomposed by income source, can be represented as the combined influence of the share of each source k (S_k) in total income, the source Gini (G_k) corresponding to the distribution of income from source k and the Gini correlation of income from source k (R_k) with the distribution of total income. As noted by Stark, Taylor and Yitzhaki (1986), the relation between these three terms has a clear and intuitive interpretation. If an income source represents a large share of total income it may potentially have a large impact on inequality. However, if it is perfectly equally distributed ($G_k = 0$), it cannot influence inequality even if its magnitude is large. On the other hand, if this income source is large and unequally distributed (S_k and G_k are large), it may either increase or decrease inequality, depending upon where the recipients of this income are placed in the income distribution. If the income source is unequally distributed and is tilted disproportionately towards those at the top of the income distribution (R_k is positive and large), its contribution to inequality will be positive. However, if it is unequally distributed but targets poor households (individuals), the income source may have an equalizing effect on the income distribution.

Further, Lerman and Yitzhaki (1985) show that, by using this particular method of Gini decomposition, one can estimate the effect of small changes in a specific income source on inequality, holding income from all other sources constant. Such decomposition has been tried and its implication for inequality has been studied for GCS and SCS. The last column of Table 3.6 refers to the impact that a 1 per cent change in the respective income source will have on inequality. Four additional elements are included in the table: the share of each income source in total income (S_k), the source of Gini (G_k), the Gini correlation of income from source k with the distribution of total income (R_k) and the share of each income source in total inequality.

If we see the result for 1981 for the GCS (Appendix 3.3), we find that a 1 per cent increase in tertiary income, other things remaining constant, increases the Gini coefficient of total income by 0.049 per cent. Tertiary income had the second largest share in total income (0.337) and is unequally distributed (0.179), and the Gini correlation between tertiary income and total income is the highest (0.919) compared to the other two sectors, indicating that tertiary income favours the rich more than any other income source. An income source may be unequally distributed and yet may favour the poor.

This is the case for income from the primary sector for the year 1981. Primary sector incomes have an equalizing effect on the distribution of total income in 1981. This is chiefly due to two factors. The source of Gini is the lowest for this sector and Gini correlation (0.647) between primary sector income and total income again is the lowest compared to other sectors. The primary sector for the GCS continued to have a positive impact on inequality all through the period of our study. In other words, in spite of the fact that Gini for primary sector increased from 0.172 in the year 1994 to 0.196 in 2004, primary sector income had an equalizing effect on the distribution of total income. This was possible as income from primary sector had a lesser bias towards the rich in the income scale.

Tertiary sector income had an equalizing effect on the distribution of total income over the last five years of the pre-reform period (1989–93) and the same scenario continued up until the first two years of the post-reform period. The equalizing effect of tertiary sector income, which accounts for the highest share in income, was found last in 1997. The Gini correlation was originally very high in the post-reform period. Because of the low source of Gini in the initial years

Table 3.6 Gini decomposition of sectoral inequality (1994–2004)

Source	Year	GCS					SCS				
		S_k	G_k	R_k	Share	% change	S_k	G_k	R_k	Share	% change
Primary	1994	0.367	0.172	0.836	0.282	−0.085	0.376	0.116	0.549	0.231	−0.145
Secondary	1994	0.241	0.273	0.929	0.327	0.086	0.161	0.240	0.747	0.279	0.118
Tertiary	1994	0.392	0.196	0.949	0.391	−0.002	0.463	0.150	0.731	0.490	0.027
SDP	1994		0.187					0.104			
Primary	1995	0.365	0.168	0.855	0.285	−0.080	0.371	0.115	0.592	0.224	−0.148
Secondary	1995	0.247	0.271	0.911	0.331	0.084	0.170	0.279	0.750	0.314	0.144
Tertiary	1995	0.388	0.195	0.937	0.384	−0.004	0.459	0.157	0.729	0.462	0.004
SDP	1995		0.184					0.113			
Primary	1996	0.342	0.170	0.730	0.223	−0.120	0.354	0.112	0.595	0.197	−0.156
Secondary	1996	0.256	0.281	0.945	0.357	0.101	0.192	0.307	0.793	0.392	0.200
Tertiary	1996	0.402	0.204	0.978	0.420	0.019	0.455	0.152	0.711	0.411	−0.044
SDP	1996		0.191					0.119			
Primary	1997	0.349	0.183	0.806	0.265	−0.084	0.355	0.098	0.421	0.136	−0.219
Secondary	1997	0.246	0.293	0.917	0.339	0.093	0.183	0.282	0.829	0.397	0.214
Tertiary	1997	0.406	0.197	0.965	0.396	−0.009	0.462	0.138	0.789	0.467	0.005
SDP	1997		0.194					0.108			
Primary	1998	0.321	0.171	0.713	0.209	−0.112	0.337	0.059	0.495	0.093	−0.245
Secondary	1998	0.254	0.273	0.959	0.355	0.101	0.189	0.268	0.886	0.418	0.230
Tertiary	1998	0.425	0.202	0.953	0.436	0.011	0.474	0.129	0.857	0.489	0.015
SDP	1998		0.187					0.107			
Primary	1999	0.318	0.164	0.792	0.221	−0.097	0.339	0.052	0.551	0.098	−0.240
Secondary	1999	0.251	0.266	0.950	0.339	0.088	0.183	0.257	0.895	0.425	0.241
Tertiary	1999	0.431	0.204	0.939	0.440	0.009	0.478	0.125	0.792	0.477	−0.001
SDP	1999		0.187					0.099			
Primary	2000	0.301	0.169	0.751	0.202	−0.099	0.334	0.071	0.550	0.133	−0.201
Secondary	2000	0.250	0.263	0.911	0.318	0.068	0.175	0.281	0.798	0.401	0.226
Tertiary	2000	0.449	0.212	0.955	0.481	0.032	0.491	0.108	0.861	0.466	−0.025
SDP	2000		0.189					0.098			
Primary	2001	0.291	0.189	0.771	0.224	−0.067	0.327	0.100	0.653	0.182	−0.145
Secondary	2001	0.240	0.259	0.915	0.300	0.061	0.191	0.278	0.686	0.311	0.119
Tertiary	2001	0.470	0.209	0.916	0.476	0.006	0.482	0.126	0.979	0.507	0.025
SDP	2001		0.189					0.117			
Primary	2002	0.293	0.176	0.764	0.211	−0.081	0.330	0.104	0.793	0.240	−0.089
Secondary	2002	0.230	0.257	0.940	0.297	0.067	0.181	0.283	0.555	0.251	0.070
Tertiary	2002	0.478	0.209	0.920	0.492	0.014	0.490	0.124	0.948	0.509	0.019
SDP	2002		0.187					0.113			
Primary	2003	0.260	0.183	0.689	0.169	−0.091	0.325	0.111	0.732	0.234	−0.091
Secondary	2003	0.244	0.272	0.914	0.312	0.069	0.179	0.284	0.610	0.276	0.097
Tertiary	2003	0.496	0.218	0.929	0.518	0.022	0.497	0.118	0.955	0.496	−0.001
SDP	2003		0.194					0.112			
Primary	2004	0.270	0.196	0.557	0.155	−0.115	0.320	0.120	0.563	0.197	−0.123
Secondary	2004	0.236	0.271	0.981	0.331	0.095	0.189	0.293	0.745	0.375	0.186
Tertiary	2004	0.494	0.219	0.903	0.513	0.020	0.496	0.111	0.888	0.442	−0.054
SDP	2004		0.190					0.110			

of the post-reform phase, the tertiary sector income used to have a marginal equalizing effect. As in the later years of the post-reform period the source of Gini from tertiary sector increased considerably, we find the equalizing impact of tertiary sector income vanishing. Though the tertiary sector has grown at a faster pace in most of the states and its share in overall SDP has increased in the post-reform period, income originating from this sector had an inequalizing impact on the distribution of income for most part of the post-reform period. The increasing contribution to overall inequality from the tertiary sector in the post-reform period is a challenge for the growth paradigm currently being pursued in India. For the SCS, the very high source Gini, coupled with a high Gini correlation, implied that the tertiary sector had an inequalizing effect throughout the pre-reform period. In the post-reform period, source Gini from the tertiary sector has been significantly reduced; but Gini correlation has remained on the high side. The interplay of these two opposing forces, depending on their relative strengths, has meant the tertiary sector has a slight equalizing effect for five out of the 11 years in the post-reform period. Interestingly, the secondary sector, which used to have an equalizing effect in the pre-reform period, started having an inequalizing effect in the post-reform period. This is because both source Gini and the Gini correlation for the secondary sector have deteriorated in the post-reform period.

3.4   Convergence analysis

Convergence: the state of the debate

The literature on regional catch-up or convergence has been enriched by the seminal contributions of Barro and Sala-í-Martin (1991). The two notions of convergence that are used extensively in empirical works are sigma (σ) convergence and beta (β) convergence. In simple terminology, σ convergence requires cross-sectional disparity of per capita income to decline over time. Beta convergence, on the other hand, requires poorer economies to grow faster than wealthier ones. The idea that initially poorer regions might grow faster has its formal conceptualization in the neoclassical growth model of Solow (1956). The key assumption that drives the convergence result in neoclassical models is that of diminishing returns to reproducible capital.

The relatively less well-off economies are generally endowed with lesser stocks of physical capital, and hence higher marginal rates of return on capital. Therefore, for any given rate of investment, the relatively worse-off regions will have faster growth in the transition phase. Here it is pertinent to note that such β-convergence implied by the Solow model is conditional and perceptible only after other factors, which may cause variation in steady states, have been accounted for. Anything that drives apart investment rates in rich and poor regions will, *ceteris paribus*, drive their steady-state income levels apart, even as each region is converging to its diverging steady state. In contrast to this, one can define a stronger kind of convergence that takes place unconditionally or absolutely, where initially poorer states grow faster, notwithstanding differences in initial conditions. In terms of the Solow (1956) model, if one postulates that all regions in the long run have no tendency to display variation in the rates of investment, capital depreciation, population growth, and so forth, then such a model would generate unconditional or absolute convergence to a common steady state per-capita income. Subsequently, Mankiw, Romer and Weil (1992) have suggested that in an augmented Solow model, where growth is expressed explicitly as a function of the determinants of the ultimate steady state, the initial level of income is a 'natural' way to study convergence. Let us now examine whether the theoretical construct on convergence holds in the empirical plane.

Though a large number of studies have empirically tested the convergence phenomenon across nations, we will confine ourselves here to the studies on the Indian states/regions (see Table 3.7). While some studies have investigated convergence in the cross-sectional dimension (Bajpai and Sachs 1996 and 2002), others have used panel estimates (Aiyar 2001; Trivedi 2002). A typical pattern adopted in most of the studies is to test for convergence in various subperiods. Unconditional convergence found in some studies for the 1960s are based on the sign of the coefficient of initial per capita income, but they are often not statistically significant. However, most of the studies find evidence in support of statistically significant conditional (β) convergence. Of late, it has become popular to apply convergence style regressions to factors other than income to study inequality.[3]

It has been established in the literature that beta convergence is a necessary but not a sufficient condition for sigma convergence (Barro

72

Table 3.7 Select convergence studies for Indian states

Study	Period	States	Main results
Cashin and Sahay (1996)	1961–91	20	Slow absolute and conditional convergence. Weak impact of internal migration.
Sachs and Bajpai (1996)	1961–90	19	Convergence of per capita income only during the sub-period 1961-71 and divergence during the sub-periods 1972-82 and 1983-93
Nagaraj, Varoudakis and Véganzonès (1998)	1970–94	17	Absolute divergence but conditional convergence. Share of agriculture, infrastructure, and political and institutional factors matter for convergence.
Rao, Shand and Kalirajan (1999)	1965–95	14	Absolute and conditional divergence, faster in early 1990s. Private investment matters.
Dasgupta, Maiti, Mukherjee, Sarkar and Chakrabarti (2000)	1961–96	21	States of India do not converge in per capita SDP terms but converge in shares of different sectors in the SDP.
Aiyar (2001)	1971–96	19	Conditional convergence; infrastructure, private investment and non-measured institutional factors matter.
Ahluwalia (2002a)	1981–99	14	Gini coefficient of per capita SDP (weighted by population) increased in the 1990s compared to the 1980s. Convergence not allowed for, but private investment matters for growth.
Singh and Srinivasan (2002)	1991–99	14	No clear evidence of conditional convergence or divergence. Financial variables matter for growth.
Sachs, Bajpai and Ramiah (2002)	1980–98	14	Absolute divergence for all states (and for rich group but not poor group) for 1990–8; qualitative discussion of possible conditioning factors (social and geographic variables).
Trivedi (2002)	1960–92	16	There is no evidence of unconditional convergence, but there is clear and robust evidence of conditional convergence after holding constant proxies for educational and non-educational human capital and physical capital.

and Sala-ì-Martin 1995). Other things being equal, β convergence may eventually lead to σ convergence. However, if other things are not equal, perhaps because each region is subject to random disturbances, then β convergence need not imply a reduction in the dispersion of income levels over time. Hence, conditional β convergence, as implied by the Solow model, is consistent with σ divergence. For instance, anything that drives apart steady-state incomes in rich and poor regions will lead to σ divergence, although each region might still be (conditionally) converging to a diverging steady state. A complete analysis of the convergence behaviour would require us to adopt the scheme of investigation shown in Figure 3.2. Technical details of estimation issues have been addressed in Appendix 3.7.

Following Figure 3.2, we have studied both the sigma and beta convergence for the GCS and SCS. In view of the econometric issues involved (Appendix 3.3), conditional convergence has been studied using both Least Square Dummy Variable (LSDV) and Generalized Method of Moments (GMM) estimates. In the two-way fixed effects model, all the conditioning variables are subsumed under the state-specific fixed effects instead of explicitly modelling a few conditioning variables.[4] In spite of the superiority of GMM estimates, the LSDV estimates are also computed to study the dispersion of fixed

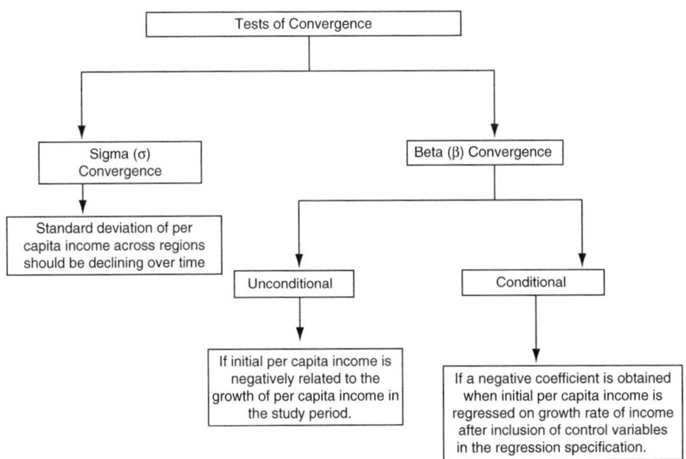

Figure 3.2   Scheme of convergence analysis

effects across the states which in effect represent the steady state incomes.

Results of the convergence analysis

Sigma (σ) convergence requires cross-sectional disparity of per capita income to decline over time. To examine σ convergence, the standard deviation of logarithm of SDP per capita and logarithm of per capita income of different sectors are computed and their movement over time is studied. Figure 3.3 depicts the evidence on sigma convergence. The standard deviation of the sectoral dispersion of output for the GCS and the SCS can be seen from the figure. The dispersion of per capita NSDP has increased over the last two decades, suggesting absence of σ convergence for the general category states. Thus the gulf between the richest and poorest states in the GCS has widened in the post-reform period and the spatial dispersion has become more pronounced for the secondary and tertiary sectors in the second half of the 1990s. For the special category states, the standard deviation of per capita state income has also increased but by a lesser degree than that for the GCS. As far as sectoral dispersions are concerned, one finds that dispersion of per capita income originating from the secondary sector has increased substantially, while that for the tertiary sector has actually declined in the post-reform period.

Given the broad evidence against sigma convergence in the post-reform period, we now move on to see whether beta convergence holds for the Indian states. As indicated in Figure 3.3, we first tested for unconditional convergence both in the cross-section and the panel dimension based on a linear version of the original Barro and Sala-i-Martin specification. The specification broadly involves regressing 'growth in income' on 'initial income'. Barro and Sala-i-Martin used average annual growth rates to study convergence. Average annual growth rates based on end points do not make use of all the available data points. In contrast, the compound annual growth rates (CAGR) make use of all the available data points and as such are derived from a richer information set and thus more reliable. Hence, we have used CAGR-based figures to comment on beta convergence. The broad synoptic view of the results from the regression exercises is presented in Table 3.8.

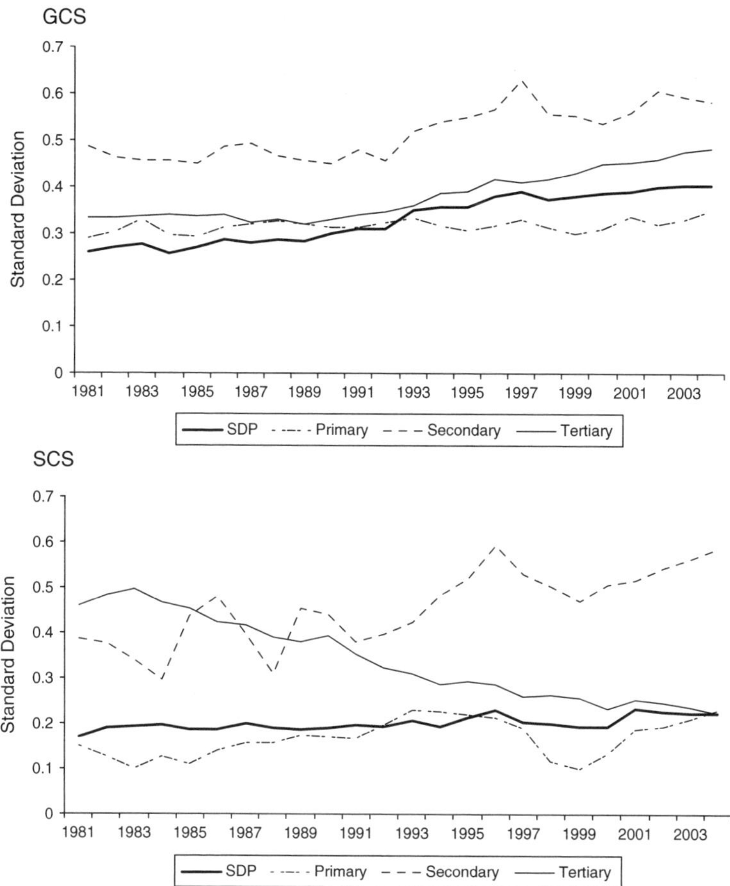

Figure 3.3   Standard deviation of per capita income: GCS and SCS

The CAGR-based regressions indicate lack of absolute convergence in per capita state income both for the general and the special category states. Further, we find no evidence of absolute convergence for any of the subsectors in the GCS. The panel unconditional convergence estimations (based on a reasonably large number of observations) provide some interesting insights. First, as was the case for cross-section estimates, there is no evidence of absolute convergence for either the GCS or the SCS in either the pre- or the post-reform

Table 3.8   Absolute convergence scenario across states and sectors

Category	Period	Cross-section		Panel	
		General Category States	**Special Category States**	**General Category States**	**Special Category States**
Agriculture	1981–93	No	Yes	Yes	Yes
	1994–2004	No	No	Yes	No
Primary	1981–93	No	Yes	Yes	Yes
	1994–2004	No	Yes	Yes	No
Manufacturing	1981–93	No	Yes	No	Yes
	1994–2004	No	No	Yes	No
Secondary	1981–93	No	Yes	No	Yes
	1994–2004	No	No	No	No
Tertiary	1981–93	No	Yes	No	Yes
	1994–2004	No	No	No	No
SDP	1981–93	No	No	No	No
	1994–2004	No	No	No	No

periods for total income. However, unlike the cross-section results, the panel estimates provide evidence in favour of absolute convergence in both the subperiods and for the entire period for the agriculture and primary sector incomes. Though evidence is in favour of convergence for the manufacturing segment in the post-reform period, the same does not hold for the secondary sector. Again there is no convergence for the tertiary sector in any of the periods under study. The positive implication for equality of the growth in primary sector income (as indicated by the Gini decomposition) is also corroborated by the evidence with regard to absolute convergence for the primary sector in the panel dimension for the GCS.

For the special category states, the cross-section convergence estimates reveal the following. First, there are signs of absolute convergence in the primary sector in the two subperiods. For the entire 1981–2004 period, the negative sign on the coefficient of initial income in the primary sector is obtained but is not statistically significant. Though there was absolute convergence taking place in the 1981–93 period for the secondary and the tertiary sectors, the same did not hold good for the 1994–2004 period. If we turn our attention to the panel estimates, we find that absolute convergence took place for the secondary and the tertiary sectors in the pre-reform period. The convergence of the 1980s has turned into divergence in the post-reform period in these two sectors.

Conditional β convergence

When control variables are accounted for in the regression specification, different states do not converge to a single steady state income; rather, each of them converges to its own steady state income. To examine whether conditional convergence is present, the two-way fixed effects model was estimated using equations for total as well as sectoral incomes. The results (see Table 3.9) confirm the presence of conditional convergence in total income for both the general and special category states in all the periods. The results are discussed in some detail for the GCS and the SCS.

Looking first at the GCS, the dispersion of individual cross-section effects obtained from the LSDV estimates for total income or NSDP has come down in the post-reform period compared to the pre-reform period. As the individual cross-section effects represent the steady state income, the decline in dispersion can be seen as the poorer states catching up with their richer counterparts in the post-reform period. The LSDV estimates, however, indicate a slowing down of the speed of convergence in the post-reform period for all subsectors and also for the NSDP as compared to the pre-reform period. Seen from the inequality perspective, the results of LSDV estimates (Table 3.9) are reassuring in the sense that the dispersion of steady state incomes across states has declined in the post-reform period.

Turning now to the SCS, conditional convergence is found in case of NSDP for both the subperiods. It holds for the primary and secondary sectors also. The standard deviation of fixed effects from the LSDV estimates for NSDP has also declined. This signifies, on the whole, that poorer states are catching up with their richer counterparts within the special category states. As far as the speed of convergence is concerned, it has slowed down for the primary and secondary sectors and also for the NSDP. The speed of convergence, however, has significantly improved for the tertiary sector in the post-reform period. In other words, the special category states converged to their

Table 3.9 Panel conditional convergence: two-way fixed effects results

Variable		Major States				Special Category States			
		Coefficient	P-value	R square	SD of fixed effects	Coefficient	P- value	Rsquare	SD of fixed effects
1981–93	Primary	−0.817	<0.0001	0.529	0.242	−0.440	<0.0001	0.414	0.067
	Secondary	−0.554	<0.0001	0.539	0.260	−0.254	0.001	0.384	0.101
	Tertiary	−0.296	<0.0001	0.616	0.100	−0.073	0.218	0.528	0.021
	SDP	−0.729	<0.0001	0.555	0.210	−0.266	0.000	0.456	0.053
1994–2004	Primary	−0.811	<0.0001	0.509	0.249	−0.086	0.160	0.323	0.027
	Secondary	−0.493	<0.0001	0.506	0.282	−0.157	0.042	0.302	0.093
	Tertiary	−0.131	0.001	0.840	0.068	−0.226	0.001	0.634	0.053
	SDP	−0.447	<0.0001	0.566	0.173	−0.171	0.015	0.511	0.038
1981–2004	Primary	−0.608	<0.0001	0.455	0.181	−0.232	<0.0001	0.269	0.036
	Secondary	−0.223	<0.0001	0.402	0.117	−0.108	0.010	0.245	0.049
	Tertiary	−0.036	0.105	0.685	0.022	−0.038	0.123	0.548	0.013
	SDP	−0.195	<0.0001	0.424	0.069	−0.100	0.009	0.397	0.021

steady state incomes in the tertiary sector at a faster pace in the post-reform period compared to the pre-reform period.

The advantage of the LSDV estimates is that the fixed effects estimated from the convergence regressions allow us to comment on the evolution of steady state incomes of the states over time. As can be seen from Table 3.10, the fixed effect estimates are significant at less than the 1 per cent level of significance. The following points are worth noting. First, the steady state incomes for all the states have increased in the post-reform period. Second, the steady state incomes of states with initial high income in the pre-reform period have increased substantially in the post-reform period as compared to states with low initial income in the pre-reform period. Third, except for Bihar, Orissa, Rajasthan and Uttar Pradesh, all other states in the general category could attain the implied steady state income, obtained from the LSDV estimates for the 1981–93 period, by the year 1994. Within the special category states, only Himachal Pradesh and Meghalaya could reach the steady state income by the year 1994.

Two factors seem to have influenced the evolution of the steady state incomes over the years: the initial per capita income of the states, and their growth performance. The distance that the states had to travel to bridge the gap between their steady state income and the initial income has increased significantly in the post-reform period. This increase has been by a much higher proportion for states such as Gujarat, Karnataka, Kerala and West Bengal, which had high per capita income and which have also performed quite well in the post-reform period. The growth impulses generated in states during the post-reform period have been of a higher order for states which had higher incomes to begin with and which had also grown faster. For relatively low-income states, such as Bihar, Orissa, Rajasthan and Uttar Pradesh, the gap between the initial income and the steady state income has been of a very low order in the post-reform period. This suggests that growth has an inertia which propels a state which is doing well to do even better. By contrast, the laggard states are trapped in a vicious cycle of low growth. A similar picture emerges if we analyse the evolution of steady state incomes of the special category states. Himachal Pradesh, Tripura and Nagaland have seen a substantial rise in their steady state incomes in the post-reform period and these are the top performing states in the special category.

Table 3.10 Steady state income of states

	1981–93					1994–2004				
	Estimate	Pr>|t|	Steady state income	Initial income	Difference	Estimate	Pr>|t|	Steady state income	Initial income	Difference
Andhra Pradesh	6.445	<0.0001	6,904	4,586	2,318	4.201	<0.0001	12,175	7,416	4,759
Bihar	6.150	<0.0001	4,608	3,363	1,245	3.837	<0.0001	5,388	3,750	1,638
Gujarat	6.673	<0.0001	9,445	6,480	2,965	4.355	<0.0001	17,188	9,796	7,392
Haryana	6.787	<0.0001	11,030	7,549	3,481	4.352	<0.0001	17,057	11,079	5,978
Karnataka	6.480	<0.0001	7,244	4,980	2,264	4.253	<0.0001	13,678	7,838	5,840
Kerala	6.463	<0.0001	7,077	5,666	1,412	4.238	<0.0001	13,209	7,983	5,227
Madhya Pradesh	6.402	<0.0001	6,510	5,113	1,398	4.084	<0.0001	9,374	6,572	2,802
Maharashtra	6.729	<0.0001	10,194	7,145	3,050	4.388	<0.0001	18,496	12,183	6,313
Orissa	6.253	<0.0001	5,309	4,149	1,160	3.961	<0.0001	7,113	4,896	2,217
Punjab	6.884	<0.0001	12,608	8,465	4,143	4.385	<0.0001	18,367	12,710	5,657
Rajasthan	6.395	<0.0001	6,444	4,284	2,160	4.135	<0.0001	10,497	6,182	4,315
Tamil Nadu	6.549	<0.0001	7,965	5,305	2,660	4.295	<0.0001	15,019	8,955	6,064

Uttar Pradesh	6.287	<0.0001	5,555	4,095	1,461	3.968	<0.0001	7,216	5,151	2,066
West Bengal	6.415	<0.0001	6,624	4,984	1,640	4.190	<0.0001	11,883	6,756	5,127
Arunachal Pradesh	2.373	0.00	7,510	4,113	3,397	1.622	0.01	12,981	8,733	4,248
Assam	2.319	0.00	6,140	4,611	1,529	1.547	0.01	8,376	5,715	2,661
Himachal Pradesh	2.379	0.00	7,679	5,760	1,919	1.662	0.01	16,386	7,870	8,516
Jammu & Kashmir	2.445	0.00	9,849	6,004	3,844	1.649	0.01	15,159	6,543	8,616
Manipur	2.340	0.00	6,630	4,416	2,215	1.588	0.01	10,617	5,841	4,776
Meghalaya	2.313	0.00	5,998	5,547	451	1.586	0.01	10,529	6,893	3,636
Nagaland	2.267	0.00	6,120	5,920	200	1.633	0.01	13,814	9,129	4,684
Tripura	2.353	0.00	6,965	3,998	2,967	1.635	0.01	14,035	5,534	8,501

Note: incomes are in rupees.

Keeping in view the fact that the lagged dependent variable is used as a regressand in the estimation, the GMM estimation of the convergence coefficients has also been computed to obtain more efficient estimates. The GMM estimates (Table 3.11) indicate convergence for both subperiod time periods and for all subsectors, and for both the GCS and the SCS. The GMM estimator, however, provides a different picture of the speed of convergence across the two decades as compared to the LSDV estimator. We now provide the scenario for the general and the special category states.

For the GCS, the convergence coefficient implying the speed of convergence has slowed down for NSDP in the post-reform period. At the sectoral level, while the speed of convergence has improved for the secondary sector, it has declined for the primary and the tertiary sectors in the post-reform period. Compared to the LSDV estimates, the GMM estimates indicate a substantially lower speed of convergence for the secondary and the tertiary sectors in the post-reform period.

In the SCS, the speed of convergence for the NSDP or overall state income as suggested by the GMM estimates has declined in the post-reform period. There has also been a decline in the speed of convergence in the post-reform period for the income from the primary sector. It has, however, increased for the secondary and the tertiary sectors. If we compare the GMM with the LSDV estimates, we find the latter overestimates the speed of convergence for all the sectors as well for the NSDP, except for the primary sector during the pre-reform period. Further, the speed of convergence, as suggested by the more efficient GMM estimates, is much slower for the tertiary sector and NSDP than the same suggested by the LSDV estimates in the post-reform period. Interestingly, the speed of convergence for the primary sector as suggested by the GMM estimates is double the figure obtained from the LSDV estimates (see Table 3.12).

Another indicator of the growth dynamics at the state level is the estimate of the time required by a state to cover half the distance between its initial income and the steady state income. As per the GMM estimates, the general category states would have covered half the distance to their steady state income in 3.70 years in the pre-reform period. This has increased to 15.7 years in the post-reform period. The time taken to cover half the distance of steady state income for the GCS, while it has come down for the primary and

Table 3.11 Panel conditional convergence: GMM estimations

Period	Variable	Major States			Special Category States		
		Coefficient	P-value	P-value of Sargan Test	Coefficient	P-value	P-value of Sargan Test
1981–93	Primary	0.02	0.00	0.45	0.32	0.00	0.4
	Secondary	0.84	0.00	0.48	0.86	0.00	0.35
	Tertiary	0.98	0.00	0.52	1.03	0.00	0.34
	SDP	0.93	0.00	0.52	0.01	0.00	0.43
1994–2004	Primary	0.02	0.10	0.51	0.88	0.00	0.15
	Secondary	0.56	0.00	0.49	0.51	0.00	0.52
	Tertiary	1.01	0.00	0.28	0.93	0.00	0.53
	SDP	0.96	0.00	0.43	0.94	0.00	0.53

Table 3.12 Speed of Convergence

Period	Sector	GCS				SCS			
		LSDV		GMM		LSDV		GMM	
		Implied β	Time	Implied β	Time	Implied β	Time	Implied β	Time
1981–93	Primary	1.7	0.41	3.77	0.18	0.58	1.2	1.16	0.6
1981–93	Secondary	0.81	0.86	0.18	3.87	0.29	2.37	0.15	4.53
1981–93	Tertiary	0.35	1.97	0.02	40.43	0.08	9.14	0.03	20.04
1981–93	SDP	1.31	0.53	0.19	3.7	0.31	2.24	0.09	7.52
1994–2004	Primary	1.67	0.42	3.91	0.17	0.07	9.84	0.13	5.42
1994–2004	Secondary	0.68	1.02	0.59	1.18	0.17	4.06	0.67	1.04
1994–2004	Tertiary	0.14	4.94	0.01	105.62	0.26	2.71	0.07	9.41
1994–2004	SDP	0.59	1.17	0.04	15.77	0.19	3.7	0.06	11.81

Note: Time refers to the time in years required to cover half the distance between initial income and steady state income.

secondary sectors, has more than doubled for the tertiary sector in the post-reform period. For the special category states, although the time required has increased in the post-reform period to cover half the distance between initial income and the steady state income, it is lower than the time required for the general category states. Though the time required has slightly increased for the primary sector, it has come down substantially for the secondary and the tertiary sector in the post-reform period for the special category states.

3.5 Concluding observations

In this chapter we have attempted to study the distributional aspects of growth in the post-reform period using a host of approaches. Given the lack of information on state level poverty from the 61st round of NSS for the year 2004–5 and the methodological controversy associated with the 1999–2000 estimates of poverty, we have studied inequality in per capita income across the states in both the general category and the special category. We have undertaken rank analysis and convergence analysis. The results of the rank analysis broadly indicate a lack of noteworthy changes in the rank of the states in the post-reform period. The concordance index indicates an absence of mobility of the states falling under GCS in the post-reform period.

For the SCS, there has been some mobility across the states in both the pre- and the post-reform periods. We find that there is nothing peculiar associated with the post-reform period as far as the mobility in income position of either category of the states is concerned. If the GCS are exhibiting immobility in PCI ranks in the post-reform period, it is a characteristic observed since the pre-reform days. The movement of the four inequality indices, such as the Entropy, Kakwani, Meheran and Theil indices, indicates a worsening of inequality over the years both for the general and the special category states. The extent of the rise in inequality has been much lower for the special category states than for the general category states. Much of the rise in inequality indices was noticed in the pre-reform period rather than in the post-reform period and this was even more the case for the general category states. Sectoral decomposition of inequality reveals that Gini coefficient for the tertiary sector has increased in the post-reform period. An increase in inequality in the tertiary sector, which has emerged as the largest contributor to SDP in the post-reform period, does not convey a very desirable development. Growth in the primary sector, however, has an equalizing impact on the distribution of income in the post-reform period.

The convergence analysis attends to the following two issues: (1) whether there has been a tendency for the cross-sectional disparity to decline over time (sigma convergence), and (2) whether relatively worse-off states have grown faster than their richer counterparts (beta convergence) in the post-reform period. The dispersion of per capita NSDP has increased over the last two decades, suggesting absence of sigma convergence for the general category states. Thus the gulf between the richest and the poorest states in the GCS has widened in the post-reform period and the spatial dispersion has become more pronounced for the secondary and tertiary sectors in the second half of the 1990s. For the special category states, the standard deviation of per capita state income has also increased but by a lesser degree than that for the GCS. As far as sectoral dispersion is concerned, one finds that for the SCS dispersion of per capita income originating from the secondary sector has increased substantially, while that for the tertiary sector has actually declined in the post-reform period.

Beta convergence was studied both in the absolute and in the conditional sense and also in the cross-section and the panel dimension for the GCS and the SCS separately. As far as absolute convergence is concerned, except for the income from the primary sector, there was no tendency for the income from the other sectors as well as for the overall SDP to grow at a faster pace for the relatively worse-off states compared to the better-off ones in the post-reform period in the GCS category. In the SCS category there was no evidence that the relatively poorer states in any of the sectors was catching up with the richer states in the post-reform period. Conditional convergence analysis, however, has something positive to convey. The steady state income for all the states has increased in the post-reform period. The steady state income of the high-income states in the pre-reform period has increased substantially in the post-reform period as compared to the states having low income in the pre-reform period. Except for Bihar, Orissa, Rajasthan and Uttar Pradesh, all other states in the general category could meet or exceed the implied steady state income obtained from the LSDV estimates for the 1981–93 period by the year 1994. Among the special category states, only Himachal Pradesh and Meghalaya could do so by 1994.

Two factors seem to explain the evolution of the steady state income over the years: first, the initial per capita income of the states and second, the growth performance of the states in the study period. The distance that the states had to travel to bridge the gap between their steady state incomes and the initial incomes has increased significantly in the post-reform period. This increase has been by a much larger proportion for states such as Gujarat, Karnataka, Kerala and West Bengal which had high per capita income and which have also performed quite well in the post-reform period. The growth impulses generated in the states during the post-reform period have been of a higher order for the high income and better performing states. For relatively low-income states, such as Bihar, Orissa, Rajasthan and Uttar Pradesh, the gap between the initial income and steady state incomes has been quite small in the post-reform period. This suggests that growth has an inertia which propels a state which is doing well to do even better. By contrast, the laggard states are caught in a vicious cycle of low growth. A similar picture emerges if we analyse the evolution of steady state incomes of the special category states also. Himachal Pradesh, Tripura and Nagaland have seen substantial rise in their steady state incomes in the post-reform period, and these are also the top-performing states in the special category.

There has been a decline in the dispersion of steady state income across both categories of states in the post-reform period. The speed of convergence of overall state income, however, has slowed down in the post-reform period for both the GCS and the SCS. Another indicator of the growth dynamics at the state level is the estimate of the time required by a state to cover half the distance between its initial income and the steady state income. Results indicate that the general category states would have covered half the distance between their initial incomes and their steady state incomes in 3.70 years in the pre-reform period. This has increased to 15.7 years for the post-reform period. The time taken to cover half the distance between their initial and steady state incomes for the GCS has come down for the primary and the secondary sectors, while more than doubling for the tertiary sector in the post-reform period. The time required to cover half the distance between their initial and steady state incomes is found to be lower in the case of special category states compared with the general category states in the post-reform period.

Appendix 3.1   Kendall's Coefficient of Concordance

Take k columns with n items each and rank each column from 1 to n. The null hypothesis is that the rankings disagree.

The null and the alternative hypothesis are:

$$\begin{cases} H_0 : Disagreement \\ H_1 : Agreement \end{cases}$$

We first compute a sum of ranks SR_i for each row. Then $S = \sum (SR)^2 - n\left(\overline{SR}\right)^2$, where

$$\overline{SR} = \frac{(n+1)\,k}{2}$$

is the mean of all the SR elements.

If H_0 is disagreement, S can be checked against a table for this test. If $S > S_\alpha$, reject H_0. For n too large for the table use

$$\chi^{2(n-1)} = k\,(n-1)\,W = \frac{S}{{}^1\!/_{12}\,kn\,(n+1)},$$

where

$$W = \frac{S}{{}^1\!/_{12}\,k^2\,(n^3 - n)}$$

is the Kendall Coefficient of Concordance and must be between 0 and 1.

To do a test of the null hypothesis of disagreement ($\alpha = 0.05$), look up S_α in the table giving 'Critical values of Kendall's S as a Measure of Concordance'. Suppose in a particular case $n=31$ and $k=3$, we get $W=0.10$, and wish to test the null. In cases where n is too large for the table, we can use $\chi^2 = k\,(n-1)\,W = 3\,(30)\,(0.10) = 9.000$ as an approximation.

Using a χ^2 table, we find that $\chi_\alpha^{2(n-1)} = \chi_{0.05}^{2(30)} = 43.733$. Since 9 is below the table value, we do not reject H_0.

Appendix 3.2   Construction of Rank Concordance Index

Boyle and McCarthy (1997) have proposed a multi-annual version (*RCt*) and a binary version (*RCat*) of the measure. The first is defined as

$$RC_t = \text{Variance} \sum_{t=0}^{T} AR(Y)_{it} \, / \, \text{Variance} \left\{ (T+1)^* AR(Y)_{i0} \right\}$$

The binary measure, on the other hand, can be obtained by considering the ranks in years *t* and 0 and is given by

$$RC_{at} = \text{Variance} \left\{ AR(Y)_{it} + AR(Y)_{i0} \right\} / \text{Variance} \left\{ 2^* AR(Y)_{i0} \right\}$$

Clearly, the multi-annual measure, extending over the whole period, contains all possible pairs of years for which the binary measure could be computed. The intuitive interpretation of this measure is not difficult. First of all, let us note that the multi-period measure can be calculated for every value of T: that is, $T = 0$, 1, 2, and so on. Second, the denominator gives the variance of the sum of the rankings if the relative position of the states remained unchanged in every period from 0 to T. This is obtained by multiplying the base period ranking by $(T + 1)$ and then calculating the variance of the product across states. The numerator, on the other hand, measures the interstate variation of the sum of the actual rankings of the states over the period from 0 to T. Now, it can be shown that the variance of the sum of rankings (i.e., denominator of RC_t) is greatest if the states did not have any change in the ranking over time. The variance in the numerator, however, could be zero since the rankings may change in such a manner that the sum becomes the same for all the states. Hence, the value of the rank concordance measure will lie between zero and unity. The closer the value of the measure to zero, the greater is the extent of mobility within the distribution. The index of concordance indicates the mobility of the ranks over the years. Suppose we want to construct the rank index for the period 1994–2004 for the 14 general category states under our study. The steps involved in the construction of a year-based index would involve the following.

1   The states have to be ranked each year for all the years under study, say, 1994–2004. This gives us 11 sets of rankings for the 14 states, one set of rankings for each of the 11 years.
2   Now sort the data by state. This gives the rank of a state for every year in a chronological order. The cumulative sums of the ranks are then obtained for each state for the 11-year period.
3   The cumulative sum of ranks obtained for each state is now sorted by year (i.e., the cumulative sums of ranks for different states for a particular year are taken as a block and the variance of the cumulative rank sums are then computed for every year). In this fashion, we will get 11 variances for 11 years.
4   The rank concordance is computed with reference to a base year. If 1994 is the base year, then, the index for different years is obtained using the formula:

$$RCI = RKSVAR/(T)^2 * (RKSVAR\_BASE)$$

where RKSVAR denotes the variance of cumulative sum of ranks for the states and RKSVAR_BASE is the variance of cumulative sum of ranks for the base year.

Appendix 3.3　Gini decomposition of sectoral inequality (1981–93)

Table 3A.1　Gini decomposition of sectoral inequality (1981–93)

Source	Year	Major States					Special States				
		S_k	G_k	R_k	Share	% Change	S_k	G_k	R_k	Share	% Change
Primary	1981	0.457	0.158	0.647	0.326	−0.131	0.476	0.079	0.416	0.180	−0.296
Secondary	1981	0.214	0.250	0.812	0.303	0.089	0.141	0.150	−0.099	−0.024	−0.165
Tertiary	1981	0.337	0.179	0.919	0.386	0.049	0.432	0.255	0.807	1.020	0.589
SDP	1981		0.144					0.087			
Primary	1982	0.462	0.169	0.692	0.363	−0.099	0.478	0.067	0.644	0.208	−0.270
Secondary	1982	0.208	0.246	0.839	0.288	0.080	0.138	0.158	−0.130	−0.029	−0.166
Tertiary	1982	0.338	0.179	0.933	0.379	0.041	0.437	0.268	0.922	1.095	0.657
SDP	1982		0.149					0.099			
Primary	1983	0.439	0.182	0.676	0.355	−0.085	0.459	0.053	0.547	0.130	−0.329
Secondary	1983	0.215	0.242	0.814	0.278	0.063	0.142	0.163	−0.082	−0.019	−0.160
Tertiary	1983	0.352	0.182	0.928	0.389	0.038	0.452	0.276	0.957	1.165	0.714
SDP	1983		0.152					0.103			
Primary	1984	0.451	0.165	0.666	0.360	−0.090	0.469	0.062	0.614	0.179	−0.291
Secondary	1984	0.215	0.246	0.829	0.320	0.104	0.135	0.142	−0.064	−0.012	−0.148
Tertiary	1984	0.341	0.181	0.766	0.344	0.003	0.443	0.258	0.937	1.064	0.621
SDP	1984		0.137					0.101			
Primary	1985	0.443	0.161	0.736	0.349	−0.094	0.458	0.052	0.803	0.200	−0.258
Secondary	1985	0.215	0.246	0.860	0.303	0.088	0.140	0.176	−0.174	−0.045	−0.185

Table 3A.1 (Continued)

Source	Year	Major States					Special States				
		S_k	G_k	R_k	Share	% Change	S_k	G_k	R_k	Share	% Change
Tertiary	1985	0.349	0.179	0.909	0.378	0.029	0.450	0.251	0.959	1.133	0.683
SDP	1985		0.150					0.096			
Primary	1986	0.424	0.174	0.635	0.295	−0.129	0.460	0.068	0.529	0.186	−0.274
Secondary	1986	0.224	0.263	0.892	0.331	0.107	0.142	0.211	0.076	0.025	−0.117
Tertiary	1986	0.357	0.179	0.956	0.384	0.027	0.438	0.232	0.899	1.027	0.588
SDP	1986		0.159					0.089			
Primary	1987	0.407	0.177	0.587	0.271	−0.136	0.438	0.083	0.511	0.187	−0.252
Secondary	1987	0.226	0.269	0.913	0.356	0.129	0.141	0.186	0.411	0.108	−0.033
Tertiary	1987	0.372	0.172	0.929	0.381	0.009	0.455	0.229	0.845	0.881	0.427
SDP	1987		0.156					0.100			
Primary	1988	0.381	0.181	0.627	0.273	−0.108	0.417	0.083	0.251	0.089	−0.327
Secondary	1988	0.234	0.252	0.902	0.336	0.102	0.154	0.155	0.402	0.099	−0.055
Tertiary	1988	0.388	0.170	0.951	0.397	0.009	0.452	0.212	0.895	0.887	0.435
SDP	1988		0.158					0.097			
Primary	1989	0.407	0.177	0.749	0.346	−0.061	0.410	0.090	0.359	0.134	−0.276
Secondary	1989	0.233	0.246	0.880	0.322	0.090	0.149	0.214	0.588	0.191	0.041
Tertiary	1989	0.365	0.165	0.917	0.352	−0.013	0.457	0.207	0.771	0.742	0.285
SDP	1989		0.156					0.098			
Primary	1990	0.396	0.174	0.808	0.338	−0.057	0.411	0.089	0.516	0.186	−0.225
Secondary	1990	0.231	0.244	0.898	0.307	0.076	0.145	0.209	0.349	0.104	−0.041
Tertiary	1990	0.377	0.171	0.938	0.366	−0.011	0.469	0.215	0.840	0.836	0.367

SDP	1990		0.165					0.101			
Primary	1991	0.384	0.173	0.825	0.327	−0.057	0.404	0.088	0.629	0.215	−0.188
Secondary	1991	0.242	0.253	0.870	0.318	0.075	0.157	0.198	0.502	0.150	−0.007
Primary	1991	0.384	0.173	0.825	0.327	−0.057	0.404	0.088	0.629	0.215	−0.188
Secondary	1991	0.242	0.253	0.870	0.318	0.075	0.157	0.198	0.502	0.150	−0.007
Tertiary	1991	0.376	0.171	0.946	0.364	−0.012	0.458	0.190	0.810	0.677	0.219
SDP	1991		0.168					0.104			
Primary	1992	0.377	0.174	0.804	0.311	−0.066	0.399	0.103	0.666	0.270	−0.129
Secondary	1992	0.235	0.245	0.927	0.314	0.079	0.155	0.205	0.506	0.160	0.004
Tertiary	1992	0.389	0.176	0.946	0.381	−0.008	0.464	0.171	0.815	0.639	0.175
SDP	1992		0.170					0.101			
Primary	1993	0.378	0.186	0.851	0.324	−0.054	0.378	0.121	0.584	0.239	−0.138
Secondary	1993	0.239	0.269	0.923	0.320	0.082	0.159	0.208	0.640	0.191	0.032
Tertiary	1993	0.385	0.184	0.945	0.362	−0.023	0.468	0.164	0.788	0.544	0.077
SDP	1993		0.185					0.111			

Appendix 3.4   Absolute convergence cross-section dimension

Table 3A.2   Absolute convergence cross-section dimension

Variable		Major States				Special Category States			
		Coefficient	T-stat.	Significance	Centred R square	Coefficient	T-stat.	Significance	Centred R square
1981–93	Agriculture	−0.001	−0.134	0.897	0.001	−0.139	−4.195	0.005	0.75
	Primary	0.000	−0.042	0.967	0.355	−0.121	−3.617	0.011	0.69
	Manufacturing	−0.006	−0.713	0.489	0.040	−0.035	−1.806	0.120	0.35
	Secondary	−0.001	−0.227	0.823	0.004	−0.061	−1.578	0.165	0.29
	Tertiary	−0.004	−0.457	0.655	0.416	−0.038	−3.185	0.018	0.63
	SDP	0.016	1.982	0.070	0.246	−0.041	−1.189	0.279	0.19
1994–2004	Agriculture	0.004	0.381	0.709	0.011	−0.100	−1.354	0.224	0.23
	Primary	−0.001	−0.111	0.913	0.001	−0.134	−2.261	0.064	0.46
	Manufacturing	0.009	1.081	0.300	0.088	0.030	0.383	0.714	0.02
	Secondary	0.001	0.188	0.853	0.002	−0.100	−1.802	0.121	0.35
	Tertiary	0.019	1.526	0.152	0.162	0.091	5.424	0.001	0.83
	SDP	0.002	−0.039	0.969	0.377	−0.046	−1.023	0.345	0.15

Appendix 3.5 Absolute convergence panel dimension

Table 3A.3 Absolute convergence panel dimension

Variable		GCS				SCS			
		Coefficient	T-stat.	Significance	Centred R square	Coefficient	T-stat.	Significance	Centred R square
1981–93	Agriculture	−0.135	−3.030	0.002	0.052	−0.223	−3.319	0.001	0.104
	Primary	−0.139	−3.113	0.002	0.055	−0.151	−2.417	0.017	0.058
	Manufacturing	−0.020	−1.286	0.200	0.009	−0.134	−2.205	0.029	0.049
	Secondary	−0.009	−0.625	0.532	0.002	−0.058	−1.581	0.117	0.025
	Tertiary	−0.001	−0.138	0.890	0.000	−0.028	−2.408	0.017	0.058
	SDP	−0.004	−0.194	0.845	0.000	−0.041	−1.189	0.279	0.190
1994–2004	Agriculture	−0.092	−2.460	0.015	0.042	0.005	0.115	0.908	0.000
	Primary	−0.088	−2.373	0.018	0.039	−0.040	−0.984	0.327	0.012
	Manufacturing	−0.041	−1.928	0.055	0.026	0.035	−0.818	0.415	0.008
	Secondary	−0.018	−1.197	0.233	0.010	−0.041	−0.932	0.353	0.011
	Tertiary	0.018	2.900	0.010	0.057	−0.019	−0.889	0.376	0.010
	SDP	0.030	0.270	0.786	0.000	0.001	0.067	0.946	0.000

Appendix 3.6   Ranking of states (1981–93)

Table 3A.4   Ranking of states (1981–93)

States	1981	1982	1983	1984	1985	1986	1987	1988	1989	1990	1991	1992	1993	Average rank	Standard deviation of ranks	Worse years cases
Andhra Pradesh	10	7	9	9	9	10	10	9	7	7	6	7	9	8.4	1.39	6
Bihar	14	14	14	14	14	14	14	14	14	14	13	14	14	13.9	0.28	12
Gujarat	4	4	4	3	3	4	4	4	3	4	4	5	4	3.8	0.55	10
Haryana	2	2	2	2	2	2	2	2	2	2	2	2	3	2.1	0.28	1
Karnataka	9	8	8	6	6	8	6	6	6	6	9	6	6	6.9	1.26	5
Kerala	5	6	5	11	7	6	8	8	9	8	7	8	7	7.3	1.65	6
Madhya Pradesh	7	9	7	7	10	9	11	10	11	11	10	11	11	9.5	1.61	7
Maharashtra	3	3	3	4	4	3	3	3	4	3	3	3	2	3.2	0.55	3
Orissa	12	13	13	12	13	12	12	13	12	12	14	13	13	12.6	0.65	8
Punjab	1	1	1	1	1	1	1	1	1	1	1	1	1	1.0	0.00	0
Rajasthan	11	11	11	8	11	11	9	12	8	9	8	10	8	9.8	1.48	7
Tamil Nadu	6	5	6	5	5	5	5	5	5	5	5	4	5	5.1	0.49	2
Uttar Pradesh	13	12	12	13	12	13	13	11	13	13	12	12	12	12.4	0.65	6
West Bengal	8	10	10	10	8	7	7	7	10	10	11	9	10	9.0	1.41	7
Arunachal Pradesh	7	6	6	6	6	5	4	4	3	4	3	2	2	4.5	1.66	6
Assam	5	5	5	5	5	6	6	6	7	6	6	7	7	5.8	0.80	8
Himachal Pradesh	3	2	3	3	4	3	2	2	2	2	2	3	3	2.6	0.65	7
Jammu & Kashmir	1	3	2	2	2	2	3	5	5	5	5	5	5	3.5	1.56	6
Manipur	6	7	7	7	7	7	7	7	6	7	7	6	6	6.7	0.48	9
Meghalaya	4	4	4	4	3	4	5	3	4	3	4	4	4	3.8	0.55	10
Nagaland	2	1	1	1	1	1	1	1	1	1	1	1	1	1.1	0.28	1
Tripura	8	8	8	8	8	8	8	8	8	8	8	8	8	8.0	0.00	0

Appendix 3.7 Issues in convergence estimation: cross-section and panel data models

The cross-section model

Barro and Sala-i-Martin (1995) have proposed the non-linear specific-ation (3.1) to compute the speed of convergence:

$$(\ln Y_{iT} - \ln Y_{i0})/T = a - (1 - e^{-\beta T})/T \ln Y_{i0} + u_{it} \tag{3.1}$$

where Y_{i0} is the per capita income of a set of economies i at the beginning of a period of time length T, and Y_{iT} is the income at the end of the period. The parameter ß denotes the speed of convergence. The left-hand term refers to the average growth rate of per capita income Y_i in period T. Convergence would imply that the growth rate of income is negatively related to the initial per capita income Y_{i0}. The coefficient $(1 - e^{-\beta T})/T$ declines over time, reflecting the dynamics in a neoclassical growth model. The speed of convergence, ß, indic-ates the rate at which the economy converges towards its steady state income.[5] In specification (3.1) all states have the same steady state income. If different steady state incomes across economies are assumed, (i.e., in the case of conditional convergence), the specifica-tion becomes:

$$(\ln Y_{iT} - \ln Y_{i0})/T = a - (1 - e^{-\beta T})/T \ln Y_{i0} + X_i + u_{it} \quad 0 < \beta \tag{3.2}$$

where X_i represents a set of variables (conditional variables or growth determinants) which influence the general level of growth and hence the steady state. In practice, for X_i, either stock variables at the beginning of the period are considered, such as the level of education in the working population, or flow variables in the period T (e.g., the average rate of investment).[6]

Instead of estimating the convergence coefficient from the non-linear specifications (3.1) or (3.2), empirical studies often use a linear[7] specification (3.3):

$$(\ln Y_{iT} - \ln Y_{i0})/T = a - b \ln Y_{i0} + X_i + u_{it} \quad 0 < b \tag{3.3}$$

The panel data model

The cross-section approach to convergence involves loss of inform-ation as it takes into account only the end points in the time scale, ignoring the information content of the in-between time points. Panel data estimation uses several observations in time and, as such, is derived from a much richer set of information than cross-section analyses. Consequently, panel data estimation procedures have been suggested. When pooled data are used, tests for absolute convergence usually take the form:

$$(\ln Y_{i,t} - \ln Y_{i,t-1}) = a - b \ln Y_{i,t-1} + u_{i,t} \quad 0 < b \qquad (3.4)$$

According to this equation, the annual growth rate of per capita income, $\ln Y_{i,t} - \ln Y_{i,t-1}$ should be negatively related to the previous level of income (i.e., $\ln Y_{i,t-1}$) if neoclassical convergence dynamics is present. This would suggest that not only that poor countries grow faster than rich countries, but that they all also converge to the same per capita SDP.

The cross-section analysis has recently been criticized on econometric grounds. Conditional convergence analysis argues that one must account for steady state income differences when investigating income convergence. It is very possible that the number of factors which determine the steady state are not quantifiable. In addition, data on certain quantitative indicators that have a bearing on the steady state may not be available. The cross-section regression analysis neglects unobservable factors which determine regional differences of the production function and consequently lead to different steady state incomes. The neglect of potential steady state determinants clearly leads to an omitted variable bias. From the perspective of panel data econometrics (Hsiao 1986; Baltagi 1995), a cross-section analysis which does not account for individual-specific effects of the single economy delivers inconsistent estimates.[8] However, the omitted variable bias can be tackled through a fixed effect specification in the panel data context.[9] The panel data specification of a fixed effects model can be represented as:

$$\ln Y_{i,t} - \ln Y_{i,t-1} = -c \ln Y_{i,t-1} + X_{i,t-1}\delta + \eta_i + \zeta_t + \varepsilon_{i,t} \quad 0 < c \quad (3.5)$$

The individual fixed effect η_i replaces the common intercept. Thus the fixed effect η_I represents the individual steady state income. $X_{i,t-1}$ is a vector of growth determinants and δ is the coefficient vector. ζ_t is a time-specific effect, ruling in period t. It is most useful to include a time-specific effect in order to capture aggregate shocks which may be present in a particular period. The error term $\varepsilon_{i,t} \sim N(0, \sigma^2)$ is a random disturbance. According to the specification (3.5), the annual growth rate of per capita income $(\ln Y_{i,t} - \ln Y_{i,t-1})$ should be negatively related to the level of income $\ln Y_{i,t-1}$. Regions are expected to exhibit a higher growth rate when their income level is low, but it should decline when income rises. This relation is represented by the common coefficient c. The region-specific fixed effect, present over the whole sample period, is captured through η_i. Hence the model operates with a variable intercept instead of a common one, which was used in the cross-section analysis.[10] The term ζ_t represents the time-specific effect affecting all regions in period t. Consequently, in econometric terms one uses a two-way fixed effects model to estimate convergence (Hsiao 1986; Baltagi 1995). The region-specific fixed effect η_i determines the region's steady state income. This fixed effect is a concept similar to taking explanatory variables or country dummy variables in the conditional convergence analysis. However, whereas conditional convergence analysis traditionally identifies groups of individual units as those which are characterized by the same size of a conditional variable, one can now allow for continuous individual conditional effects. This implies that each region is converging towards its own steady state.[11] The commonly applied LSDV estimator, however, is consistent only for a large number of observations over time (Nickell 1981). Otherwise, an upward bias of the estimated convergence coefficients results. Therefore, one often needs to apply a kind of first difference estimator to estimate the convergence coefficient in panel data models. The specification (3.5), in fact, constitutes a dynamic panel data model, where the dependent variable is partly explained by its past value. As the right-hand side of equation (3.5) contains a lag of the dependent variable, the problem of a correlation of error terms arises with the common estimation procedure of fixed effects models (i.e., the LSDV). Such static panel data estimation methods lead to biased estimates with dynamic panel data models. To overcome this problem, LSDV estimation is effected by applying Ordinary Least Squares on a transformed series, where the individual time series mean is subtracted from each observation to sweep out the individual effects and avoid the dummy variable trap. However, Nickell (1981) shows that the bias approaches zero if T goes to infinity. For a small number of observations in time[12], the LSDV estimate involves rather considerable bias. To cope with this problem, first differencing is used to eliminate the fixed effect, and lags (two and above) of the dependent variable are used as instruments[13]. Anderson and Hsiao (1981) proposed an instrumental variable estimation procedure whereby, in a first step, first differences of the series are taken in order to remove the individual fixed effects:

$$(Y_{i,t} - Y_{i,t-1}) = d(Y_{i,t-1} - Y_{i,t-2}) + (X_{i,t-1} - X_{i,t-2})d \quad\quad (3.6)$$

$$+ (\eta_i - \eta_i) + (X_t - X_{t-1}) + (\varepsilon_{i,t} - \varepsilon_{i,t-1})$$

Equation (3.6) has the problem that that the errors $(\varepsilon_{i,t} - \varepsilon_{i,t-1})$ are correlated with $(Y_{i,t-1} - Y_{i,t-2})$. Anderson and Hsiao use a lag of the variable, either the lagged observation $Y_{i,t-2}$ or the lagged difference $(Y_{i,t-2} - Y_{i,t-3})$, as an instrument for $(Y_{i,t-1} - Y_{i,t-2})^{14}$. In the Anderson and Hsiao scheme of estimation, one obtains a consistent estimator for a dynamic panel data model but not necessarily an efficient estimator[15]. Arellano and Bond (1991) argue that additional instruments[16] can be gained by using all possible orthogonality conditions $E(Y_{i,t-2}, e_{i,t} - e_{i,t-1}) = 0$, $E(Y_{i,t-3}, e_{i,t} - e_{i,t-1}) = 0$, and so on. Arellano and Bond (1991) have demonstrated significant gains in estimation efficiency when the estimation procedure uses all available lags as instruments[17].

4
State Finances

Fiscal consolidation has been a key policy concern ever since India embarked on the path of economic reform in the early 1990s. The stress on fiscal consolidation is premised on the hypothesis that the economic crisis of 1991 was an outcome of poor fiscal management during the 1980s (Srinivasan 2003; Bajpai and Sachs 1999).[1] The build-up to the economic crisis seen from the fiscal perspective runs along the following lines. Fiscal expansion helped India break out from its low Hindu rate of growth in the 1980s. This fiscal expansion, however, was backed by borrowed funds rather than by the government's own revenue and that fact was reflected in the rising fiscal deficit figures throughout the 1980s. Fiscal deficit is not a problem in itself if the returns on the use of the borrowed funds exceed the cost of borrowing. This, however, was not the case in India where a large part of the deficit financed the day-to-day expenditure of government instead of creating productive assets. Continued high levels of fiscal deficit to finance revenue expenditure create macroeconomic imbalances and, as such, have the potential of culminating in a full-scale macroeconomic crisis. Thus it is no coincidence that in the year 1991, when the Indian economy was hit by a macroeconomic crisis, fiscal deficit for the general government was more than 11 per cent of GDP, and inflation (fuelled by high fiscal deficits) was in double digits. Hence, a principal concern in the overall economic reform process was to rein in the fiscal slippage and restore order in government finances through fiscal stabilization.

Notwithstanding the continuity in commitment towards fiscal consolidation for almost 15 years, government finances have remained out of shape at the level of both central government and state governments. Competitive populism and political expediency have contributed to high levels of fiscal deficit, even though successive governments echoed the need for fiscal consolidation. In the absence of self-restraint by the government, the panacea for the persistently high fiscal deficit was sought in promulgation of the FRBM Act, 2003, which became effective from 5 July 2004. The FRBM Act mandates the central government to eliminate revenue deficit by March 2009 and reduce fiscal deficit to 3 per cent of GDP by March 2008. The central government has further encouraged the state governments to enact their own fiscal responsibility legislation and many of them have followed suit. The move towards a rule-bound fiscal regime is a landmark development in Indian federation in recent times. The anchor chosen for fiscal rule in India is the observed fiscal deficit numbers as a proportion of GDP. The observed fiscal deficit figures, however, contain a structural and a cyclical component. Neglect of this distinction may, at times, prompt policy action which could be counterproductive. This point can be further illustrated. The three years from 1994–5 to 1996–7 are often referred to as the golden years of economic reform in India when the economy grew at an average of 7.5 per cent per annum. This was the best growth ever recorded in a row since India became independent. These three years also witnessed fiscal deficit figures coming down successively from 5.7 per cent in 1994–5 to 4.88 per cent in 1996–7. Since 1996–7 growth momentum has not been steady, and neither has central government's attempt at fiscal consolidation. This raises the question of whether the growth trajectory of the economy has any relevance for the fiscal outcome. In other words, one is interested to know how government's fiscal operations have been conditioned by the cyclical position of the economy.

Fiscal imbalances often have the danger of translating into reserve losses, unstable exchange rates and balance of payments crises. Apart from these broad concerns, fiscal imbalances arising out of an expansionary fiscal policy have important consequences for the price situation in an economy. The impact on prices is likely to be felt as an expansionary fiscal policy adds to aggregate demand. An expansionary fiscal policy during an economic boom acts like adding fuel to fire in raising the price level. This chapter makes an attempt to delve into certain less discussed, though important, aspects of fiscal policy-making in India and tries to gauge the inflationary consequences of such a policy. But before doing so, a brief look at the fiscal performance at the central and state government levels would set the stage for further discussion.

The rest of this chapter is schematized as follows. Section 4.1 provides a synoptic view of the evolution of public finances in India both at the level of the central and the state governments with a focus on the post-reform period. It also provides a comparative perspective on the fiscal performance of the different states in the post-reform period. The fiscal reform initiatives in the states in recent times are addressed in section 4.2. Section 4.3 explores the cyclical character of the fiscal policy pursued at the federal level in the post-reform period. This section also attempts to decompose the fiscal deficit of the states into their structural and cyclical components, which is then the subject of discussion in section 4.4. The fiscal stance of the Indian states and the associated inflationary consequences of the fiscal policy are also discussed in section 4.4. The last section, section 4.5, presents concluding observations.

4.1   Evolution of public finances

The state of public finance in any federal set-up is an outcome of the fiscal conduct of the government at different tiers of governance. In India, the federal set-up consists of the centre and the states. In keeping with the philosophy of a welfare state, the Constitution of India has drawn the contours within which the centre and different state governments are to conduct their fiscal operations. The Constitution has laid down the functions and also the sources of finance for the different tiers of government to discharge their responsibilities. In addition, the Constitution provides for the setting-up of a Finance Commission in every five years to address vertical imbalances in the revenue accounts of the central government and the state governments (Singh 2006). In addition to the constitutional provisions, the Planning Commission – an extra constitutional innovation dating from the early 1950s – also plays a key role in shaping the financial health of the states by way of resource transfer from the centre to states for planned development.

Evolution of the central government finances since the initiation of economic planning in 1951 may be classified into five broad phases: Phase I (1951–81); Phase II (1982–91); Phase III (1991–6); Phase IV (1997–2002); and Phase V (2003 onwards). It may be noted that the first two phases relate to the pre-reform period, while the later three phases reflect the developments during the reform process which started in July 1991. The first phase was a period of surplus in the revenue account. Fiscal deficit and debt were maintained at reasonable levels in this phase, though monetization of deficit and debt were predominant. This period was, however, characterized by a high marginal rate of taxation, a predominance of public investment neglecting commercial considerations and financial repression. The second phase may be truly called the decade of fiscal deterioration as the major fiscal variables were in disarray. The fiscal deterioration eventually destabilized the balance between the budget and the economy which was reflected in accumulation of large debt, a high debt–service ratio and double-digit inflation. Furthermore, the increasing chasm between the income and expenditure of the government led to a widening of the gap between the income and expenditure of the economy as a whole, resulting in a bulging of the current account deficit in the balance of payments. It was widely recognized that a fiscal situation was unsustainable. Accordingly, a fiscal adjustment programme laying stress on reduction of fiscal deficit has been pursued by the central government since July 1991.

Concerted efforts to restore fiscal balance beginning in July 1991 in terms of a fiscal adjustment programme constitutes the third phase. These, *inter alia*, comprised tax and non-tax reforms, expenditure management and institutional reforms. These initiatives resulted in a significant fall in the fiscal deficit and in public debt as a proportion of GDP until 1996–7, but the trends reversed shortly thereafter. This reversal was largely on account of downward rigidity in revenue expenditure, a fall in tax buoyancy, a slowdown in Public Sector Undertaking (PSU) restructuring and continuation of uneconomic user charges, particularly at the state level. The 1997–2002 phase was marked by the Fifth Pay Commission awards which resulted in a ballooning of revenue expenditure. The 1997–2002 phase also marks the historic move to end the automatic monetization of government's deficit, and the introduction of the Ways and Means Advances (WMA) scheme to meet government's temporary mismatch in revenue and expenditure. The year 2003 witnessed the enactment of the FRBM Act which commits the central government to reducing its deficits to a particular level within a defined time frame. The fiscal operations after 2004 are guided by the FRBM precept.

For a complete picture of the government finances in a country such as India with a federal set-up, the fiscal conduct of the state governments assumes equal, if not more, importance. While central government finances were in a complete mess at the time of the economic crisis, the finances of the state governments were also not in good shape, although they were less conspicuous. In fact, the states had started to stray away from the path of fiscal austerity after 1987–8 when they recorded a deficit in their revenue account on a sustained basis. In the crisis year, 1991, state governments' revenue deficits had reached 0.93 per cent of GDP and the fiscal deficit was 3.3 per cent. Though the fiscal deficit of the state governments could be contained within 3 per cent of GDP until 1997–8, it received a major wake-up call with the implementation of the Fifth Pay Commission's recommendations for a wage hike for government employees.[2] Further, the states' contribution to the combined fiscal deficit had increased over the decade.

The fiscal posture of state governments has broadly followed the pattern seen in case of the central government, albeit, with a lag. For instance, the surplus on revenue account for the states had turned into deficit just as was the case for the centre, but slightly later. Systemic reforms in taxation and expenditure management were adopted by the states, once the centre vouched for them. There has been severe fiscal stress in respect of finances of state governments since the mid-1980s. Unlike for the central government, the revenue account of the states was in surplus up to 1986–7. The fiscal stress emanates from an inadequacy of receipts to meet the expenditure requirements. The low and declining buoyancies in tax and non-tax receipts, constraints on internal resource mobilization due to losses incurred by state Public Sector Undertakings and a decelerating rate of resources transfer from the centre have contributed to a worsening of state finances. A survey of worsening state finances as set out in the Reserve Bank of India (RBI) *Report on State Finances: A Study of Budgets, 2002–03* (2003) reveals that the following factors were responsible for the deterioration in state finances: (1) a reluctance to raise additional resources (Kurian 1999); (2) a competitive reduction in taxes, absence of service tax and agricultural income tax (Rao 2002); (3) sluggishness in central transfer, reflecting the precariousness of the centre's own finances (Chakraborty 1999); (4) inappropriate user charges (Mohan 2000); and (5) impact of pay revisions (Acharya 2002). It is important to recognize that there are large disparities across the states in terms of level of income and the tax and expenditure policies pursued by respective governments. Accordingly, the impact of various factors is likely to vary across the states. Reflecting the fiscal stress, the expenditure for development activities, which are directly related to growth, suffered (RBI 2002b).

We now present the movement with regard to three important fiscal indicators since the 1980s when the symptoms of fiscal imbalance were first noticed in India (see Figure 4.1). Be it fiscal deficit or primary deficit, one does not find a sustained improvement in the post-1991 crisis period either for the states or for the centre. For the centre, revenue deficit as a proportion of fiscal deficit (which was around 25 per cent of the fiscal deficit in 1980–1), had deteriorated to 42 per cent in the crisis year, 1990–1. Since then, this ratio has successively increased to around 80 per cent (of fiscal deficit). With the exception of 1984–5, the revenue account was in surplus until 1986–7 for the states. After that, revenue deficit persisted and by 1990–1 it was 28 per cent of the fiscal deficit which, by 2003–4, had scaled up to 50 per cent of the fiscal deficit. The interest payment component of the revenue deficit has taken a major toll on the overall fiscal scenario. Accumulated debt over the period has reared its ugly head in the shape of rising interest payments for past fiscal profligacy. Thus it is no surprise that debt sustainability has emerged as a major fiscal concern (Rajaraman, Bhide and Pattanaik 2005). Since 1996–7, the states have been borrowing more and more to meet their day-to-day expenditure. Borrowing for purposes other than interest payments (i.e., the primary deficit account) turned into surplus in 2003–4 for the central government. Primary deficit for the states, however, was at a very high level, 1.5 per cent of GDP, in the same year, 2003–4.

Shankar Acharya, having a ringside view of economic policy-making in India, in his detailed analysis of the impact of the Fifth Pay Commission on the finances of the Centre and the states finds that employee compensation increased from 1.6 per cent of GDP in 1996–7 to 2.3 per cent in 1999–2000 for central government, and that for the states increased from 3.8 per cent to 4.7 per cent of GDP over the same period. The Fifth Pay Commission (FPC)-induced

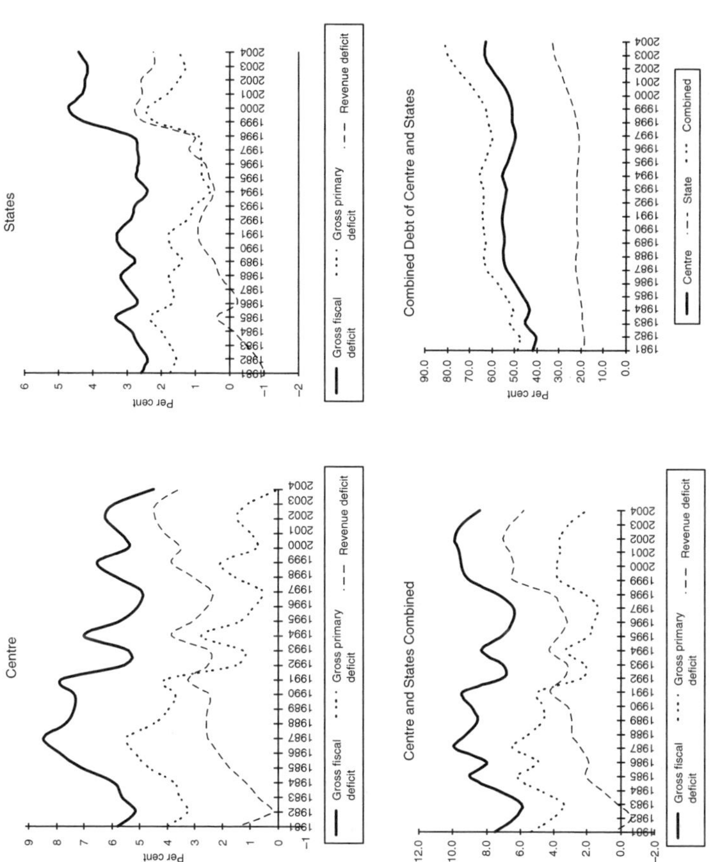

Figure 4.1 Select fiscal indicators for the centre and the states

increase in salaries and the wage component constituted about half of the worsening in states' revenue deficit and over 40 per cent of the widening in fiscal deficit between 1996–7 and 1999–2000. For the combined government sector, employee compensation rose from 5.4 per cent of GDP in 1996–7 to 6.9 per cent in 1999–2000. This rise in the magnitude of employee compensation accounted for over half of the worsening in the consolidated revenue deficit and for almost half of the deterioration in consolidated fiscal deficit during this period. Shankar Acharya concludes that, 'whatever else may be happening, the FPC effects constitute the single largest adverse shock to Indian public finances in the last decade, with corresponding negative consequences for aggregate savings and investment in the economy'.

While it is certainly true that the state finances have undergone a deterioration, especially since the second half of the 1990s, it is a matter of investigation how the fiscal health of different states has evolved over the years. Has it been the case that the worsening of state finances is all-pervasive, or is it largely confined to a few states? This has been examined by studying the intertemporal movement in the Composite Index of Fiscal Health (CIFH) brought out by the Office of the Comptroller and Auditor General of India. The CIFH has been computed for the post-1990 period up to 2004 (see Table 4.1). We will comment on the intertemporal movement in the CIFH and two of its important constituents:[3] the Composite Resource Mobilization Index (CRMI) and the Composite Index of Expenditure Management (CIEM). Based on the index values for the GCS and the SCS, the following observations can be made. Seen in terms of the CIFH, we find a deterioration in fiscal health during 1995–2000 compared to the base period 1990–5 for the GCS. During the 2000–4 period, a marginal improvement is noticed compared to 1995–2000, but that is below the level recorded in 1990–5. In other words, the financial health of the GCS has deteriorated during 1995–2004 as compared to the 1990–5 period. For the SCS, the index has improved during 1995–2000 compared to 1990–5. In the recent period of 2000–4, there is again a sign of deterioration. The extent of the decline in the CIFH during 2000–4 for the SCS has been so severe that it is worse than the scenario prevailing in 1990–5. The performance of the GCS on the resource mobilization front has substantially improved in the more recent period of 2000–4 compared to the earlier periods.

Table 4.1 Composite index of fiscal health

State	Fiscal health			Resource management			Expenditure management		
	1990–5	1995–2000	2000–4	1990–5	1995–2000	2000–4	1990–5	1995–2000	2000–4
Andhra Pradesh	0.43	0.28	0.28	0.25	0.1	0.6	0.35	0.31	0.36
Assam	0.3	0.28	0.29	0.36	0.45	0.64	0.25	0.22	0.26
Bihar	0.16	0.13	0.2	0.32	0.19	0.54	0.14	0.11	0.14
Goa	0.75	0.66	0.45	0.75	0.54	0.73	0.87	0.74	0.72
Gujarat	0.53	0.32	0.33	0.96	0.48	0.37	0.41	0.46	0.48
Haryana	0.54	0.37	0.37	0.64	0.5	0.67	0.38	0.47	0.52
Karnataka	0.49	0.39	0.36	0.47	0.39	0.82	0.4	0.42	0.42
Kerala	0.37	0.23	0.25	0.5	0.43	0.68	0.24	0.28	0.27
Madhya Pradesh	0.36	0.25	0.27	0.27	0.31	0.59	0.37	0.33	0.32
Maharashtra	0.58	0.31	0.24	0.28	0.4	0.39	0.45	0.42	0.4
Orissa	0.3	0.14	0.23	0.2	0.26	0.64	0.29	0.25	0.23
Punjab	0.35	0.2	0.32	0.48	0.34	0.8	0.28	0.28	0.35
Rajasthan	0.35	0.23	0.24	0.41	0.29	0.59	0.34	0.33	0.32
Tamil Nadu	0.47	0.31	0.34	0.4	0.42	0.75	0.39	0.35	0.36

Table 4.1 (Continued)

State	Fiscal health			Resource management			Expenditure management		
	1990–5	1995–2000	2000–4	1990–5	1995–2000	2000–4	1990–5	1995–2000	2000–4
Uttar Pradesh	0.16	0.11	0.18	0.22	0.27	0.46	0.12	0.11	0.21
West Bengal	0.18	0.14	0.11	0.25	0.07	0.29	0.15	0.11	0.12
GCS	*0.38*	*0.21*	*0.22*	*0.32*	*0.31*	*0.49*	*0.29*	*0.27*	*0.29*
Arunachal Pradesh	0.67	0.48	0.45	0.45	0.59	0.76	0.29	0.63	0.55
Himachal Pradesh	0.43	0.48	0.29	0.41	0.52	0.57	0.35	0.58	0.41
Jammu & Kashmir	0.34	0.4	0.4	0.46	0.58	0.78	0.13	0.22	0.4
Manipur	0.38	0.4	0.31	0.27	0.38	0.46	0.31	0.41	0.28
Meghalaya	0.39	0.4	0.37	0.33	0.34	0.54	0.32	0.34	0.4
Mizoram	0.6	0.4	0.35	0.46	0.59	0.69	0.67	0.53	0.46
Nagaland	0.49	0.31	0.39	0.24	0.53	0.63	0.28	0.3	0.39
Sikkim	0.66	0.68	0.64	0.79	0.85	0.92	0.64	0.62	0.68
Tripura	0.28	0.47	0.37	0.39	0.36	0.53	0.19	0.27	0.38
SCS	*0.4*	*0.46*	*0.38*	*0.41*	*0.54*	*0.74*	*0.28*	*0.43*	*0.41*

Note: GCS and SCS refer to averages.
Source: Comptroller and Auditor General of India (2005).

The expenditure management aspect has more or less remained stable with a minor improvement during 2000–4 compared to the 1995–2000 period.

In spite of an improvement in resource mobilization efforts and containment of expenditure, the CIFH shows deterioration for the GCS as they have really fared poorly on the basis of an index of management of fiscal imbalances and of management of fiscal liabilities. In spite of a marked improvement in the resource mobilization index, the CIFH for the SCS has suffered a decline on account of the poorer performance of expenditure management, management of fiscal imbalances and management of fiscal liabilities. At the level of states, CIFH exceeds 0.3 for Goa, Gujarat, Haryana, Karnataka, Punjab and Tamil Nadu. It was below the cluster average for Bihar (though there was an improvement during 2000–4 relative to the base figures), Uttar Pradesh and West Bengal. In case of SCS, the index value suffered only a moderate deceleration from an average of 0.398 during 1990–5 to an average of 0.381 during 2000–4. Himachal Pradesh, Manipur, Meghalaya, Mizoram and Tripura had index values lower than their cluster average. If one were to assess the fiscal health of the Indian federation in 2001–2, a decade after the introduction of the reforms, it would have been found to be languishing as before. This raises a vital question as to what went wrong with India's fiscal sector reforms. Before we take up that it would be instructive to have a look at the attempts at fiscal sector reforms at the state level.

4.2 Major fiscal reform initiatives at the state level

At the state level, the prelude to rule-based fiscal policy was the setting-up of the State Fiscal Reform facility (2000–1 to 2004–5) by the centre in pursuance of the recommendations of the Eleventh Finance Commission (EFC). Under this arrangement, 28 states entered into a medium-term fiscal reform programme (MTFRP) which set up targets for broad fiscal indicators (deficit, revenue and expenditure), besides public sector enterprise reforms, power sector reforms and budgetary reforms. The Twelfth Finance Commission (TFC) has discontinued this facility beyond 2005 and instead has suggested a 'debt consolidation and waiver' scheme. In addition, state governments have opted for fiscal rules of their own through legislation. The Reserve Bank of India, which acts as the debt manager for the states, has framed a model fiscal legislation scheme for the use of the states. While only five states – Karnataka, Punjab, Kerala, Tamil Nadu and Uttar Pradesh – had enacted their fiscal responsibility legislation[4] by the end of the financial year 2004–5, another ten – Orissa, Maharastra, Rajasthan, Gujarat, Himachal Pradesh, Haryana, Chhattisgarh, Tripura, Madhya Pradesh and Andhra Pradesh – had joined the league by October 2005. Bihar promulgated an Ordinance to this effect in February 2006. Thus, the Indian states have adopted a unique blend of co-ordination approach (MTFRP) and autonomous approach (FRL) in providing statutory backing for their fiscal reform process.

Another significant development has been the implementation of Value Added Tax (VAT) in the majority of states. Twenty-five states introduced the VAT system of commodity taxation as from 1 April 2005. The switch to the VAT system from the erstwhile sales tax system is seen as a major breakthrough in taxation reforms in the context of states pursuing a competitive sales taxation system. VAT has been introduced to simplify the tax administration and to remove the cascading effects of the sales tax. To encourage the states to adopt the VAT system, central government has extended technical and financial support to the states.

What went wrong in improving state finances?

The various fiscal indicators show that the fiscal health of the country has actually deteriorated, despire the attempts at fiscal consolidation during the reform process. The deterioration in the fiscal situation is not an outcome of the reform process but rather of inadequate reform measures. There is a near consensus amongst public finance experts, both within and outside the government, as to what needs to be done. But public expenditure in a democracy is a sensitive issue on which governments prefer to go slow. In a federal set-up, systemic changes require a consensus-based approach by all the stakeholders which takes time. A glaring example is the implementation of VAT system of commodity taxation. It has taken more than five years from conceptualization to implementation of VAT, and still a number of states have yet to join the VAT system of taxation.

The need for fiscal rules is appreciated in view of the fiscal degeneration. While it is important to appreciate the need for fiscal rules, it is equally important to be alive to the nuances of a fiscal rule. Critics of fiscal rules point to the potentially harmful consequences of having deficit ceilings, especially during downturns. The government's efforts to meet deficit targets by cutting spending and raising taxes during economic slowdowns, may only aggravate the recession. As fiscal deficit targets are expressed without adjusting for cyclical conditions, the need to stabilize the budget over the cycle may be conducive to a procyclical fiscal policy (i.e., one which may unnecessarily increase the amplitude and persistence of economic fluctuations).

To what extent these concerns are justified can only be tested from what the data have to suggest. As FRL is a relatively new concept in the Indian context, the hypothesis that a fiscal deficit ceiling constrains the stabilization initiatives of government is something that only time will tell. But pending that, how fiscal policy has behaved with respect to the economic cycles, especially during the recent times, can act as a pointer to the possible limiting influence that a FRL would exert on the stabilization initiatives of the fiscal authority.

4.3   The cyclical character of fiscal policy

The standard Keynesian viewpoint for macroeconomic stabilization is to have a fiscal policy which is countercyclical: that is, it should be expansionary in times of economic slowdowns to engineer a faster recovery, and contractionary during boom periods. This Keynesian viewpoint came under attack from the 1950s onwards and especially during the 1980s, when a certain section of economists held that fiscal policy could turn out to be useless, and even harmful, as recessions might be 'self-correcting'; there could be long and uncertain time lags in the implementation of fiscal measures and institutional constraints might restrict the timely use of fiscal policy. Given these opposing viewpoints many countries have provided for an acyclical fiscal policy, where there is no room for active fiscal interventions and discretionary fiscal policy should be neutral. Acyclical fiscal policy under a targeted fiscal deficit scenario might induce a procyclical fiscal policy. For instance, during an economic slowdown the necessity to abide by the deficit rule may force governments to cut expenditures drastically when aggregate demand is already weak and may aggravate the situation. In this context it would be interesting to explore the cyclical behaviour of the fiscal policy pursued in India.

An enquiry into the cyclical sensitivity of fiscal policy requires that the fiscal variables under study are cyclically adjusted. There is a vast body of fiscal literature that explicitly recognizes how to net out the cyclical effects from the observed fiscal deficit numbers. The fiscal literature in the Indian context, however, is relatively silent on this finer aspect. To establish the true intent of the government when it has been pressing hard for fiscal stabilization, it is essential that the impact of cyclical forces be netted out to get the structural component of the deficit. The structural deficit, in simple terms, would mean how the deficit figures would have evolved had the economy moved along the trend path unfettered by any cyclical upturns or downswings. On netting out the cyclical component, if one is still confounded by relatively higher deficit figures, it could be an outcome of the drag from the past and/or a purely discretionary policy action. Persistent fiscal drag would imply that the institutional structure and spending priorities, as well as the weak tax base, are responsible for the fiscal fragility. A higher discretionary component in the fiscal deficit figures would indicate that fiscal authorities to have chosen the soft option of raising government's expenditure commitments without a concomitant attempt at removing the maladies of the taxation system. Thus, to appreciate the true character and content of the fiscal policy pursued by the central government and the state governments, it becomes necessary to disentangle the impact of fiscal drag to get an idea of the discretionary fiscal policy action. Such an attempt has been made here to decompose the deficit into a structural and a cyclical component using the methodology suggested by Price and Muller (1984). The Price and Muller approach decomposes the structural deficit into three components: base year budget balance, fiscal drag, and discretionary fiscal policy action. For our purpose, we will concentrate on the decomposition of deficit into a structural and a cyclical component.

Having netted out the cyclical influence from the deficit numbers, the cyclical character of the fiscal policy is inferred by regressing the structural primary deficit on the output gap. Following the standard practice in the literature (Bohn 1998; Wyplosz 2002; Gali and Perotti 2003), a debt stabilization motive is also incorporated by including the debt to SDP ratio in the regression specification. The fiscal literature is not unanimous on the exact specification for estimating the cyclical character of fiscal policy. While the traditional approach consists of regressing the recorded (or cyclically-adjusted) budget balance on the output gap to estimate the sensitivity of fiscal stance to the business cycle, the OECD uses a specification where changes in the cyclically-adjusted primary budget balance are regressed against changes in the cyclical component of the primary budget balance. Gali and Perotti (2003) provide a useful discussion on the alternative specification to estimate the cyclicality of the fiscal policy. Here the regression specification suggested by Cimadomo (2005) as given in (4.1) has been estimated, which is along the lines of the traditional approach:

$$CAPB_{i,t} = \alpha + \beta_1 CAPB_{i,t-1} + \beta_2 DEBT_{i,t-1} + \beta_3 OG_{i,t-1} + \epsilon_{i,t} \qquad (4.1)$$

where *CAPB* is the cyclically-adjusted primary balance, *DEBT* is the outstanding debt as a percentage of SDP, and *OG* is the Output Gap, while i and t stand for the cross-section and time dimension respectively.

Model (4.1) is a dynamic panel data model. A dynamic panel model poses a number of econometric issues. The major problem that arises when introducing a lagged dependent variable as an explanatory variable is that the error term and the lagged dependent variable are correlated, with the lagged dependent variable being correlated with the individual specific effects that are subsumed into the error term. This implies that standard estimators are biased and, as such, an alternative method of estimating such models is required. The standard procedure to obtain consistent estimates in such a situation is to adopt an instrumental variable procedure where different lags of the dependent variable are used as instruments. Although a number of candidates are possible, the Arellano and Bond (1991) approach is adopted as this generates the most efficient estimates. While using lagged dependent variables as instruments, overall instrument validity is ascertained using a Sargan test of overidentifying restrictions.

The primary balance is defined in terms of deficit, or the excess of spending over revenue. A negative β_3 coefficient would suggest an (aggregate) countercyclical fiscal stance and a positive coefficient, procyclicality. We have estimated two variants of (4.1): the first is a plain vanilla model with 'output gap' as the only explanatory variable, and the second is an extended model with 'output gap' and 'the lagged debt' as an additional explanatory variable. As the results

Table 4.2   Evidence on cyclicality of fiscal policy

Model	Explanatory variable	General Category States	All states
Plain vanilla	SDPD(-1)	0.50	0.07
		(0.00)	(0.00)
	OG(-1)	0.02	0.04
		(0.07)	(0.00)
	P-value of Sargan Test	0.42	0.48
Extended	SDPD(-1)	0.29	0.06
		(0.08)	(0.00)
	OG(-1)	0.05	0.05
		(0.00)	(0.00)
	DEBT(-1)	0.04	−0.01
		(0.17)	(0.36)
	P-value of Sargan Test	0.28	0.47

Notes: Dependent variable is the structural primary balance.
'All states' includes 14 general category and five special category states.
Estimation is for the period 1991–2004.
Figures in parentheses indicate *p*-values.

indicate (Table 4.2), fiscal policy has been procyclical in the Indian states between 1991 and 2004.

A procyclical fiscal policy during a boom has potential consequences for higher inflation. The next issue we address is whether the fiscal stance of the states had any consequences for the inflation recorded in the states. Though the fiscal stance can be expressed through the change in the cyclically adjusted primary balance, there are established methodologies to infer about the fiscal stance of the government. Before we attempt to establish the empirical link between the fiscal stance and inflation, a discussion on the significance of the concept of the fiscal stance would be worthwhile.

4.4   Fiscal stance: significance and consequence for inflation

The fiscal stance is best described through the discretionary fiscal policy which is the deliberate attempt by the government to adjust the fiscal position. However, to ascertain the fiscal policy stance, the effect of the business cycle on the fiscal accounts has to be considered.

The fiscal impulse indicators evaluate the discretionary variation in the fiscal balance (Chand 1993). Fiscal impulse refers to the change in the fiscal balance and it is seen as a measure of the impact of fiscal policy on aggregate demand. This concept is traditionally related to the structural fiscal balance which excludes the effect of the business cycle and provides an estimate of discretionary fiscal policy. One method of assessing the stance and thrust of fiscal policy is to measure the total impulse or initial stimulus to aggregate demand arising from the fiscal policy during a given period. A positive (negative) measure of fiscal impulse (MFI) will imply a more expansionary (contractionary) fiscal stance compared to the previous year. The changes in MFI will capture the changes in both discretionary decisions on expenditure and revenue policies as well as the estimated effects of the automatic stabilizers.

Measuring the adjustment in the public balance due to the deliberate intervention of the government requires distinguishing between the cyclically adjusted and the actual balance. Public expenditures and revenues have country-specific cyclical components. Therefore, when economic activity is contracting, a deterioration of the fiscal accounts may occur for reasons other than a fiscal impulse, such as the presence of automatic stabilizers. These are expenditure and taxation items already built in to stimulate economic activity during recessions and to temper it in periods of economic overheating. For developed countries, one of the most important built-in stabilizers is unemployment compensation. When economic activity slows down, the expenditure on unemployment insurance increases, stimulating the economy. However, when economic activity is above potential, such unemployment insurance expenditure decreases. In India there were no provisions for unemployment benefit that would have a macroeconomic impact prior to the enactment of the National Rural Employment Guarantee[5] (NREG) Act, 2005. It is important for the central bank (Reserve Bank of India) to be aware of the intended adjustments of the fiscal authority, given its implications for demand management.

For the formulation of monetary policy it is necessary to be aware of the cyclical position of the economy as well as of the fiscal stance which can be evaluated by the fiscal impulse. Deviations above potential growth may result in higher inflation (Alesina *et al.* 2001). When the economy is growing above its potential and the fiscal impulse is positive, it is more difficult for the monetary authority to control inflation. For instance, when the Mexican economy in the year 2000 grew at 3.4 percentage points above the potential and the fiscal impulse was 2 per cent of GDP, monetary policy had to be tightened six times because of aggregate demand[6] pressures.

Fiscal policy stance

To measure the fiscal impulse of discretionary policies accurately, it is necessary to take into consideration the business cycle. Methodologies pursued by the International Monetary Fund (IMF) and the OECD have been adopted to measure fiscal impulse for 19 Indian states. The fiscal impulses have been derived for 14 GCS and 5 SCS for the period 1990–1 up to 2003–4 for which actual (account) fiscal data are available. The variables used are gross fiscal deficit (GFD) expenditure (revenue expenditure plus capital outlay and net lending) and revenue receipts. Potential GDP has been calculated using a Hodrick–Prescott filter, which is the standard technique in the literature to fit a smooth trend to the data.[7] States which have undergone a division in the year 2000 to create new states are treated as undivided, and the necessary adjustments in the data for these states have been made. For instance, revenue receipts for Uttar Pradesh in the year 2004 would be inclusive of the figures for Uttaranchal and the remaining Uttar Pradesh. The SDP for the states have been projected up to 2008–9 and then the Hodrick–Prescott filter has been applied to this extended SDP series to tackle the end point problem. For the IMF methodology, the base year has been defined as that year for which the difference between actual and potential real SDP is minimized.[8]

Going by the IMF methodology, the cyclically neutral budget is derived under the assumption of unitary elasticities of expenditure and revenue with respect to the potential and actual output respectively.[9] The OECD methodology, however, explicitly takes into account income elasticities of revenues and expenditures in the computation of the fiscal impulse measure. The fiscal impulse measured by the IMF and OECD methodologies reveal more or less similar patterns of fiscal stance (see Figure 4.2) for the different states. In certain cases there is a difference in results produced by the two methodologies which can be appreciated if one looks at methods of computing fiscal impulses suggested by them. While

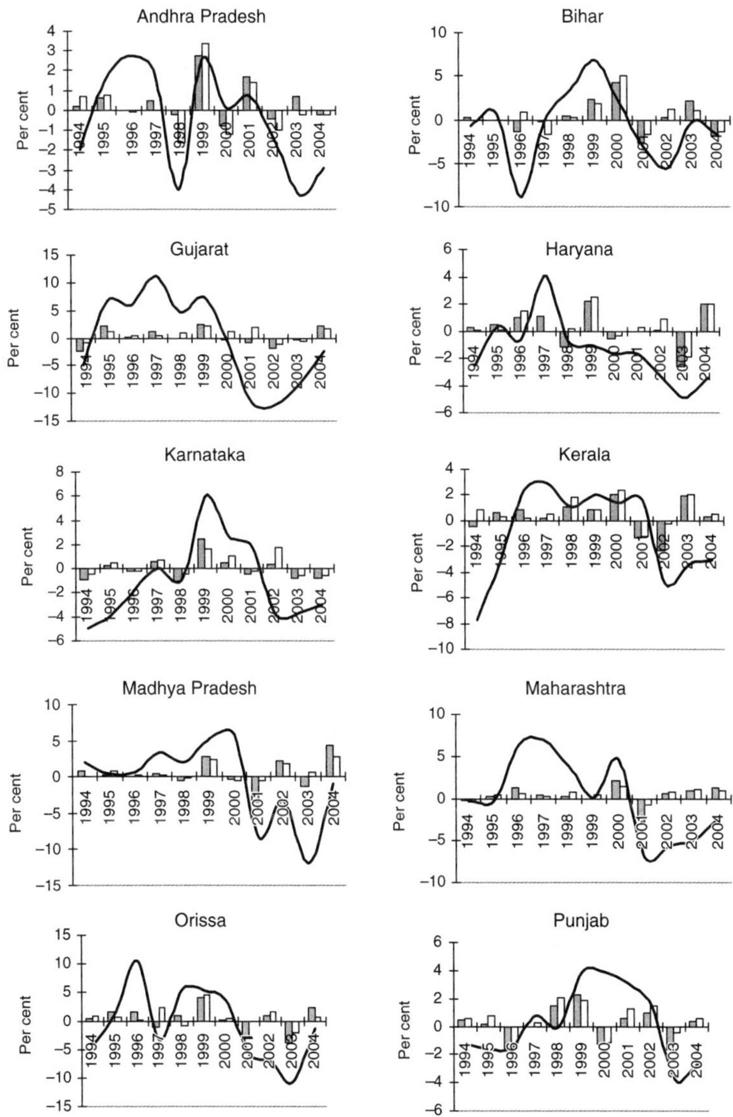

Figure 4.2　Fiscal stance and output gap

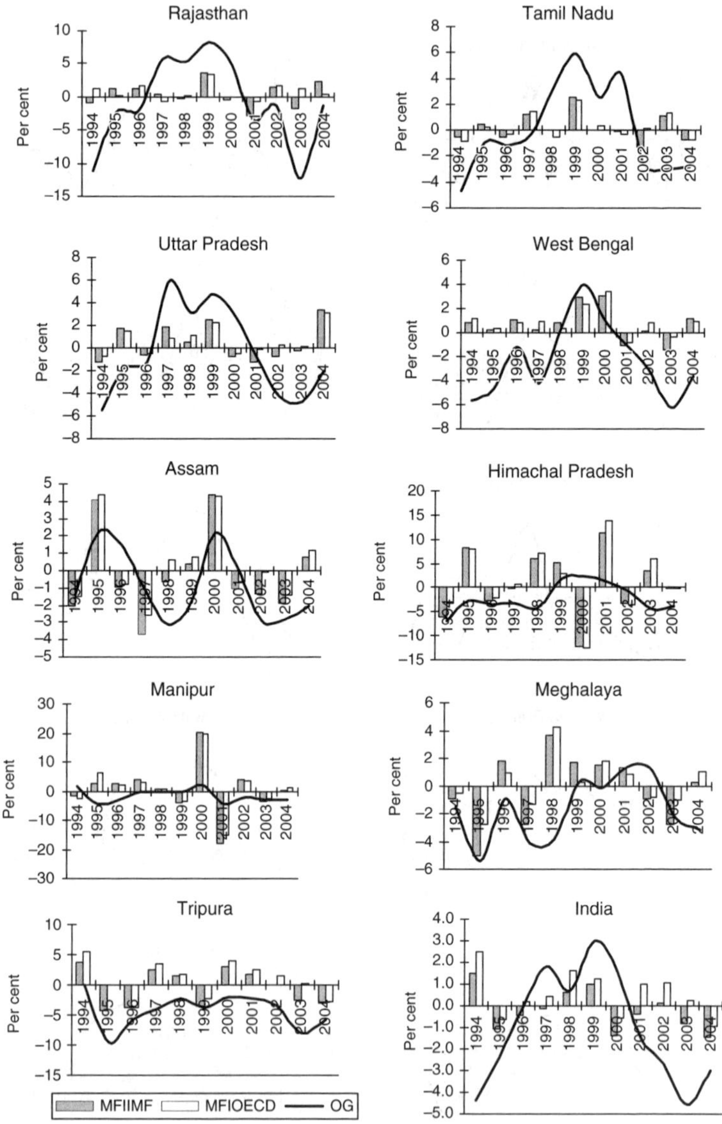

OG = Output gap defined as the deviation of actual output from potential output and expressed as per centage of potential output

MFIIMF = Measure of fiscal impulse computed using IMF methodology

MFIOECD = Measure of fiscal impulse measured using OECD methodology

Figure 4.2 (Continued)

the OECD method is based on receipts and expenditure elasticities, the IMF methodology is sensitive to the choice of base year. The noteworthy aspect is that an expansionary fiscal stance is suggested by the OECD methodology for the majority of the states in all the years between 1991 and 2004, except for the year 2001. The IMF methodology, however, suggests that the majority of the states was pursuing an expansionary fiscal policy in 9 out of the 14 years. Most of the states were pursuing an expansionary fiscal policy as suggested by both the methods beginning with the late 1990s.

Fiscal stance and inflation

During 1994–7, the best period of the reforms from a growth perspective, we find that the majority of the states were experiencing actual growth which was higher than their potential, and during these years the majority of the states were also found to be pursuing an expansionary fiscal policy as suggested by the IMF and the OECD methodologies. Economic theory suggests that positive output gap, coupled with an expansionary fiscal policy, adds to the inflationary pressures in the respective states.

Let us now proceed to examine the validity of the above hypothesis for the Indian states. We find there was deterioration in output gap compared to the previous year for the majority of the states during 2001–3. In the year 2004, the output gap had again improved over that of 2003 for as many as 16 out of the 19 states. While the implementation of pay revision in most of the states after 1996–7 and the overall economic slowdown in the late 1990s could partially explain the expansionary fiscal stance in the late 1990s, the continuance of an expansionary stance in the later years of the study period appears perplexing. This is even more true when fiscal consolidation was the expressed intention at the policy level, given the overall picture of an expansionary fiscal stance.

To enquire into the inflationary aspect, the period 1993–4 to 2003–4 is considered. Inflation in the states has been proxied by the CPI for Industrial Workers (CPIIW). Table 4A.2 provides the source of prize information for the states. To ascertain the impact of the fiscal stance and the output gap on inflation in a more rigorous manner, panel data regression models have been used. Apart from using lagged value of inflation in model (4.2) as one of the regressors, we have accounted for the effect of money supply on inflation as a control variable. Equation (4.2) describes the specification of the model:

$$INF_{i,t} = \alpha\, INF_{i,t}(-1) + \beta\, M3G_{i,t} + \theta MFI_{i,t} + \zeta\, OG_{i,t} + \epsilon_{i,t} \qquad (4.2)$$

where *INF* is inflation as measured by the variation in CPIIW, *M3G* is the growth of the money supply, *MFI* is the measure of fiscal impulse (either by the IMF or the OECD method), *OG* is the measure of output gap, *INF(-1)* is the lag of the dependent variable, ϵ is the error term and α, β, θ, ζ are the coefficients to be estimated.

Due to the lagged dependent variable in equation (4.2), an estimation is performed by the Arellano and Bond (1991) methodology which allows us to obtain consistent estimates of the model parameters. Table 4.3 brings out certain interesting results. First of all, the fiscal stance positively contributes to inflation in the states. The coefficient of fiscal stance turns out to be positive, quite high and statistically significant. The positive coefficient of the output gap suggests that fiscal policy has been procyclical for the Indian states. This attests robustness to our earlier inference about the

Table 4.3 Dynamic panel data estimation results

Variable	Coefficient	SE	*t*-ratio	*P*-value
MFI measured by IMF methodology				
INF(-1)	0.35	0.15	2.30	0.02
MFI	0.90	0.29	3.15	0.00
OG	0.21	0.06	3.66	0.00
M3G	0.47	0.05	10.16	0.00
p-value of Sargan Test is 0.34				
MFI measured by OECD methodology				
INF(-1)	0.17	0.12	1.35	0.18
MFI	0.69	0.32	2.15	0.03
OG	0.30	0.06	5.27	0.00
M3G	0.52	0.04	13.98	0.00
p-value of Sargan Test is 0.22				

Notes: Regression is based on the information for 15 states inclusive of one SCS, i.e., Assam. Price information is not available for the rest of the SCS. First column refers to explanatory variables. The dependent variable is inflation.

procyclicality of fiscal policy based on the relationship between the cyclically adjusted primary balance and output gap. The results remain insensitive to the use of MFI computed either by the IMF or the OECD methodologies. This adds credence to the empirical findings.

4.5   Concluding observations

This chapter made an attempt to explore the cyclical character of fiscal policy pursued in the Indian states during the reform period. We find that the fiscal policy at the level of the states has been procyclical. Given the adverse implications of a procyclical fiscal policy during economic downturns, there is a need to redesign the recently formulated FRLs at the centre and in the states. The FRLs should not be constraining factors in macroeconomic stabilization. There is a need for policy sensitization to tackle phases of economic slowdown by incorporating enabling provisions in the FRLs. This chapter further attempted to examine the fiscal stance of the 16 major states for the period 1990–1 to 2003–4. Fiscal stance was defined by the measure of fiscal impulse. Fiscal impulse was estimated following two methodologies as suggested by IMF and OECD. With growing emphasis on fiscal consolidation at the state level, one would expect that states are adopting a non-expansionary fiscal policy. The results obtained, however, are indicative of an expansionary fiscal policy pursued by the majority of the states in the period after the mid-1990s. More importantly, the expansionary fiscal policy had a significant impact on inflation in the states. This suggests that fiscal consolidation would have a beneficial impact on controlling inflation.

Appendix 4.1   Computation of fiscal impulse

International Monetary Fund methodology

$$FI_{IMF} = (MFI/Y)^*100$$

$$MFI = -\Delta B - (G_0/Y_0^p)\,\Delta Y^p + (T_0/Y_0^p)\,\Delta Y$$

where FI_{IMF} is the measure of the fiscal impulse (percentage of SDP); MFI is the absolute measure of the fiscal impulse; T represents government revenues; G represents government expenditures; ΔB is the actual budget balance (first difference) $(B = T - G)$; $g_0 = G_0$, the base year expenditure ratio; Y_0 is the base year SDP; Y_0^p is the potential output during the base year; Y is the output (SDP); ΔY^p is the potential output in nominal prices (first difference); and ΔY is the actual output in nominal prices (first difference). The subscript '0' refers to the base year values of any variables.

OECD methodology

$$FI_{OECD} = (FI/Y)^*100$$

$$FI = \Delta G_{ADJ} - \Delta T_{ADJ}$$

$$T_{ADJ} = T - [\mu_T\{(T_{-1}/G_{-1})(Y - Y^p)\}]$$

$$G_{ADJ} = G - [\mu_G\{(T_{-1}/G_{-1})(Y - Y^p)\}]$$

where FI_{OECD} is the fiscal impulse (percentage of SDP); FI is the fiscal impulse (absolute number); G_{ADJ} is the adjusted expenditure; T_{ADJ} is the adjusted budgetary income; μ_T is the income elasticity of revenue; μ_G is the income elasticity of expenditure; G_{-1} is the government expenditure in the previous period; T_{-1} is the government revenue in the previous period; Y is the output GDP or SDP; Y^p is the potential output; and Δ is the first difference operator.

Appendix 4.2   Decomposition of primary deficit

Table 4A.1   Decomposition of primary deficit (%)

Year	PD	SD	CD	PD	SD	CD	PD	SD	CD	PD	SD	CD
	Andhra Pradesh			Bihar			Gujarat			Haryana		
1990–1	1.07	1.18	−0.11	3.01	3.01	0	4.15	4.26	−0.11	0.98	0.98	0.00
1991–2	1	1.02	−0.02	1.96	1.95	0.01	3.47	3.65	−0.18	0.3	0.31	0.00
1992-3	1.57	1.69	−0.12	0.27	0.2	0.06	0.56	0.57	−0.01	0.54	0.52	0.02
1993–4	1.4	1.42	−0.02	−0.03	−0.04	0.01	−1.06	−1.01	−0.04	0.26	0.26	0.01
1994–5	1.58	1.57	0.01	−0.5	−0.49	−0.01	0.16	0.12	0.04	0.18	0.18	0.00
1995–6	1.11	1.09	0.02	−0.22	−0.33	0.11	0.58	0.55	0.03	1.44	1.44	0.00
1996–7	1.08	1.06	0.02	−0.98	−0.98	0	0.87	0.82	0.05	1.08	1.08	0.00
1997–8	0.29	0.32	−0.03	−0.9	−0.88	−0.03	1.41	1.4	0.02	0.8	0.79	0.00
1998–9	2.66	2.65	0.02	0.73	0.77	−0.05	3.19	3.16	0.03	2.85	2.85	0.00
1999–2000	1.5	1.5	0	4.46	4.48	−0.01	3.66	3.66	0	1.58	1.58	0.00
2000–1	2.51	2.5	0	3.34	3.32	0.02	4.48	4.53	−0.05	1.41	1.4	0.00
2001–2	1.41	1.42	−0.01	2.65	2.61	0.04	1.9	1.95	−0.05	1.84	1.84	0.00
2002–3	0.92	0.94	−0.02	3.21	3.21	0	0.8	0.83	−0.03	−0.71	−0.72	0.01
2003–4	0.33	0.34	−0.01	1.49	1.48	0.01	2.01	2.01	−0.01	1.09	1.09	0.00
	Karnataka			Kerala			Madhya Pradesh			Maharashtra		
1990–1	0.49	0.58	−0.09	2.78	2.9	−0.12	1.42	1.41	0.01	1.1	1.19	−0.18
1991–2	1.25	1.24	0.01	1.56	1.59	−0.03	0.99	1	−0.01	0.66	0.77	−0.11
1992–3	2.23	2.27	−0.03	0.81	0.86	−0.05	0.32	0.33	−0.02	1.33	1.37	−0.04

Table 4A.1   (Continued)

Year	PD	SD	CD	PD	SD	CD	PD	SD	CD	PD	SD	CD
	Karnataka			Kerala			Madhya Pradesh			Maharashtra		
1993–4	1.3	1.33	−0.03	0.94	1.01	−0.07	0.22	0.21	0.01	0.67	0.67	0.00
1994–5	1.34	1.36	−0.02	0.91	0.93	−0.02	0.56	0.56	0	0.85	0.85	0.00
1995–6	0.73	0.74	−0.01	0.98	0.96	0.01	0.73	0.73	0	1.33	1.3	0.03
1996–7	1.13	1.13	0	0.99	0.97	0.01	0.74	0.73	0.01	1.4	1.37	0.03
1997–8	0.3	0.3	0	2.28	2.27	0	0.2	0.19	0	1.81	1.8	0.01
1998–9	1.7	1.69	0.02	2.79	2.78	0.01	2.46	2.45	0.01	1.81	1.81	0.00
1999–2000	2.38	2.38	0.01	4.13	4.13	0	1.72	1.71	0.01	2.81	2.79	0.01
2000–2001	1.75	1.75	0	2.32	2.32	0	−0.03	−0.02	−0.01	1.57	1.6	−0.03
2001–2002	2.92	2.93	−0.01	1.08	1.09	−0.02	1.54	1.55	0	1.67	1.69	−0.02
2002–2003	1.66	1.66	−0.01	2.52	2.53	−0.01	1.51	1.53	−0.02	2.42	2.44	−0.02
2003–2004	0.6	0.6	−0.01	2.47	2.48	−0.01	3.77	3.77	0	2.88	2.88	0.00
	Orissa			Punjab			Rajasthan			Tamil Nadu		
1990–1	2.17	2.42	−0.25	4.95	5.09	−0.15	0.19	0.19	0	1.93	1.9	0.03
1991–2	2.9	2.91	−0.01	3.55	3.61	−0.06	0.66	0.7	−0.03	1.81	1.78	0.03
1992–3	1.23	1.31	−0.08	3.29	3.34	−0.05	1.33	1.35	−0.02	2.22	2.2	0.02
1993–4	1.18	1.23	−0.05	1.49	1.5	−0.01	1.77	1.85	−0.07	0.7	0.69	0.01
1994–5	1.67	1.66	0.02	1.58	1.6	−0.01	1.75	1.76	−0.01	0.59	0.59	0.00
1995–6	1.72	1.65	0.07	−0.32	−0.31	−0.01	2.83	2.84	−0.01	−0.05	−0.05	0.00
1996–7	1.97	2.73	−0.03	−0.38	−0.39	0	1.66	1.64	0.02	1.09	1.09	0.00
1997–8	1.58	1.55	0.03	1.29	1.29	0	1.02	1.01	0.01	0.35	0.35	0.00
1998–9	4.02	5.41	0.03	2.62	2.61	0.02	3.97	3.95	0.02	2.25	2.25	0.00

	Uttar Pradesh			West Bengal			Assam			Himachal Pradesh		
1999–2000	6.49	6.48	0.02	0.91	0.9	0.02	3.23	3.22	0.01	2.11	2.12	0.00
2000–1	2.68	2.71	−0.03	2.37	2.35	0.01	1.23	1.24	−0.01	1.38	1.39	−0.01
2001–2	2.68	2.72	−0.04	2.53	2.53	0.01	2.12	2.13	0	0.85	0.85	0.00
2002–3	−0.2	−0.1	−0.06	1.35	1.36	−0.02	2.12	2.15	−0.03	1.68	1.68	0.00
2003–4	1.32	1.33	−0.01	1.5	1.5	−0.01	2.48	2.49	0	0.53	0.53	0.00
1990–1	2.98	3.95	−0.97	2.68	2.68	0	2.79	2.78	0.01	5.28	5.3	−0.02
1991–2	1.61	1.85	−0.24	0.73	0.71	0.01	1.33	1.33	0	2.02	2.03	−0.01
1992–3	2.18	3.59	−1.41	0.1	0.14	−0.04	−1.51	−1.49	−0.02	3.11	3.14	−0.03
1993–4	1.23	2.7	−1.48	0.94	0.98	−0.04	−3.35	−3.34	−0.01	−1.2	−1.09	−0.11
1994–5	1.66	2.07	−0.4	1.03	1.06	−0.03	0.69	0.68	0.02	6.83	6.86	−0.03
1995–6	0.93	1.17	−0.25	1.46	1.47	−0.01	0.85	0.84	0.01	3.52	3.56	−0.04
1996–7	1.39	0.5	0.89	1.77	1.79	−0.02	−2.31	−2.31	−0.01	3.34	3.37	0.03
1997–8	1.97	1.53	0.44	1.63	1.63	0	−2.18	−2.16	−0.02	9.39	9.43	−0.04
1998–9	3.74	3.15	0.59	3.6	3.59	0.01	−0.71	−0.71	−0.01	10.88	10.87	0.01
1999–2000	2.58	2.26	0.32	5.91	5.91	0	2.22	2.21	0.01	−3.33	−3.35	0.02
2000–1	1.49	1.6	−0.11	4.05	4.06	0	2.14	2.14	0	7.7	7.69	0.01
2001–2	0.82	1.33	−0.51	3.53	3.54	−0.01	1.15	1.17	−0.01	3.14	3.14	0.00
2002–3	1.32	1.83	−0.51	1.75	1.76	−0.01	−0.87	−0.86	−0.01	7.28	7.3	−0.02
2003–4	3.14	3.33	−0.19	1.93	1.94	−0.01	−0.13	−0.12	−0.01	5.08	5.09	−0.01

128

Table 4A.1 (Continued)

Year	PD	SD	CD	PD	SD	CD	PD	SD	CD	PD	SD	CD
	Manipur			**Meghalaya**			**Tripura**			**India**		
1990–1	1.11	1.14	−0.03	2.29	2.28	0.03	3.65	3.44	0.22	4.53	4.55	−0.02
1991–2	3.85	3.85	0	4.28	4.25	0.03	2.99	2.81	0.17	1.65	1.67	−0.02
1992–3	−2.4	−2.4	−0.02	5.15	5.16	−0.01	−2.3	−2.32	0.02	1.35	1.38	−0.03
1993–4	−5.3	−5.31	0.01	3.59	3.61	−0.01	2.41	2.42	0	3.01	3.03	−0.02
1994–5	0.73	0.75	−0.02	−0.58	−0.54	−0.05	1.82	1.97	−0.15	1.49	1.5	−0.01
1995–6	2.89	2.91	−0.01	0.08	0.08	−0.01	−2.39	−2.31	−0.07	0.95	0.95	0.00
1996–7	5.37	5.38	0	−1.48	−1.45	−0.03	0.42	0.46	−0.04	0.58	0.58	0.00
1997–8	5.03	5.03	0	2.63	2.65	−0.02	2.3	2.32	−0.02	1.68	1.67	0.01
1998–9	0.61	0.61	0	2.65	2.65	0	−0.58	−0.55	−0.03	2.22	2.21	0.01
1999–2000	18.7	18.73	0	3.45	3.44	0	2.31	2.32	−0.01	0.82	0.82	0.00
2000–1	1.96	1.98	−0.01	3.65	3.64	0	4.16	4.17	−0.01	1.02	1.03	−0.01
2001–2	4.45	4.46	0	2.23	2.22	0	4.75	4.76	−0.02	1.61	1.61	0.00
2002–3	−0.2	−0.15	−0.01	0.22	0.23	−0.01	3.73	3.77	−0.04	1.21	1.22	0.00
2003–4	1.75	1.7	−0.01	0.66	0.67	−0.01	0.1	0.13	−0.02	−0.03	−0.03	0.00

Notes: PD = primary deficit; SD = structural component of primary deficit; CD = cyclical component of primary deficit. 0 means the percentage is negligible or nil.

Appendix 4.3   Decomposition of deficit: estimation procedure

The GFD is the sum of a structural deficit (SD) and a cyclical deficit (CD) component. The structural component can be further decomposed into three more constituents:

$$SD = A + B + K \tag{4.3}$$

where A, B and K stand for base year balance, discretionary policy action and the fiscal drag respectively.

The following steps are involved in computing the different constituents of the GFD.

Step 1: choice of receipt, expenditure and deficit indicators

While revenue receipt is considered for the receipt indicator, GFD expenditure is considered for the expenditure indicator. GFD expenditure is revenue expenditure inclusive of capital outlay and net lending. The difference between the GFD expenditure and revenue receipts gives the GFD figure.

Step 2: estimation of potential output (Y_t^*)

Potential GDP has been calculated using a Hodrick–Prescott (HP) filter which is the standard technique in the literature to fit a smooth trend to the data. In the present study GSDP at current market prices is taken as the actual output, Y_t, and the trend output, Y_t^*, is considered as the potential output. To overcome the end point problem associated with the Hodrick–Prescott filter, both real and nominal SDP figures have been projected for the 2005–8 period based on an auto-regressive model and then the Hodrick–Prescott filter has been applied on the elongated series.

Step 3: estimation of revenue and expenditure elasticity with respect to output

A double log specification is used to obtain the revenue and expenditure elasticities. The relevant equations are:

$$\text{Log}(GFDE) = a_1 + E_g{}^* \log(GSDP) \tag{4.4}$$

$$\text{Log}(RR) = a_2 + E_r{}^* \log(GSDP) \tag{4.5}$$

The coefficients E_g and E_r are the expenditure and revenue elasticities with respect to GSDP.

Step 4: choice of base year

The base year is an important variable in the calculation of structural deficit since the base year balance is a part of the structural balance along with discretionary policy action and fiscal drag. The base year is chosen to be that year for which the difference between the real actual GSDP (*RGSDP*) and real potential[10] GDP (RPGSDP) is zero or very small, and the expenditure and revenue are more or less in balance. Following this procedure, let Y_0 be the base year GSDP, R_0 base year receipt and G_0 base year expenditure respectively. From this information, we can derive the base year balance, A, as $A = G_0 - R_0$.

Step 5: derivation of the discretionary policy action (B)

The balance arising out of discretionary policy action, B, is the difference between discretionary policy induced revenues, G_{dt}, and discretionary policy induced expenditure, R_{dt}.

$$B = G_{dt} - R_{dt} \tag{4.6}$$

G_{dt} and R_{dt} are further derived as

$$G_{dt} = G_t - G_{at} \tag{4.7}$$

and

$$R_{dt} = R_t - R_{at} \tag{4.8}$$

where G_t and R_t are the actual expenditures and receipts underlying the actual GFD figure, and G_{at} and R_{at} are expenditure and receipts of deficit indicators which are responsive to change in output Y. Thus

$$G_{at} = G_0 + g_0{}^* E_g (Y_t - Y_1) \tag{4.9}$$

and

$$R_{at} = R_0 + r_0{}^* E_r (Y_t - Y_1) \tag{4.10}$$

where $g_0 = G_0/Y_0$ and $r_0 = R_0/Y_0$ and Y_1 is the output in the beginning year

Step 6: estimation of fiscal drag

Fiscal drag (K) is the product of potential change in output (F) and the built-in budget balance (C). Taking the potential (trend) level of output Y_t^*, in year t as worked out in Step 2, and assuming r to be the exponential rate of growth (e^{rt}) of the trend output, Y_t^*, the potential change in output may be measured as:

$$F = Y_1(e^{rt} - 1) \tag{4.11}$$

where $e^{rt} = Y_t^*/Y_1$.

The built-in budget balance, C, is the result of the passive policy which holds the tax rates and expenditure programmes unchanged. The estimation of C is done as follows:

$$C = (g_0{}^*E_g - r_0{}^*E_r) \tag{4.12}$$

Thus fiscal drag:

$$K = C.F \tag{4.13}$$

Step 7: estimation of structural and cyclical balance

The equation for structural balance (SD) may be written as:

$$SD = A + B + K$$

Substituting the values for A, B and K we get:

$$SD = (G_0 - R_0) + (G_{dt} - R_{dt}) + [(g_0{}^*E_g - r_0{}^*E_r)\{Y_1(e^{rt} - 1)\}] \tag{4.14}$$

The cyclical balance, CD, may be worked out as follows:

$$(g_0{}^*E_g - r_0{}^*E_r)(Y_t - Y_t^*) \tag{4.15}$$

Table 4A.2 Price information from states

Centre	State
Hyderabad	Andhra Pradesh
Guwahati	Assam
Munger-Jamalpur	Bihar
Ahmedabad	Gujarat
Faridabad	Haryana
Bangalore	Karnataka
Alwaye	Kerala
Bhopal	Madhya Pradesh
Mumbai	Maharashtra
Rourkela	Orissa
Ludhiana	Punjab
Jaipur	Rajasthan
Saharanpur	Uttar Pradesh
Kolkata	West Bengal
Chennai	Tamil Nadu

Price for a state is proxied by the price information from a centre within the state.
Source: RBI Bulletin, various issues.

5
Analytics of Credit–Output Behaviour for Indian States

Enduring growth in an emerging economy such as India's invariably requires that the economy be set on a trajectory of higher savings and also ensuring that the savings realized are channelled into productive investment. In this scheme of growth, the banking system has a dual role to play: it acts as a mobilizer of savings as well as being an allocator of credit for production and investment. Prior to the economic reforms of the early 1990s, banks were fulfilling this mandate under the direct control of the government. The motivation for state control of banking activities can be appreciated if one traverses the broad agenda of economic policy-making since Independence. Under the broad rubric of growth, balanced regional development has been one of the avowed objectives of economic policy in India since the early days of planning. To pave the way for a more balanced pattern of development and to meet socially desirable objectives as set out in the Five-Year Plans, it was necessary to ensure that availability of credit did not act as a constraint on growth. Further, there was a need to augment the savings of the economy to attain higher growth rates. This was attempted through mobilization of savings by widening the reach of the banking system throughout the country. In this context, the nationalization of banks in the late 1960s was a major landmark.

Prior to nationalization, banks were controlled by big industrial houses and their reach was limited to urban areas; they mostly financed industry. For instance, 64.3 per cent of the aggregate credit in the banking system was going to finance industry as of March 1966.[1] Bank nationalization was a conscious attempt on the policy front to expand the reach of banking beyond the mainstream. The objective behind bank nationalization was broadly twofold: first, to inculcate banking habits in the people so that deposit mobilization became smoother, simpler and faster; second, to ensure that credit needs of the different sectors and regions are adequately addressed for balanced development and in a timely fashion. If one were to assess the success of bank nationalization in extending the reach of banking, it can be gauged from the increase in commercial bank branches from 4,158 to 11,010 between 1968–9 and 1975–6. Out of the total increase of 6,852 branches during this period, about 68 per cent were opened in rural and semi-urban areas. Thus nationalization of banks served the purpose of extending the scope of banking to the rural hinterlands. Rapid branch expansion helped to mobilize untapped rural savings. Consequently, gross savings in the Indian economy increased from 11.9 to 16.2 per cent during this period. Subsequently, the number of offices of scheduled commercial banks has increased to more than 66,000. In addition, there has been significant improvement in the various indicators of financial development. As far as credit disbursal during the post-nationalization period is concerned, the share of the priority sector in total bank credit increased from 15 per cent in 1969 to 25 per cent in June 1971, and further to 34 per cent in March 2004.

In essence, after nationalization, commercial banks in India were viewed as instruments of economic and social development rather than purely as profit-seeking commercial ventures. Commercial banks were entrusted with the task of nurturing entrepreneurial talent by providing finance through their expanded branch network. Banks were given a mandate to cater to the needs of planned development by channelling the flow of credit to agriculture, rural artisans, housing loans for weaker sections, the retail trade and other priority sectors which did not have access to capital markets earlier. This mandate was operationalized through the monetary and credit policy of the central bank (RBI). Consequently, credit policy in India evolved with credit rationing as an integral part of it and the credit needs of the different sectors were prioritized. The rationing of credit was schematized with food credit as the top priority, followed by prescribed priority sector lending, sectoral limits for credit deployment and selective credit controls. Sectoral credit targets became the proximate target for monetary policy which operated through the allocation of non-food commercial bank credit. The underlying idea was that the adequate and timely availability of credit to a large section of people can contribute to a growth process which will be broadly based. The interest rate structure was administered and given importance of second order in the conduct of monetary policy. The pursuit of social banking, however, had its pitfalls too. Directed lending, coupled with administered interest rates, not only distorted the interest rate mechanism but also adversely affected the viability and profitability of the banks (Reddy 2004). With economy-wide changes effected through structural reform measures, it was natural that the financial system was repositioned to meet the challenges of an open economy.

In keeping with the economy-wide reforms, financial sector reforms were initiated in India in 1992–3 to promote a diversified, efficient and competitive financial system. The banking sector being the dominant segment in India's financial system, a number of measures specific to the banking system were initiated to improve its long-term viability as a commercial entity. The freedom to price banking products on commercial considerations, relaxation in various balance sheet restrictions in the form of statutory pre-emptions (exposing the banking sector to increased competition by allowing entry of new private sector banks) and the introduction of prudential norms relating to income recognition, asset classification and capital adequacy were some of the ingredients of the banking sector reforms. The early initiatives in the banking reforms were geared towards removing the functional and operational constraints impinging upon banks' operations and, subsequently, providing them with greater operational autonomy to take decisions based on commercial considerations. With the gradual relaxation of administered controls, banks and financial institutions were expected to evolve as truly commercial entities.

Alongside these structural reforms in the banking sector, the RBI has broadened its monetary policy framework. The use of broad money as an intermediate target has been de-emphasized and a multiple indicator approach has been adopted. In the multiple indicator approach, in addition to interest rates, information on credit expansion, fiscal position, trade, capital flows, inflation rate and the exchange rate is juxtaposed with output data for drawing policy perspectives. The twin objectives of 'maintaining price stability' and 'ensuring availability of adequate credit to productive sectors of the economy to support growth' continue to govern the stance of monetary policy.

Notwithstanding the various banking sector reforms and the recommendation of the Narasimham Committee on Banking Sector Reforms in 1998 to relax the norms for priority sector lending targets, the banking system has not been absolved of its responsibilities to finance the priority sector. Further, in the Plan process, credit targets for important sectors are specified. For instance, the Tenth Five-Year Plan envisaged a substantial jump in credit flow to agriculture, from Rs 229,956 crores achieved in the 9th Plan period to Rs736, 750 crores (Government of India (2006)). In recent times, the Indian Finance Minister in his 2004–5 Budget proposed doubling the credit available to the agriculture sector by March 2007. All these indicate that credit expansion is still taken seriously in policy-making in India. If credit is seen as an instrument for growth, and balanced regional development as the policy objective, it is a matter of interest to investigate how balanced has been the flow of credit over time and across the states to attain this policy objective. Further, it would be interesting to decipher whether there has been any perceptible change in the credit deployment pattern across the states in the post-reform scenario, when balance sheet restrictions to a great extent have been withdrawn.

Prior to economic and banking sector reforms, balance sheet restrictions in the form of Cash Reserve Ratio (CRR) and Statutory Liquidity Ratio (SLR) investment used to lock up around 63 per cent of NDTL (net demand and time liabilities) of the banks. On top of that, given the priority sector target of 40 per cent, banks were left with very few funds to explore business opportunities. With relaxation of balance sheet restrictions, it was expected that banks' commercial ingenuity would be vented and in the process that credit growth would get a boost. Despite the relaxations in the balance sheet restrictions for quite a long stretch of time, particularly between 1999–2000 and 2003–4, the investment portfolio, especially in the (government securities) G-Sec segment, was quite high. The very high SLR holdings of banks (at close to 39 per cent at an aggregate level, as compared to the regulatory prescription of 25 per cent) was attributed to banks' preference to minimize credit risk while increasing profitability (Mohan 2003). It may be argued that the reforms brought in stringent asset recognition norms in keeping with the best international practices but, given the legal constraints in asset recovery,[2] banks preferred lazy or narrow banking. However, it is interesting to observe that the period of higher preference for investment was also marked by an economic slowdown.[3] This leads one to ponder whether banks preferred investment to advances not because investments were relatively more profitable, but more because there was not enough absorptive capacity in the face of the slowdown. There is credence to lend support to such a view. With economic growth picking up in recent times, there has been a phenomenal upsurge in credit growth too. While the Indian economy grew at more than 8 per cent in 2004–5 and 2005–6, credit growth has been of the order of more than 30 per cent in 2005–6 on top of a high credit growth of 26 per cent in 2004–5. The phenomenon of lower credit growth during the times of economic slowdown and high growth during the times of economic boom raises a more fundamental question about whether credit follows output in the Indian economy or whether it is the other way round. This leads us to the issue of causality between credit and output.

An idea about the causality between credit and output becomes pertinent especially for states with a very low CD ratio, where the debate on low credit off-take becomes an issue of contention between the banking system and the state government concerned. While the state governments cry foul at being neglected by the banking system, the banking system blames it on the lack of credit absorption capacity in the state.[4] The recently submitted Expert Group Report (chaired by Y.S.P. Thorat) has revisited the issue of the credit-absorptive capacity of states in detail (NABARD, 2006). One issue which stands out in the debate, which is worth pondering, is that banks (being commercial entities with an eye on profit) would certainly not like to miss viable business opportunities, if there are any. The empirical evidence with regard to causality between credit and output at the state level will throw some light on the relative strengths of the contrasting viewpoints.

Against this backdrop, the present chapter will address two broad issues: first, the temporal and spatial pattern of growth and credit allocation over the last two decades, and second, the nature of the relationship between bank credit and growth at the regional level. The rest of the chapter is schematized as follows. Section 5.1 reviews the relationship between bank credit and growth, from both a historical and a theoretical perspective. The major changes in the pattern of growth and credit allocation over the last two decades are dealt in section 5.2. The empirical framework to facilitate a study of the causality between credit and output is discussed in section 5.3. The econometric findings are discussed in section 5.4, and section 5.5 presents some concluding observations.

5.1 Review of the literature

There is much more to bank credit than that meets the eye. From the early days of Adam Smith, there has been a continuing and intense debate on the role of financial intermediaries in the development process. Adam Smith, in *An Inquiry into the Nature and Causes of Wealth of Nations* (1776), was sceptical about banks' ability to create capital. Nonetheless, he perceived banks' role in augmenting the productivity of capital stock in the economy and thereby promoting growth. Dunning McLeod, writing some 80 years after Adam Smith, attributed a much more positive role to the banks in promoting growth. He not only disagreed with the view that banks do not create capital but added that, by lending, banks bring unutilized resources into production; extend the market by providing credit facilities; and, more importantly, promote venture capitalists through their cash credit facilities. Schumpeter, another great economic thinker, in *Theory of Economic Development* (1912) argued that financial intermediaries help the growth process in a variety of ways, such as mobilizing savings, evaluating projects, managing risks, monitoring managers and facilitating transactions. Further, in his analysis of business cycles, bank credit plays a crucial role in accentuating/moderating the phases of business cycles.

Over the last 50 years, the literature on finance and development has proliferated on both the theoretical and the empirical planes. Two broad schools of thought – the financial structuralist and financial repressionist – have been expounded in the literature that deals with the relationship between financial intermediaries and growth. The financial structuralists stress the quantity aspects of financial variables, such as the volume of credit, that positively affect growth. The financial repression school, on the other hand, discusses how financial repression, especially in the form of below-equilibrium real interest rate and domestic currency overvaluation, retard growth.

Patrick (1966) provides a useful reference framework for the study of the causal relationship between bank claims and growth. Patrick makes a distinction between the 'demand-following approach' and the 'supply-leading approach' to financial development. Demand following is defined as a situation where financial development is an offshoot of the developments in the real sector. Markets expand with growth and require more, and more efficient, financial services to maintain the pace of growth. In the case of supply leading, financial development precedes and stimulates the process of economic growth. The supply of financial services and instruments creates demand for them. Patrick suggested that in the early stages of economic development, a supply-leading relation is more likely to hold since a direct stimulus is needed to collect savings to finance investment for growth; while, at a later stage, when the financial sector is more developed, the demand-following relation will be more prevalent. The two alternative hypotheses suggested by Patrick have been empirically tested by several authors. Gupta (1984) found support for the supply-leading hypothesis in a study of 14 developing countries. Both Jung (1986) and St. Hill (1992), using data on 56 countries (of which 37 were less developed countries, or LDCs), found moderate support for the supply-leading hypothesis in LDCs, while the demand-following hypothesis appeared to fit more closely the situation in developed nations. These results are suggestive of the pattern of financial development envisaged by Patrick.

Although the question of causality remains unresolved until now, the answer to this question has far-reaching policy implications and has, therefore, been a recurring subject of debate in the literature on financial markets and economic development. It is often argued that only for the supply-leading hypothesis is there a need to direct attention to developments in the financial sector. When financial development arises spontaneously as the economy grows (demand-following approach), the emphasis should be more on developments in the real economy. However, such a theoretical dichotomy is difficult to defend in the face of continuous interaction between the real and the financial sectors in practice. Even when the evidence is suggestive of the demand-following approach, financial policy needs to be fine-tuned to let the demand-following scheme run its full course.

Again, there has been a revival of finance and economic development linkage through the endogenous growth theory over the past 15 years. In the endogenous growth theory framework, bank finance has the scope to influence economic growth by increasing the productivity of capital, lowering the intermediation cost or augmenting the savings rate. The role of financial institutions is to collect and analyse information so as to channel investible funds into activities that yield the highest returns (Greenwood and Jovanovich 1990). Although in a pure neoclassical framework the financial system is irrelevant to economic growth, in practice an efficient financial system has the potential for improving growth rates (RBI 2001b). It can simultaneously lower the cost of external borrowing, raise the return to savers and ensure efficient allocation of resources.

Martin Fase (2001) presents an empirical examination of the relationship between financial intermediation and economic growth. Employing data from aggregated balance sheets for financial institutions in the Netherlands for the years 1900–2000, and conducting estimations and causality tests, Fase shows that financial intermediation encourages economic growth. Employing GMM panel estimators on a panel data set from 74 countries and a cross-sectional instrumental variable estimator on data from 71 countries, Levine, Loayza and Beck (2000) find that the exogenous component of financial intermediary development is positively associated with economic growth. Robert G. King and Ross Levine (1993a) have studied the empirical link between a range of indicators of financial development and economic growth. They found that indicators of the level of financial development, such as the size of the formal financial intermediary sector relative to GDP, the importance of banks relative to the central bank, the percentage of credit allocation to private firms and the ratio of credit issued to private firms to GDP, are strongly and robustly correlated with growth, the rate of physical capital accumulation and improvements in the efficiency of capital allocation. Indeed, the predetermined components of these financial development indicators significantly predict subsequent values of the growth indicators. Gregorio and Guidotti (1995) examined the empirical relationship between long-run growth, financial development (proxied by the bank credit to the private sector) and GDP for a large cross-country sample (sample of 98 countries for 1960–85), and found a positive effect of financial development on long-run growth of real per capita GDP. Goldsmith (1969) used the ratio of assets of the financial intermediaries to GNP as a proxy for financial development under the implicit assumption that the size of the financial system is positively correlated with the quality and provision of financial services. Using the data on 35 countries from 1860 to 1963, his results indicated a rough 'parallelism' between economic and financial development.

Empirical studies of the credit–output relationship for the Indian economy are at variance with each other. Industry level studies generally confirm the positive impact of unanticipated changes in credit on the level of output. On the other hand, it has been shown that within a rational expectations framework, credit shocks do not have any significant impact on firm level output in India because monetary policy is predictable. Employing the bivariate Vector Auto Regression (VAR) model, Reserve Bank of India (2001b) found two-way Granger causality between GDP growth and real bank claims growth for the Indian economy over the period 1972–2000. Further, in the *Report on Currency and Finance, 2000-01* (Reserve Bank of India (2002b), using a simultaneous equations framework, it was found that the demand for non-food credit is predominantly influenced by output represented by an index of industrial production (IIP), not only contemporaneously but also by 1-month and 2-months lagged outputs. Causality analysis reveals bi-directional causality in the Granger sense between cyclical movements of non-food credit and overall industrial production as well as with latter's components (i.e., basic goods, capital goods and consumer goods production).

On a re-examination of the causal relationship between credit[5] and output, employing a bivariate VAR, RBI (2004) finds evidence of bi-directional causality between output (proxied by IIP) and credit (proxied by real non-food credit) during 1994–2004. While the relationship between bank credit and growth has been studied to some extent at the sectoral/disaggregated level, similar studies relating financial development to growth at the aggregate level are rather few. Misra (2003) has analysed the causality between credit and output in the spatial dimension for the period 1981–2000. This study, based on an error correction framework, finds evidence in favour of uni-directional causality from output to credit for the majority of the states. This study suggests that credit flow to different states is guided by the credit absorptive capacity of the states. Misra (2003) undertook the causality analysis for the individual states; the study had the limitation of a small sample size. With developments in panel data econometrics, causality between output and credit can be studied in a panel error correction framework. As the panel data analysis is based on a broader and richer information set, the results from panel tests have greater power than individual time series tests. Here we have extended the period of analysis up to 2004 and tested for causality both in the time series and the panel dimension. Before we discuss the econometric methodology to study causality, we chronicle some of the stylized facts about credit and output behaviour in the Indian economy since the 1980s.

5.2 Pattern of growth and credit allocation

Growth in credit and output at the aggregate level over the last two decades (Table 5.1) reveals that nominal output has grown at a slower rate in the post-reform period; but we have already seen that real output grew at a faster rate after the reforms. Both these observations are consistent as the post-reform period in India is marked by a relatively lower rate of inflation compared to the pre-reform period. Certain other observations follow from Table 5.1. First, overall credit growth has marginally improved in the post-reform period. Second, although deceleration in the nominal per capita output growth is found in all the sectors, it has been sharper in the case of the primary and secondary sectors. Third, credit has grown much higher than output in both the periods. Fourth, credit growth in the secondary sector, while it has decelerated rather like the tertiary sector, has gathered further momentum. Primary sector credit growth has more or less remained the same in both the pre- and the post-reform

Table 5.1 Growth of output and credit (%)

Variable	1980–1 to 1992–3		1993–4 to 2003–4		1980–1 to 2003–4	
	Output	**Credit**	**Output**	**Credit**	**Output**	**Credit**
Primary	10.04	12.49	6.52	12.79	9.78	10.64
Secondary	12.69	14.66	8.85	12.79	12.02	13.80
Tertiary	13.54	15.49	12.31	18.25	13.53	15.52
All sectors	12.15	14.66	10.01	15.21	12.07	14.09

Note: Output figures are represented by GDP at factor cost and at current prices, and credit figures are all-India credit outstanding for all sectors at current prices. Both the credit and output figures are in per capita terms.

Table 5.2   Average share in output and credit (%)

Sector	1980–1 to 1992–3		1993–4 to 2003–4	
	Output	**Credit**	**Output**	**Credit**
Primary	33.83	16.35	26.82	10.81
Secondary	21.15	45.74	21.08	45.44
Tertiary	45.02	37.91	52.10	43.75

periods. Fifth, the gap between the credit growth and output growth has widened substantially in the post-reform period.

If we consider the share of different sectors in output and credit (Table 5.2), the following pattern emerges at the aggregate level. The primary sector has witnessed a decline in both the share of credit and output. While the decline in the share of the primary sector in output has been of the order of seven percentage points, the same for credit has been 5.5 percentage points in the post-reform period compared to the pre-reform period. The secondary sector's share in output and credit has more or less remained the same in both the periods at around 21 and 45 per cent respectively. The share of the tertiary sector in output, which was around 45 per cent during 1981–93, has increased to 52 per cent in the latter period. The 7 per cent gain in the share in output is matched by a corresponding increase in this sector's share of the total outstanding credit of around 6 per cent (from 38 to 44 per cent). So, at the all-India level, the service sector turns out to be the most vital sector. While agriculture is undergoing a decline, industry seems to be caught by inertia. But the all-India scenario shadows the detailed picture at the state level. What is happening to the share of different regions in the all-India aggregate output and aggregate credit over the two decades can be seen from Table 5.3.

Shares in output and credit

The following points emerge from the state level analysis with respect to the changing share of output and credit in the post-reform period. On the output front, 13 out of 22 states have increased their share in GDP in the post-reform period. Of these, four belong to the SCS and the rest to the GCS. However, only five states[6] could improve their share in all-India outstanding credit for all sectors in the post-reform

Table 5.3 Changing share of states in output and credit

Increased share in output and credit	Andhra Pradesh, Karnataka, Maharashtra, Tamil Nadu and Meghalaya
Increased share in output and decreased share in credit	Gujarat, Haryana, Kerala, Rajasthan, Mizoram, Nagaland and Sikkim
Increased share in credit and decreased share in output	None
Decreased share in output and credit	Bihar, Himachal Pradesh, Punjab, Madhya Pradesh, Orissa, Uttar Pradesh, West Bengal, Arunachal Pradesh, Assam, Tripura, Manipur

Note: The shares in credit (total credit outstanding for all sectors in the economy) and output (GSDP at current market prices) are expressed as a percentage of all-India outstanding credit for all sectors and GDP at factor cost and current market prices respectively.

period. Only five states could improve their share of output as well as credit. But when it comes to decline in the share of both credit and output, as many as 11 states share this attribute. Further, five of these belonged to the SCS. Thus the SCS have broadly lost out in the post-reform period compared to their GCS counterparts.

Changing share of different regions in output and credit across sectors

Going further down to the level of states, Appendix 5.5 shows the changing share of different sectors in output and credit in the post-reform period. The following points emerge from Appendix 5.5: first, the share of the primary sector in total credit outstanding for all sectors in the state has gone down for all the GCS. Amongst the SCS, only for Arunachal Pradesh and Sikkim is there an increase in the primary sector's share in overall credit, and for the remaining states there was a decline in the post-reform period. As far as the primary sector's share in SDP is concerned, all states, except Nagaland, experienced a decline. Second, except for Bihar, Maharashtra, Tamil Nadu and West Bengal in the GCS category, and Mizoram, Sikkim and Nagaland in the SCS category, the secondary sector's contribution to SDP has increased in the post-reform period. Third, as far as the secondary sector's share in total credit for the state is concerned, only

Haryana and Punjab in the GCS category and Manipur, Meghalaya and Sikkim in the SCS category experienced an increase. For the remaining states, there has been a decline in the share of credit of the secondary sector. Fourth, the share of the service sector in SDP has gone up for all the 23 states studied in the post-reform period. The share of the tertiary sector in total credit has also gone up for all the states studied, except for Sikkim. Thus, at the state level, the broad picture that emerges is one of the prominence of the tertiary sector both in output and credit. The primary sector is losing out both in credit and output shares. The secondary sector is saddled with inertia.

As far as the growth in sectoral credit and output (Appendix 5.6) is concerned, we find that primary sector growth for all the GCS has declined in the post-reform period. Among the SCS, only Himachal Pradesh and Tripura experienced an accelerated growth of the primary sector in the post-reform period compared to the pre-reform period. The rest of the SCS also experienced decelerated primary sector growth during the post-reform period. Growth of credit for the primary sector was noticed for Kerala, Maharashtra, Punjab, Rajasthan and Uttar Pradesh in the GCS category, and for Himachal Pradesh in SCS category. Further, the secondary sector grew at a faster pace in the post-reform period only in Kerala and West Bengal in the GCS category, and Tripura and Sikkim in the SCS category. For all other states, growth of the secondary sector was slower in the post-reform period. An acceleration of credit growth in the secondary sector was noticed for Haryana and Karnataka in the GCS category and only for Himachal Pradesh in the SCS category. For the tertiary sector, growth has accelerated for Haryana, Karnataka, Kerala and West Bengal under the GCS category and Meghalaya and Tripura in the SCS category. However, credit growth to the tertiary sector was more pervasive in the GCS, and only in case of Andhra Pradesh, Bihar, Madhya Pradesh and Uttar Pradesh was there a decline in the post-reform period. Amongst the SCS, credit growth to the tertiary sector slowed for a number of states, such as Manipur, Meghalaya, Nagaland and Tripura.

5.3 Econometric methodology

What we try to explore here is the causal relationship between credit and output. The most widely accepted nomenclature for causality in econometrics is Granger causality. We discuss the framework for Granger causality both in the time series and in the panel dimension.

Time series approach

According to Granger (1969), Y is said to Granger-cause X if and only if X is better predicted by using the past values of Y than by not doing so with the past values of X being used in either case. If Y causes X and X does not cause Y, it is said that uni-directional causality exists from Y to X. If Y does not cause X and X does not cause Y, then X and Y are statistically independent. If Y causes X and X causes Y, it is said that feedback exists between X and Y. Essentially, Granger's definition of causality is framed in terms of predictability.

Granger (1969) originally suggested the Granger test, which was improved by Sargent (1976). To implement the Granger test, a particular autoregressive lag length k (or p) is assumed and equations (5.1) and (5.2) are estimated by Ordinary Least Squares (OLS):

$$X_t = \lambda_1 + \sum_{i=1}^{k} a_{1i} X_{t-i} + \sum_{j=1}^{k} b_{1j} Y_{t-j} + \mu_{1t} \tag{5.1}$$

$$Y_t = \lambda_2 + \sum_{i=1}^{p} a_{2i} X_{t-i} + \sum_{j=1}^{p} b_{2j} Y_{t-j} + \mu_{2t} \tag{5.2}$$

In the above system of equations, the F-test is carried out for the null hypothesis of no Granger causality: that is, $H_0 : b_{i1} = b_{i2} = \ldots = b_{ik} = 0, i = 1, 2$ (where the F-statistic is the Wald statistic for the null hypothesis). If the F-statistic is greater than a certain critical value for an F distribution, then we reject the null hypothesis that Y does not Granger-cause X (equation 5.1), which means Y does Granger-cause X. The definition of the Granger causality, however, is based on the hypothesis that X and Y are stationary or I(0) time series, and a stationary series is one which has both a stable mean and standard deviation. If d differences have to be made to get a stationary process, then it can be defined as integrated of order d. Granger (1981, 1983) proposed the concept of cointegration, and Engle and Granger (1987) have made further refinements.

If several variables are all I(d) series, their linear combination may be cointegrated: that is, their linear combination may be stationary. Although the variables may drift away from equilibrium for a while, economic forces may be expected to act so as to restore equilibrium, and thus they tend to move together in the long run irrespective of short run dynamics. If the series at hand appear to contain a (or at least a) unit root in their autoregressive representations, it is not proper to apply the fundamental Granger method for variables of I(1). The classical approach for dealing with integrated variables is to difference them to make them stationary. Hassapis *et al.* (1999) show that in the absence of cointegration, the direction of causality can be decided upon via standard *F*-tests in the first differenced VAR.

The VAR in the first difference can be expressed as:

$$\Delta X_t = \lambda_1 + \sum_{i=1}^{k} a_{1i}\Delta X_{t-i} + \sum_{j=1}^{k} b_{1j}\Delta Y_{t-j} + \mu_{1t} \tag{5.3}$$

$$\Delta Y_t = \lambda_2 + \sum_{i=1}^{p} a_{2i}\Delta X_{t-i} + \sum_{j=1}^{p} b_{2j}\Delta Y_{t-j} + \mu_{2t} \tag{5.4}$$

However when both Y_t and X_t are truly I(1) and *cointegrated*, the bivariate dynamic relation between Y and X will be misspecified if one works with the differences of Y and X. According to Engle and Granger (1987), the test must be carried out with error-correction models (ECMs). They proved that any cointegrated series must have an error correction representation, and the converse is also true: cointegration is a necessary condition of ECMs. An ECM representation is really a restricted VAR with cointegration specification, so it is designed for the non-stationary series, which are found to be cointegrated. Here are the error correction representations:

$$\Delta X_t = \lambda_1 + \sum_{i=1}^{k} \alpha_{1i}\Delta X_{t-i} + \sum_{j=1}^{k} \beta_{1j}\Delta Y_{t-j} + \phi_1 ecm_{1t-1} + \mu_{1t}, \quad ecm_{1t-1}$$

$$= (X - \gamma Y)_{t-1} \tag{5.5}$$

$$\Delta Y_t = \lambda_2 + \sum_{i=1}^{k} \alpha_{2i}\Delta X_{t-i} + \sum_{j=1}^{k} \beta_{2j}\Delta Y_{t-j} + \phi_2 ecm_{2t-1} + \mu_{2t}, \quad ecm_{2t-1}$$

$$= (Y - \delta X)_{t-1} \tag{5.6}$$

where $ecm_{it-1}(i = 1, 2)$ is the error-correction (EC) term(s). ϕ_1 and ϕ_2 are called coefficients of adjustment and one of them must not be equal to zero according to Engle and Granger (1987). In equations

(5.5) and (5.6), all series are I(0) processes. The parameters in the ECM have the following interpretations. In equation (5.5), the coefficient of Y in the EC term (ecm_{1t-1}) is the long-run elasticity of X with respect to Y. Conversely, in equation (5.6), the coefficient of X in the EC term (ecm_{2t-1}) is the long-run elasticity of Y with respect to X.

β_{1j} and α_{2i} reflect the immediate response of X to changes in Y and the immediate response of Y to changes in X respectively. They are, therefore, the short-run elasticities (Thomas 1997). In equation (5.5), the larger the parameter ϕ_1, the faster is the adjustment of X to the previous period's deviation from long-run equilibrium. At the opposite extreme, very small values of ϕ_1 imply that X is unresponsive to the last period's equilibrium error. The same condition exists in equation (5.6). Since the ECM coefficients ϕ_1 and ϕ_2 cannot at the same time equal zero as the result of the presence of the cointegrating relationship, there must exist one direction of long-term causality between Y and X.

An advantage of the cointegration analysis with respect to the conventional causality test is that if the two variables are cointegrated then Granger causality must hold in at least one direction. If the coefficient of the error correction term is significant, a causal relationship will exist between the two variables. Standard t-tests are used to test the significance of ϕ_1 and ϕ_2. We use the augmented Dickey–Fuller (ADF) method to test the order of the series, and Johansen's method to test for cointegration.

Often the test of cointegration in the time series dimension is constrained by small sample size. In such situations, the test of cointegration in a panel context becomes more useful. Now, we discuss the methodology to study Granger causality in a panel data set.

Panel data approach

A study of causality in a panel context would require an examination of the data at hand for stationarity in the first place, followed by a test of cointegration in the panel context. Further, in the event of panel cointegration, we discuss the appropriate methods that can be employed to study causality.

Panel unit root tests

There are several techniques which can be used to test for a unit root in panel data. Specifically, we are interested in testing for non-stationarity against the alternative that the variable is trend-stationary.

One of the first unit root tests to be developed for panel data is that of Levin and Lin, as originally circulated in working paper form in 1992 and 1993. Their work was finally published, with Chu as a co-author, in 2002. The Levin, Lin and Chu (LLC) test is based on analysis of the equation:

$$\Delta y_{i,t} = \alpha_i + \delta_i t + \theta_t + \rho_i y_{i,t-1} + s_{i,t} \quad \text{where } i = 1, 2, \dots N$$

$$t = 1, 2, \dots, T \tag{5.7}$$

This model allows for two-way fixed effects (α and θ) and unit-specific time trends. The unit-specific fixed effects are an important source of heterogeneity, since the coefficient of the lagged dependent variable is restricted so as to be homogeneous across all units of the panel. The test involves the null hypothesis $H_0 : \rho_i = 0$ for all i against the alternative $H_A : \rho_i = \rho < 0$ for all i with auxiliary assumptions under the null also being required for the coefficients relating to the deterministic components. Like most of the unit root tests in the literature, Levin, Lin and Chu assume that the individual processes are cross-sectionally independent. Given this assumption, they derive conditions and correction factors under which the pooled Ordinary Least Squares estimate will have a standard normal distribution under the null hypothesis. Their work focuses on the asymptotic distributions of this pooled panel estimate of r under different assumptions about the existence of fixed effects and homogeneous time trends. The LLC test may be viewed as a pooled Dickey–Fuller (or ADF) test, potentially with differing lag lengths across the units of the panel.

The Im–Pesaran–Shin Test   Given Equation (5.7), the null and alternative hypotheses are defined as: $H_0 : \rho_i = 0 \forall_i$ and $H_A : \rho_i < 0$, $i = 1, 2 \dots, N$; $\rho_i = 0$, $i = N_1 + 1, N + 2, \dots, N$. Thus, as under the null hypothesis, all series in the panel are non-stationary processes; under the alternative hypothesis, a fraction of the series in the panel is assumed to be stationary. This is in contrast to the LLC test, which presumes that all series are stationary under the alternative hypothesis. The errors are assumed to be serially autocorrelated with different serial correlation properties and differing variances across units. Im, Pesaran and Shin propose the use of a group-mean Lagrange multiplier (LM) statistic to test the null hypothesis. The ADF regressions are computed for each unit, and a standardized statistic is computed as the average of the LM tests for each equation. Adjustment factors (available in their paper) are used to derive a test statistics that is distributed as standard normal under the null hypothesis.

Im, Pesaran and Shin also propose the use of a group-mean t-bar statistic, where the t-statistics from each ADF test are averaged across the panel; again, adjustment factors are needed to translate the distribution of t-bar into a standard normal variate under the null hypothesis. Im, Pesaran and Shin demonstrate that their test has better finite sample performance than that of Levin, Lin and Chu. The test is based on the average of the ADF test statistics calculated independently for each member of the panel with appropriate lags to adjust for autocorrelation. The adjusted test statistics, using the tables in Im, Pesaran and Shin (1995), are distributed as $N(0,1)$ under the null of a unit root, and large negative values lead to the rejection of a unit root in favour of stationarity.

Panel cointegration tests

Cointegration analysis is carried out using a panel econometric approach. Since the time series dimension is enhanced by the cross-section, the analysis relies on a broader information set. Hence, panel tests have greater power than individual tests and more reliable findings can be obtained. We use Pedroni's (1995, 1997) panel cointegration technique which allows for heterogeneous cointegrating vectors. The panel cointegration tests suggested by Pedroni (1999) extend the residual-based Engle and Granger (1987) cointegration strategy. First, the cointegration equation is estimated separately for each panel member. Second, the residuals are examined with respect to the unit root feature. If the null of no cointegration is rejected, the long-run equilibrium exists, but the cointegration vector may be different for each cross-section. Also, deterministic components are allowed to be individual-specific. To test for cointegration, the residuals are pooled either along the within or the between dimension of the panel, giving rise to the panel and group mean statistics (Pedroni 1999). In the former, the statistics are constructed by summing both numerator and denominator terms over the individuals separately, while in the latter the numerator is divided by the denominator prior to the summation. Consequently, in the case of the panel statistics the autoregressive parameter is restricted to be the same for all cross-sections. If the null is rejected, the variables in question are cointegrated for all panel members. In the group statistics, the autoregressive parameter is allowed to vary over the cross-section, as the statistics amount to the average of individual statistics. If the null is rejected, cointegration holds at least for one individual. Therefore, group tests offer an additional source of heterogeneity among the panel members.

Both panel and group statistics are based on ADF and Phillips–Perron methods. Pedroni (1999) suggests four panel and three group statistics. Under appropriate standardization, each statistic is distributed as standard normal, when both the cross-section and the time series dimension become large.

The asymptotic distributions can be stated in the form:

$$Z = \frac{Z^* - \mu\sqrt{N}}{\sqrt{v}} \tag{5.8}$$

where Z^* is the panel or group statistic and N is the cross-section dimension. μ and v arise from moments of the underlying Brownian motion functionals. They depend on the number of regressors and whether or not constants or trends are included in the cointegration regressions. Estimates for μ and v are based on stochastic simulations and are reported in Pedroni (1999). Thus, to test the null of no cointegration, one simply computes the value of the statistic so that it is in the form of (5.1) above and compares these to the appropriate tails of the normal distribution. Under the alternative hypothesis the panel variance statistic diverges to positive infinity and, consequently, the right tail of the normal distribution is used to reject the null hypothesis. Consequently, for the panel variance statistic, large positive values imply that the null of no-cointegration is rejected. For each of the other six test statistics, these diverge to negative infinity under the alternative hypothesis and, as such, the left tail of the normal distribution is used to reject the null hypothesis. Thus, for any of these latter six tests, large negative values imply that the null of no-cointegration is rejected. The intuition behind the test is that using the average of the overall test statistic allows more ease in interpretation: rejection of the null hypothesis means that enough of the individual cross-sections have statistics 'far away' from the means predicted by theory if they were to be generated under the null.

Panel Fully Modified Ordinary Least Squares

In the event that the variables are cointegrated, to get appropriate estimates of the cointegration relationship, efficient estimation techniques are employed. The appropriate estimation method is designed so that the problems arising from the endogeneity of the regressors and serial correlation in the error term are avoided. Due to the corrections, the estimators are asymptotically unbiased. In particular, Fully Modified OLS (FMOLS) is applied. In the model the asymptotic distribution of the OLS estimator depends on the long-run covariance matrix of the residual process. The estimates needed for the transformations are based on OLS residuals obtained in a preliminary step. The panel FMOLS estimator is just the average of individual parameters. The group mean FMOLS test performs best when T is larger than N.

Panel causality in the ECM framework

We have already discussed the causality issue in the time series domain. In a panel context, when we find evidence of cointegration, a moot issue is the determination of the direction of causality. The approach followed by many authors in the panel context is to test for cointegration between the variables under study. Once cointegration is found, a panel OLS is performed to obtain the residuals of the parametric relationship between the variables under study:

$$\Delta X_{it} = a_{1j} + \sum_{j=1}^{k} \alpha_{1ij}\Delta X_{i,t-j} + \sum_{j=1}^{k} \beta_{1ij}\Delta Y_{i,t-j} + \lambda_{1i}ecm_{it-1} + \mu_{1it} \qquad (5.9)$$

$$\Delta Y_{it} = a_{1j} + \sum_{j=1}^{k} \alpha_{2ij}\Delta X_{i,t-j} + \sum_{j=1}^{k} \beta_{2ij}\Delta Y_{i,t-j} + \lambda_{2i}ecm_{it-1} + \mu_{1it} \qquad (5.10)$$

The lag of the residual so obtained constitutes the ECM term in the estimation of (5.9) and (5.10). However, constructing the ECM term based on the residuals from an OLS may not be appropriate as it is FMOLS and not OLS which is the appropriate estimation technique when there is evidence of panel cointegration amongst the variables under study. As such, residuals from the panel FMOLS estimate are used to construct the ECM term in the test for Granger causality in the panel context.

First, we employ time series methods to study causality between credit and output. Subsequently, we look into the causality issue from the panel data perspective. We use the ADF method to test the order of the series and Johansen's method to test for the cointegrating relationship. The credit–growth relationship has been studied for each state to find whether any meaningful relationship exists between the two entities. Subsequently, we study causality in the panel dimension by employing the Im, Pesaran and Shin test to examine panel unit roots, Pedroni's method to test for panel cointegration and panel FMOLS.

5.4 Empirical results

Using the ADF test for the appropriate lag length, it is found that both the variables for each state contain a unit root.[7] However, both the variables are found to be stationary in their first difference: that is, they are I(1). As standard OLS would give spurious regressions if the variables under consideration were non-stationary, the next step was to test for cointegration between the two variables. Applying Johansen's cointegration tests for the appropriate lag length, the two variables were found to be cointegrated for each of the states under consideration.[8] This indicates that there exists a long-term equilibrium relationship between credit and growth for all the states. In the presence of the cointegrating relationship, an error correction representation following the Johansen framework was worked out to infer the nature of causality between the two variables. The causality results are given in Table 5.4. The direction of causality from the ECM specification indicates that, for the majority of the states under the GCS, there is evidence of bi-directional causality between credit and output. Evidence of uni-directional causality from credit to output is found for two states in the GCS category and for five states under the SCS category. Evidence of uni-directional causality from output to credit, however, is restricted to only two states, of which one belongs to the GCS and one to the SCS. Further, causality is more predominant in the long run than in the short run.

Table 5.4   Causality results based on time series ECM

Nature of causality	Direction of causality	Long run		Short run	
		GCS	SCS	GCS	SCS
Uni-directional	Credit →Output	Tamil Nadu and West Bengal	Meghalaya, Mizoram, Nagaland, Sikkim and Tripura		Sikkim
Uni-directional	Output →Credit	Uttar Pradesh	Manipur		
Bi-directional	Output ↔Credit	Andhra Pradesh, Bihar, Gujarat, Haryana, Karnataka, Kerala, Madhya Pradesh, Maharashtra, Orissa, Punjab and Rajasthan	Arunachal Pradesh, Assam and Himachal Pradesh	Andhra Pradesh Orissa, Punjab and Rajasthan	Arunachal Pradesh and Himachal Pradesh

Given the low power of the time series tests in presence of the small sample size, we look into the evidence for causality in the panel dimension. The variables under consideration were first tested for evidence regarding the panel unit root separately for the GCS and the SCS. The panel unit root tests on the credit and the output variables suggest evidence in favour of a unit root in the levels of the variables for both the GCS and the SCS as a group. As both credit and output are non-stationary, we have tested for cointegration between them in the panel context (see Table 5.5). The panel cointegration tests of Pedroni reveal that for the general category states there are reasonable grounds for rejecting the null of no-cointegration. For the special category states the null of no-cointegration could not be rejected. Thus the ECM based causality analysis would hold only

Table 5.5   Panel cointegration tests

Statistics	GCS	SCS
Panel *v-* stiatistics	1.409	−1.843
Panel *rho*-statistics	−0.273	0.537
Panel *pp*-statistics	−0.007	0.327
Panel *adf*-statistics	−1.578	0.249
Group rho-statistics	1.359	1.729
Group pp-statistics	1.153	1.305
Group adf-statistics	−1.206	0.540

Table 5.6   Panel causality tests

	Short run	Long run	Short run and long run
Output to credit	7.960(0.005)	4.565(0.033)	5.277(0.005)
Credit to output	6.039(0.014)	0.450(0.502)	3.081(0.047)

Figures in parentheses indicate the p-values of the concerned F-statistics.

for the general category states when drawing panel-based inferences. Having found evidence of panel cointegration, the residuals from the FMOLS estimates are gathered to construct the panel ECM term for doing the next round of estimations to infer the direction of causality (see Table 5.6).

The panel causality tests indicate that output Granger-causes credit both in the short run as well as in the long run, but credit Granger-causes output only in the short run. The joint F-statistics, however, provide evidence of bi-directional causality between credit and output. This tallies with the bi-directional causality found for most of the states in the GCS category.

5.5   Concluding observations

This chapter analysed the interrelationship between credit and growth. Apart from analysing the spatial and temporal pattern of growth and credit across the states, the chapter studied the issue of causality between credit and output using alternate empirical frameworks. At the aggregate level, nominal output growth has declined and credit growth has accelerated in the post-reform period. At the sectoral level, credit growth has accelerated for the tertiary sector, decelerated for the secondary and has more or less remained the same for the primary sector in the post-reform period. Not only has the growth of credit accelerated for the tertiary sector, but its share in overall credit has also seen a jump (from 38 per cent to 44 per cent). While the average share of the primary sector in both all-India credit and output has declined, that for the secondary sector has remained constant in the post-reform period. At the disaggregated state level, Andhra Pradesh, Karnataka, Maharashtra, Tamil Nadu and Meghalaya could increase their share in the all-India output and credit in the post-reform period. On the other hand, Bihar, Himachal Pradesh, Punjab, Madhya Pradesh, Orissa, Uttar Pradesh, West Bengal, Arunachal Pradesh, Assam, Tripura and Manipur experienced a decline in the share of both credit and output in the post-reform period. For Gujarat, Haryana, Kerala, Rajasthan, Mizoram, Nagaland and Sikkim, there was an increase in the share in output and a decrease in the share in credit in the post-reform period. Thus, at the state level the broad picture that emerges is one of a prominence of the tertiary sector in both output and credit at one end of the spectrum, and the primary sector losing out in both credit and output shares at the other end. The secondary sector is saddled with inertia.

The causality analysis in the time series dimension indicates evidence of bi-directional causality between credit and output for the majority of the states under the GCS category. For the SCS, for five out of nine states uni-directional causality prevails from credit to output. Causality is more of a long-run than of a short-run phenomenon. When the causality analysis was undertaken in the panel dimension, one did not find a stable long-run relationship between credit and output for the SCS. In absence of a long-run relationship, one has to go by the limited evidence obtained from the econometric analysis pursued in the time series dimension. The panel causality tests, which are more robust, indicate evidence of bi-directional causality for the GCS. The bi-directional causality is reflective of the continuous interaction between the real sector and the financial sector in practice. From the policy perspective, the present drive towards financial inclusion which purports to expand the reach of the banking sector can be a sustained phenomenon if other sectors of the economy are growing in tandem. In view of the empirical findings, it would be prudent to indict the banks for not doing enough in contributing their share towards a more broad-based growth. The structural issues need to be tacked with equal urgency, as must the drive for financial inclusion, so that credit and growth can be mutually compatible.

Appendix 5.1 Time series error correction mechanism results

Table 5A.1 Time series ECM results

State	Variable	F-statistics	$(DLPNSDP)_{t-1}$	$(DLPTCAS)_{t-1}$	$(ECM)_{t-1}$
Andhra Pradesh	DLPNSDP	2.433***	−0.107	−0.472	−0.023
			(−0.542)	(−2.084)	(−4.489)
	DLPTCAS	0.174	−0.043	0.008	0.007
			(−0.211)	(0.036)	(3.338)_
Bihar	DLPNSDP	3.393***	−0.294	0.022	−0.087
			(−1.449)	(0.183)	(−4.255)
	DLPTCAS	−0.655	0.174	0.029	0.034
			(−0.49)	(−0.138)	(−1.869)
Gujarat	DLPNSDP	1.37	−0.24	−0.307	−0.02
			(−1.126)	(−0.891)	(−3.503)
	DLPTCAS	0.702	0.123	−0.128	0.011
			(−0.929)	(−0.598)	(5.186)
Haryana	DLPNSDP	2.264	−0.297	−0.209	0.027
			(−1.404)	(−1.554)	(5.405)
	DLPTCAS	0.467	0.034	0.165	−0.024
			(0.099)	(0.754)	(−1.953)
Karnataka	DLPNSDP	−0.269	−0.025	0.032	0.066
			(−0.100)	(0.195)	(2.676)
	DLPTCAS	6.26*	−0.791	0.200	−0.121
			(−3.13)	(1.211)	(−5.058)
Kerala	DLPNSDP	1.037	0.245	−0.084	0.065
			(1.073)	(−0.529)	(2.774)
	DLPTCAS	1.696	−0.183	−0.268	−0.121
			(−0.592)	(−1.238)	(−3.948)
Madhya Pradesh	DLPNSDP	3.795**	−0.46	−0.121	−0.089
			(−2.262)	(−0.564)	(−4.003)
	DLPTCAS	0.83	−0.015	−0.106	0.039
			(−0.070)	(−0.440)	(3.438)
Maharashtra	DLPNSDP	−0.226	0.01	0.125	0.172
			(0.036)	(1.041)	(2.767)
	DLPTCAS	7.169*	−0.829	0.188	−0.38
			(−2.393)	(1.241)	(−5.298)
Orissa	DLPNSDP	4.678**	−0.439	−0.21	−0.019
			(−2.179)	(−1.317)	(−5.686)
	DLPTCAS	4.854**	−0.707	0.36	−0.0008
			(−2.910)	−1.871	(−4.296)
Punjab	DLPNSDP	2.611***	−0.083	0.05	0.12
			(−0.293)	(0.86)	(3.362)
	DLPTCAS	6.315*	−2.00	0.321	−0.42
			(−2.589)	(1.996)	(−3.573)
Rajasthan	DLPNSDP	4.574**	−0.206	−0.526	0.073
			(−0.909)	(−2.050)	−5.616
	DLPTCAS	1.749	−0.377	−0.047	−0.08
			(−1.797)	(−0.199)	(−5.579)

Table 5A.1 (Continued)

State	Variable	F-statistics	$(\text{DLPNSDP})_{t-1}$	$(\text{DLPTCAS})_{t-1}$	$(\text{ECM})_{t-1}$
Tamil Nadu	DLPNSDP	0.514	0.193 (0.859)	−0.071 (−0.390)	0.009 (2.771)
	DLPTCAS	0.559	−0.088 (−0.325)	−0.225 (−0.987)	−0.038 (−0.544)
Uttar Pradesh	DLPNSDP	2.667***	0.108 (0.545)	−0.143 (−1.116)	−0.091 (0.021)
	DLPTCAS	−0.027	−0.307 (−0.817)	0.022 (0.093)	0.095 (3.169)
West Bengal	DLPNSDP	0.79	−0.172 (−0.748)	−0.109 (−1.156)	−0.008 (−4.451)
	DLPTCAS	0.498	−0.096 (−0.445)	−0.38 (0.722)	0.007 (1.242)
Arunachal Pradesh	DLPNSDP	4.154**	−0.085 (−0.436)	−0.093 (−1.978)	−0.056 (−5.557)
	DLPTCAS	3.040***	−1.772 (−1.987)	−0.041 (−0.190)	0.014 (3.521)
Assam	DLPNSDP	0.405	−0.003 (−0.017)	0.024 (0.78)	0.011 (4.37)
	DLPTCAS	2.568***	−2.691 (−1.891)	−0.01 (−0.048)	−0.15 (−2.628)
Himachal Pradesh	DLPNSDP	2.582***	−0.157 (−0.744)	−0.16 (−2.253)	0.069 (−5.587)
	DLPTCAS	7.337*	−1.711 (−3.542)	0.139 (0.853)	−0.134 (−5.203)
Manipur	DLPNSDP	1.503	−0.322 (−1.590)	0.09 (1.434)	−0.009 (−0.703)
	DLPTCAS	4.231**	−0.605 (−1.000)	0.178 (0.954)	−0.184 (−3.059)
Meghalaya	DLPNSDP	2.398***	−0.249 (1.081)	−0.002 (−0.089)	−0.029 (−4.799)
	DLPTCAS	0.002	−0.911 (−0.383)	−0.139 (−0.543)	0.023 (1.051)
Mizoram	DLPNSDP	0.501	−0.074 (−0.330)	0.027 (0.499)	−0.054 (−3.898)
	DLPTCAS	2.104	2.017 (2.232)	−0.083 (−0.380)	−0.013 (−0.413)
Nagaland	DLPNSDP	−0.229	0.06 (0.287)	0.063 (0.813)	−0.026 (−3.406)
	DLPTCAS	4.12**	1.48 (3.166)	0.012 (0.069)	−0.051 (−1.541)
Sikkim	DLPNSDP	5.847*	−0.346 (−1.818)	0.039 (2.005)	−0.017 (−5.648)
	DLPTCAS	0.414	1.449 (0.752)	−0.062 (−0.309)	0.001 (0.197)
Tripura	DLPNSDP	1.66	0.055 (0.245)	−0.041 (−0.773)	0.171 (3.999)
	DLPTCAS	0.092	0.878 (0.966)	−0.038 (−0.177)	0.0001 (0.229)

Note: Figures in parentheses are the *t*-values. * indicates 99 per cent, ** indicates 95 per cent and *** indicates 90 per cent level of significance.

Appendix 5.2   Time series unit root tests

Table 5A.2   Time series unit root tests

State	Variable	Level	First difference
Andhra Pradesh	Output	−1.085	−4.825*
	Credit	−2.461	−4.278*
Bihar	Output	−1.454	−6.102*
	Credit	−2.298	−4.939*
Gujarat	Output	−1.955	−5.855*
	Credit	−2.768	−5.366*
Haryana	Output	−1.699	−4.013**
	Credit	−1.773	−3.727**
Karnataka	Output	−0.775	−4.489*
	Credit	−2.16	−3.449***
Kerala	Output	−1.252	−3.387***
	Credit	−1.445	−5.630*
Madhya Pradesh	Output	−0.361	−6.859*
	Credit	−1.993	−4.706**
Maharashtra	Output	−3.091	−3.935**
	Credit	−2.426	−4.300**
Orissa	Output	−3.04	−7.486*
	Credit	−1.749	−3.620***
Punjab	Output	−0.418	−3.426***
	Credit	−1.517	−4.104**
Rajasthan	Output	−1.483	−6.072*
	Credit	−1.894	−5.700*
Tamil Nadu	Output	−0.103	−3.988**
	Credit	−2.879	−5.638*
Uttar Pradesh	Output	−2.054	−4.652*
	Credit	−2.008	−4.552*
West Bengal	Output	−0.043	−4.927**
	Credit	−0.248	−3.074***
Arunachal Pradesh	Output	−1.752	−5.73*
	Credit	−2.274	−5.010*
Assam	Output	−1.467	−3.604***
	Credit	−2.492	−3.744*
Himachal Pradesh	Output	−2.022	−5.112*
	Credit	−1.781	−4.049*
Manipur	Output	−2.81	−3.795**
	Credit	−1.213	−4.149**
Meghalaya	Output	−0.45	−5.601*
	Credit	−2.277	−4.682*

Table 5A.2 (Continued)

State	Variable	Level	First difference
Mizoram	Output	−1.942	−4.773*
	Credit	−1.971	−4.316*
Nagaland	Output	−2.25	−4.780**
	Credit	−2.936	−5.601**
Sikkim	Output	−2.442	−7.03*
	Credit	−1.18	−5.716*
Tripura	Output	−0.943	−4.301**
	Credit	−2.201	−4.161*

Note: * indicates 99 per cent, ** indicates 95 per cent and *** indicates 90 per cent level of significance.

Unit root test assumes intercept and trend in the test equation. Lag length selection for the unit root tests are based on Schwarz Information Criterion.

The output variable is represented by log of per capita GSDP and credit variable by log of per capita outstanding credit to all sectors of the state.

Appendix 5.3   Time series cointegration evidence

Table 5A.3   Time series cointegration evidence

State	Trace	Maximum Eigen value	Presence of cointegration
Andhra Pradesh	27.945	23.454	✓
	(0.003)	(0.002)	
	4.491	4.491	
	(0.34)	(0.34)	
Bihar	24.36	21.46	✓
	(0.01)	(0.01)	
	2.90	2.90	
	(0.601)	(0.60)	
Gujarat	25.86	22.81	✓
	(0.01)	(0.00)	
	3.05	3.05	
	(0.57)	(0.57)	
Haryana	24.62	22.22	✓
	(0.01)	(0.00)	
	2.40	2.40	
	(0.70)	(0.00)	
Karnataka	28.68	26.27	✓
	(0.00)	0.00	
	2.41	2.41	
	(0.70)	(0.69)	
Kerala	22.31	20.19	✓
	(6.03)	(0.01)	
	2.11	9.16	
	(0.76)	(0.76)	
Madhya Pradesh	25.94	22.56	✓
	(0.01)	(0.00)	
	3.39	3.39	
	(0.51)	(0.51)	
Maharashtra	26.38	23.53	✓
	(0.01)	(0.00)	
	2.85	2.85	
	(0.61)	(0.61)	
Orissa	31.18	25.77	✓
	(0.00)	(0.00)	
	5.41	5.41	
	(0.24)	(0.24)	
Punjab	33.46	29.00	✓
	(0.00)	0.00	

Table 5A.3 (Continued)

State	Trace	Maximum Eigen value	Presence of cointegration
	3.56	3.56	
	(0.42)	(0.48)	
Rajasthan	27.71	26.16	√
	(0.00)	0.00	
	1.55	1.55	
	(0.86)	(0.86)	
Tamil Nadu	20.33	18.45	√
	(0.05)	(0.02)	
	1.88	1.88	
	(0.80)	(0.80)	
Uttar Pradesh	14.588	15.49	√
	(0.02)	(0.03)	
	0.34	2.36	
	(0.62)	(0.12)	
West Bengal	23.66	19.93	√
	(0.02)	(0.01)	
	3.73	3.73	
	(0.45)	(0.45)	
Arunachal Pradesh	29.83	23.57	√
	(0.00)	(0.00)	
	6.25	6.25	
	(0.17)	(0.17)	
Assam	30.83	22.09	√
	(0.00)	(0.00)	
	8.74	8.74	
	(0.06)	(0.06)	
Himachal Pradesh	39.44	33.30	√
	(0.00)	(0.00)	
	6.13	6.13	
	(0.18)	(0.18)	
Manipur	33.43	23.37	√
	(0.00)	(0.00)	
	10.07	10.07	
	(0.03)	(0.03)	
Meghalaya	26.09	21.82	√
	(0.01)	(0.01)	
	4.26	4.26	
	(0.37)	(0.37)	
Mizoram	21.33	15.65	√
	(0.04)	(0.05)	
	5.68	5.68	
	(0.22)	(0.22)	

Table 5A.3   (Continued)

State	Trace	Maximum Eigen value	Presence of cointegration
Nagaland	14.37	13.00	✓
	(0.02)	(0.02)	
	1.37	1.37	
	(0.28)	(0.28)	
Sikkim	31.41	22.31	✓
	(0.00)	(0.00)	
	9.10	9.10	
	(0.051)	(0.051)	
Tripura	21.63	13.57	✓
	(0.03)	(0.11)	
	8.06	8.06	
	(0.08)	(0.08)	

Note: Figures in parentheses indicate p-values.

Appendix 5.4   Panel unit root tests

Table 5A.4   Panel unit root tests

	Output		Credit	
	Level	First difference	Level	First difference
GCS	5.587	−3.090	−0.002	−3.720
	(1.000)	(0.001)	(0.499)	(0.000)
	3.229	54.706	24.395	57.731
	(1.000)	(0.002)	(0.661)	(0.001)
	9.267	188.836	24.800	139.552
	(1.000)	(0.000)	(0.639)	(0.000)
SCS	2.047	−4.733	−0.315	−2.461
	(0.980)	(0.000)	(0.376)	(0.007)
	9.510	54.910	16.129	33.415
	(0.947)	(0.000)	(0.584)	(0.015)
	26.520	232.612	22.765	99.548
	(0.069)	(0.000)	(0.200)	(0.000)

Note: Null hypothesis assumes presence of unit root.
Output variable is the log of per capita SDP and credit variable is log of per capita credit.
The unit root hypothesis assumes a constant and trend in the data.
Figures in parentheses indicate *p*-values.

Appendix 5.5 Changing share of output and credit in the states

Table 5A.5 Changing share of output and credit in the states (%)

State	Primary SDP		Primary credit		Secondary SDP		Secondary credit		Tertiary SDP		Tertiary credit		Personal and professional credit	
	1981–1993	1994–2004	1981–1993	1994–2004	1981–1993	1994–2004	1981–1993	1994–2004	1981–1993	1994–2004	1981–1993	1994–2004	1981–1993	1994–2004
Andhra Pradesh	38.38	33.07	29.24	19.36	21.13	22.23	38.19	37.43	40.49	44.7	32.57	43.21	10.02	19.69
Bihar	45.98	40.43	25.65	19.79	20.07	19.23	37.52	30.3	33.95	40.34	36.83	49.91	8.97	20.56
Gujarat	30.28	22.64	14.81	10.4	32.41	37.55	60.65	59.48	37.31	39.81	24.54	30.12	7.26	11.57
Haryana	43.10	34.02	29.73	20.47	26.65	29.73	45.2	49.87	30.25	36.25	25.07	29.66	5.62	13.69
Karnataka	38.40	29.20	22.89	16.84	25.55	26.34	42.35	40.7	36.05	44.46	34.76	42.46	12.01	20.58
Kerala	31.41	25.07	17.90	13.43	20.03	21.81	35.74	26.97	48.57	53.12	46.35	59.6	14.07	26.73
Madhya Pradesh	44.13	37.04	24.98	19.96	22.03	25.53	38.67	38.48	33.83	37.42	36.35	41.56	8.41	16.34
Maharashtra	22.30	17.26	6.84	4.10	35.46	30.75	52.19	50.83	42.24	51.99	40.97	45.07	6.14	10.3
Orissa	50.52	41.97	26.15	17.23	18.26	19.78	33.71	31.67	31.21	38.25	40.14	51.10	9.55	22.89
Punjab	46.24	41.85	30.92	19.27	21.15	23.28	35.56	38.62	32.61	34.86	33.52	42.10	6.11	14.37
Rajasthan	41.24	33.17	27.98	22.47	23.47	26.63	36.81	35.44	35.29	40.20	35.2	42.08	8.42	18.45
Tamil Nadu	23.99	18.56	16.31	10.44	36.3	31.79	49.71	46.44	39.71	49.65	33.98	43.12	9.75	18.15
Uttar Pradesh	42.27	36.80	22.58	20.54	19.91	22.67	40.56	36.46	37.82	40.53	36.86	43.00	7.93	16.86
West Bengal	32.75	32.52	8.23	5.25	26.87	20.61	61.54	54.42	40.38	46.87	30.23	40.33	6.64	14.8
Arunachal Pradesh	51.58	37.65	10.37	13.46	19.96	23.19	60.87	31.56	28.46	39.16	28.76	54.98	4.27	23.38
Assam	47.40	44.49	16.98	11.42	15.59	15.2	45.86	36.15	37.01	40.31	37.16	52.43	6.98	19.32
Himachal Pradesh	38.03	28.07	18.57	11.49	24.12	32.84	35.69	35.43	37.85	39.09	45.74	53.09	9.39	23.78
Manipur	38.58	32.05	16.38	12.48	19.55	19.89	25.46	28.39	41.87	48.06	58.16	59.13	10.55	25.11
Meghalaya	36.60	31.59	26.78	14.35	13.98	14.7	21.08	28.84	49.41	53.71	52.14	56.81	12.88	22.89
Mizoram	27.40	26.79	21.44	13.72	16.32	14.33	26.71	20.89	56.28	58.88	51.85	65.40	5.70	28.39
Nagaland	25.89	27.85	18.66	16.71	17.06	15.53	36.55	29.37	57.05	56.61	44.79	53.92	9.54	23.15
Sikkim	34.78	28.68	10.87	13.5	23.76	23.53	23.77	23.89	41.46	47.79	65.36	62.61	8.02	35.22

Appendix 5.6   Changing growth of output and credit in the states

Table 5A.6   Changing growth of output and credit in the states (%)

State	Primary SDP		Primary credit		Secondary SDP		Secondary credit		Tertiary SDP		Tertiary credit		Total credit for all sectors	
	1981–1993	1994–2004	1981–1993	1994–2004	1981–1993	1994–2004	1981–1993	1994–2004	1981–1993	1994–2004	1981–1993	1994–2004	1981–1993	1994–2004
Andhra Pradesh	10.43	8.65	13.14	12.48	14.31	9.96	16.92	12.79	13.91	12.19	19.14	18.68	16.52	15.29
Bihar	10.12	4.90	14.71	3.51	10.88	6.24	11.38	8.51	11.56	9.53	19.63	14.58	15.07	10.61
Gujarat	8.86	4.69	15.12	12.02	13.38	9.15	14.82	14.67	12.95	10.93	15.27	15.60	14.98	14.65
Haryana	10.52	4.72	10.43	13.40	13.73	10.99	12.45	13.42	13.63	14.10	13.20	18.55	11.96	15.01
Karnataka	10.59	4.51	14.99	13.93	13.68	11.15	14.21	14.91	13.96	14.37	16.27	20.88	15.08	17.26
Kerala	10.87	4.67	12.76	13.60	12.09	12.35	11.53	10.46	12.51	14.22	14.54	18.58	13.10	15.70
Madhya Pradesh	9.46	5.07	16.33	13.65	13.76	7.74	17.52	11.80	13.22	9.75	18.71	15.49	17.65	13.87
Maharashtra	10.68	4.12	11.57	14.87	12.03	6.04	14.66	13.62	14.00	11.40	13.32	18.16	13.70	15.77
Orissa	7.44	6.29	12.63	8.43	14.48	8.12	18.42	15.03	12.18	10.83	19.06	19.26	17.20	16.13
Punjab	11.67	6.43	7.25	13.51	13.65	8.69	15.01	11.63	12.17	10.23	10.63	17.51	10.98	14.53
Rajasthan	11.12	4.43	13.73	16.07	13.25	8.86	13.31	11.32	14.42	10.76	14.27	18.41	13.75	15.42
Tamil Nadu	11.45	3.46	15.45	9.71	12.87	7.99	15.90	14.42	14.51	14.11	17.87	18.90	16.47	15.89
Uttar Pradesh	9.28	6.61	13.42	13.80	14.30	6.84	13.78	9.57	12.08	9.55	16.25	16.25	14.55	13.38
West Bengal	11.26	8.98	13.88	13.17	8.67	9.94	12.16	10.34	10.86	14.39	16.43	16.87	13.52	13.16
Arunachal Pradesh	11.44	4.33	34.66	9.99	11.42	4.33	33.13	−0.61	14.93	12.33	21.51	23.31	29.41	13.03
Assam	11.31	7.08	14.13	3.06	14.54	7.55	18.75	12.12	10.71	10.25	16.86	18.98	17.13	14.82
Himachal Pradesh	8.80	9.84	11.72	14.68	15.13	13.23	16.77	19.15	13.44	13.19	16.43	20.20	15.66	19.18
Manipur	8.65	7.32	20.78	3.00	15.13	10.99	35.67	−6.28	12.91	11.29	19.61	11.80	23.29	5.73
Meghalaya	10.51	9.53	23.42	1.96	12.49	11.90	29.56	25.79	14.63	9.88	16.86	15.18	20.94	17.08
Mizoram	11.45	12.86	25.28	−7.74	12.37	5.07	21.85	−12.05	14.27	7.92	17.68	7.17	20.44	−1.11
Nagaland	17.54	7.95	43.58	2.95	15.65	9.16	37.67	2.16	13.79	12.91	22.15	24.70	28.14	16.93
Sikkim	10.64	5.20	27.94	3.31	9.85	18.81	42.62	11.16	16.76	12.42	30.90	29.23	34.05	21.50

6
Regional Rural Banks: Restructuring Strategies

The approach to banking in India underwent a sea change with the nationalization of 14 major commercial banks in 1969. Banking services, which had been the preserve of the urban population, were extended to the rural hinterlands of the country. This step was historic as more than 80 per cent of India's population lived in rural areas. The trend towards inclusive banking again got a shot in the arm in the mid-1970s when a new set of commercial banks, the regional rural banks (RRBs), were introduced to improve the efficacy of the rural credit delivery mechanism. The genesis of the RRBs can be traced to the need for a stronger institutional arrangement for providing rural credit. The Narasimham Committee (Government of India, 1975) conceptualized the creation of RRBs in 1975 as a new set of regionally oriented rural banks which would combine the local feel and familiarity of rural problems characteristic of co-operatives with the professionalism and large resource base of commercial banks. Subsequently, RRBs were set up through the promulgation of the RRBs Act, 1976.[1] With joint share holding[2] by central government, the relevant state government and the sponsoring commercial bank, the inception of RRBs was a unique effort to integrate commercial banking within the broad policy thrust towards social banking, keeping in view the local peculiarities. RRBs were supposed to evolve as specialized rural financial institutions for developing the rural economy by providing credit to small and marginal farmers, agricultural labourers, artisans and small entrepreneurs.

Over the years the RRBs, which are often viewed as the small man's bank, have developed deep roots and have become an integral part of the rural credit structure.[3] RRBs have played a key role in the development of the rural economy.[4] Their presence has expanded the institutional financing network in rural areas in terms of geographical coverage, clientele outreach and business volume. A remarkable feature of the RRBs' performance over the past three decades has been the massive expansion of their retail network in rural areas. From a modest beginning of six RRBs with 17 branches covering 12 districts in December 1975, the number of RRBs had grown to 196 with 14,446 branches operating in 518 districts across the country by March 2004. RRBs have a large branch network in the rural area forming around 43 per cent of the total rural branches of commercial banks. The rural orientation of RRBs is formidable with rural and semi-urban branches constituting over 97 per cent of their branch network. The growth in the branch network has enabled the RRBs to expand banking activities into areas previously lacking bank representation and mobilize rural savings.

The mandate of promoting banking with a rural focus, however, will be an enduring phenomenon only when the financial health of the RRBs is sound. With built-in-restrictions[5] on their operations, it is reasonable to assume that the financial health of the RRBs themselves would be a matter of concern. As regards their financial status, during the year 2003–4, 163 RRBs earned profits amounting to Rs953 crore, while 33 RRBs incurred losses to the tune of Rs184 crore. As many as 90 RRBs had accumulated losses as on 31 March, 2004. The aggregate accumulated loss of RRBs amounted to Rs2,725 crore during the year 2003–4. Of the 90 RRBs having accumulated loss, 53 RRBs had eroded their entire owned funds as also a part of their deposits. Furthermore, non-performing assets (NPAs) of the RRBs in absolute terms stood at Rs3,299 crore as on 31 March 2004. The percentage of gross NPAs was 12.6 during the year ending 31 March 2004. While 103 RRBs had gross NPAs lower than the national average, 93 had NPAs greater than the average.

To tackle the problems regarding the financial viability of RRBs, the government of India has initiated a process of restructuring RRBs through a scheme of amalgamation since September 2005. The restructuring process is an attempt to reposition the amalgamated/new entity as a stronger entity which should be able to face business challenges more effectively. The restructuring of RRBs through amalgamation, however, is both complex and delicate. It is complex as the bulk of the exercise is spread over different states involving different sponsoring banks; and it is delicate as there are transitional problems involved in addressing and redefining the role of the different stakeholders under the new dispensation.

The restructuring exercise pursued since September 2005 raises the fundamental issue of the appropriateness of the restructuring model that has been adopted. Probing further, one would be interested to know what are the factors that affect the performance of the RRBs and whether these factors have been given due consideration in the restructuring process. Thus it becomes instructive to enquire whether any discernible pattern emerges from the amalgamation, the desirability of the sort of restructuring pursued, the role of the sponsoring bank in the restructuring process and some thoughts on the possible course of restructuring in the future.

With this broad objective, the rest of the chapter is schematized as follows: section 6.1 provides a brief review of the restructuring and financial viability of RRBs suggested by different committees over the years. A bird's eye view of the spatial distribution of the performance of RRBs across the states and sponsoring banks is given in section 6.2. Section 6.3 briefly reviews the different factors identified in the literature that affect the financial performance of commercial banks and also the extant literature on factors affecting the performance of RRBs. The methodology of the empirical analysis to decipher the impact of the sponsoring bank on the performance of the RRBs (along with other factors) is discussed in section 6.4. Section 6.5 discusses the empirical results. Some reflections on the restructuring process in the light of the empirical findings are deliberated in section 6.6, while section 6.7 contains some concluding observations.

6.1   Restructuring strategies

The financial viability of RRBs has engaged the attention of the policy-makers from time to time. In fact, as early as 1981, the Committee to Review Arrangements for Institutional Credit for Agriculture and Rural Development (CRAFICARD) addressed the issue of the financial viability of RRBs. The committee recommended that 'the loss incurred by a RRB should be made good annually by the shareholders in the same proportion of their shareholdings'. Though this recommendation was not accepted, under a scheme of recapitalization financial support was provided by the shareholders according to the size of their shareholdings. Subsequently, a number of committees have come out with different suggestions to deal with the financial non-viability of RRBs. For instance, the Working Group on RRBs (Kelkar Committee) in 1984 recommended that small and uneconomic RRBs should be merged in the interest of economic viability. Five years down the line, in a similar vein, the Agricultural Credit Review Committee (Khusro Committee, 1989) pointed out that 'the weaknesses of RRBs are endemic to the system and non-viability is built into it, and the only option was to merge the RRBs with the sponsor banks. The objective of serving the weaker sections effectively could be achieved only by self-sustaining credit institutions.' The Committee on Restructuring of RRBs (Bhandari Committee, 1994) identified 49 RRBs in need of comprehensive restructuring. It recommended greater devolution of decision-making powers to the Boards of RRBs in business development and staff matters. The option of liquidation again was mooted by the Committee on Revamping of RRBs (Basu Committee, 1996).

The Expert Group on RRBs in 1997 (Thingalaya Committee) held that very weak RRBs should be viewed separately and the possibility of their liquidation should be recognized. They might be merged with neighbouring RRBs. The Expert Committee on Rural Credit (Vyas Committee I, 2001) was of the view that the sponsoring bank should ensure necessary autonomy for RRBs in their credit and other portfolio management systems. Subsequently, another committee under the chairmanship of Chalapathy Rao in 2002 (Government of India, 2002a) recommended that the entire system of RRBs be consolidated while retaining the advantages resulting from the regional character of these institutions. As part of the process, some sponsoring banks may be eased out. The sponsoring institutions may include other approved financial institutions as well, in addition to commercial banks. The Group of CMDs of Select Public Sector Banks (Purwar Committee, 2004) recommended the amalgamation of RRBs on a regional basis into six commercial banks, one each for the Northern, Southern, Eastern, Western, Central and North-Eastern Regions. Thus one finds that a host of options have been suggested, starting with vertical merger (with the sponsoring banks), horizontal merger (amongst RRBs operating in a particular region) and liquidation, by different committees that have gone into the issue of financial viability and restructuring strategies for the RRBs.

More recently, a committee under the Chairmanship of A.V. Sardesai revisited the issue of restructuring the RRBs (Sardesai Committee, 2005). The Sardesai Committee held that 'to improve the operational viability of RRBs and take advantage of the economies of scale, the route of merger/amalgamation of RRBs may be considered taking into account the views of the various stakeholders'. Mergers of RRBs with the sponsoring banks are not provided for in the RRBs Act 1976. Mergers, even if allowed, would not be a desirable way of restructuring. The Committee was of the view that merging an RRB with its sponsoring bank would go against the very spirit of setting up RRBs as local entities and providing credit primarily to weaker sections. Having discussed various options for restructuring, the Committee was of the view that 'a change in sponsor banks may *in some cases* help in improving the performance of RRBs. A change in sponsorship may, *inter alia*, improve the competitiveness, work culture, management and efficiency of the concerned RRBs' (my italics). Against this backdrop, a number of issues need further probing. The prime issue is whether any pattern is noticed for the poor performers among the RRBs: that is, are they confined to any particular region of operation or to some specific sponsoring banks? In case there is a systematic pattern, the approach to restructuring would take on a shape which is different from the restructuring in the absence of any identifiable pattern. Such an attempt to search for a specific pattern in the performance of the RRBs is made in the next section.

6.2   Performance of regional rural banks in the spatial dimension: some stylized facts

The RRBs have made impressive strides over the years on various business indicators. For instance, RRBs' deposits have grown by 18 times and advances by 13 times between 1980 and 1990. Between 1990 and 2004, deposits and advances grew by 14 times and 7 times respectively (see Table 6.1). Between the years 2000 and 2004, loans disbursed by RRBs more than doubled, reflecting the efforts made by the banks[6] to improve credit flow to the rural sector. The average per branch advances also increased from Rs25 lakh in March 1990

Table 6.1 Evolution of RRBs: select indicators (Rs crores)

Parameter	1980	1985	1990	1995	1996	1997	1998	1999	2000	2001	2002	2003	2004
No. of RRBs	85	188	196	196	196	196	196	196	196	196	196	196	196
Capital	21	46	91	166	358	705	1,118	1,380	1,959	2,049	2,143	2,141	2,221
Deposits	222	1,315	4,023	11,141	14,171	17,976	22,191	27,059	32,226	38,294	44,539	49,582	56,295
Investments	20	164	60	1,348	2,879	3,891	5,280	6,680	7,760	8,800	9,471	17,138	21,286
Advances	262	1,405	3,384	5,987	7,057	7,908	9,021	10,559	12,427	15,050	17,710	20,934	25,038
Total assets	426	2,320	6,081	14,886	18,969	24,376	29,468	35,820	42,236	49,596	56,802	62,500	70,195
Interest earned	NA	NA	480	1,158	1,421	2,033	2,624	3,281	3,938	4,619	5,191	5,391	5,535
Other income	NA	NA	113	72	89	103	136	151	207	240	370	430	697
Total income	NA	NA	593	1,230	1,511	2,136	2,760	3,432	4,145	4,859	5,561	5,821	6,231
Interest expended	NA	NA	326	851	1,065	1,462	1,773	2,131	2,565	2,966	3,329	3,440	3,363
Operating expenses	NA	NA	254	657	726	804	845	982	1,056	1,165	1,459	1,667	1,825
Provisions and contingencies	NA	NA	NA	120	171	673	72	99	96	128	163	132	289
Total expenses	NA	NA	581	1,509	1,791	2,265	2,617	3,113	3,621	4,130	4,787	5,107	5,187
Operating profit	NA	NA	12	−279	−280	−129	143	319	524	729	774	714	1,044

Notes: Total expenses are excluding provisions and contingencies. NA stands for not available. Apparent errors due to rounding of figures.

to Rs154 lakh in March 2003. When one considers the deployment of credit relative to the mobilization of resources, the credit–deposit (C–D) ratio of RRBs was more than 100 per cent during the first decade of their operations up to 1987. Though the C–D ratio subsequently became lower, of late it has shown an improvement and went up from around 39 per cent in March 2000 to 44.5 per cent in March 2004.[7]

The presence of RRBs shows wide variation across both states and sponsoring banks. Although RRBs are spread over 26 states, they have most of their presence in just seven (i.e., Andhra Pradesh, Bihar, Karnataka, Madhya Pradesh, Maharashtra, Rajasthan and Uttar Pradesh). Uttar Pradesh has the highest number of RRBs at 36, while Kerala has only two (see Table 6.2). The north-eastern states of Manipur, Meghalaya, Mizoram and Nagaland have got only one RRB. Likewise, seven sponsoring banks (Bank of Baroda, Bank of India, Central Bank of India, Punjab & National Bank, State Bank of India, United Bank of India and UCO Bank) account for more than three-fifths of the RRBs. More than 160 RRBs earned profit in March 2004 while 150 RRBs were found to be earning profits for three consecutive years beginning with the year 2000–1. More than half of these loss-making RRBs are found to be operating in four states (Bihar, Madhya Pradesh, Maharastra and Orissa). Seen at the level of sponsoring banks, three banks – Bank of India, Central Bank of India and State Bank of India – accounted for more than half of the loss-making RRBs. As a number of sponsoring banks have promoted RRBs in more than one state, it becomes natural to ask whether the presence of RRBs sponsored by a few banks whose area of operation is confined to some specific states is camouflaging the performance of better-run RRBs.

There can be three possibilities in such a situation. First, irrespective of the state, the RRBs sponsored by some banks are incurring losses; second, irrespective of the sponsoring banks, certain states are simply not conducive to better performance for RRBs; and third, there is nothing inherent in either a sponsoring bank or a particular state in which RRBs operate which contributes towards the performance of RRBs, and it is therefore due to a combination of some other factors. To answer these possibilities one needs to assess the presence of RRBs sponsored by different banks across the states and their performance. Such an attempt is made in Table 6.3, where the performance of sponsoring banks across regions is depicted. Seen from the perspective

Table 6.2 State and sponsor bank-wise distribution of RRBs

Sr. no.	State	RRBs		Sr. no.	Sponsoring bank	RRBs	
		No.	Profit-making			No.	Profit-making
1	Andhra Pradesh	16	15	1	Allahabad Bank	7	7
2	Arunachal Pradesh	1	0	2	Andhra Bank	3	3
3	Assam	5	4	3	Bank of Baroda	19	15
4	Bihar	16	8	4	Bank of India	16	10
5	Chhattisgarh	5	3	5	Bank of Maharastra	3	1
6	Gujarat	9	8	6	Bank of Rajasthan	1	0
7	Haryana	4	4	7	Central Bank of India	23	15
8	Himachal Pradesh	2	2	8	Canara Bank	8	8
9	Jammu & Kashmir	3	1	9	Corporation Bank	1	0
10	Jharkhand	6	3	10	Dena Bank	4	4
11	Karnataka	13	12	11	Indian Overseas Bank	3	2
12	Kerala	2	2	12	Indian Bank	4	4
13	Madhya Pradesh	19	14	13	J&K Bank	2	1
14	Maharashtra	10	5	14	Punjab & Sind Bank	1	1
15	Manipur	1	0	15	Punjab National Bank	19	17
16	Meghalaya	1	1	16	State Bank of Bikaner and Jaipur	3	2
17	Mizoram	1	1	17	State Bank of Hyderabad	4	4
18	Nagaland	1	0	18	State Bank of India	30	18
19	Orissa	9	3	19	State Bank of Indore	1	1
20	Punjab	5	5	20	State Bank of Mysore	2	2

21	Rajasthan	14	10	21	State Bank of Patiala	1	1
22	Tamil Nadu	3	3	22	State Bank of Saurashtra	3	3
23	Tripura	1	0	23	Syndicate Bank	10	10
24	Uttar Pradesh	36	34	24	United Bank of India	11	9
25	Uttaranchal	4	4	25	UCO Bank	11	7
26	West Bengal	9	8	26	Uttar Pradesh State Co-operative (UPSC) Bank	1	0
				27	Union Bank of India	4	4
				28	Vijaya Bank	1	1
	Total	196	150		Total	196	150

Note: Based on three consecutive years performance beginning with the year 2000–1.
Source: Statistical Tables Relating to Banks in India (various issues).

of the state in which they are operating, six out of the nine loss-making RRBs in Bihar are sponsored by the Central Bank of India, two by UCO and one by SBI. Of the 4 loss-making RRBs found in Madhya Pradesh, one each is sponsored by the State Bank of India (SBI), the Central Bank of India and UCO. Likewise, of the four loss-making RRBs found in Orissa, three are sponsored by State Bank of India and one by UCO.

It emerges from the sponsoring bank's perspective that the RRBs in which they have a stake and which are not earning profits are usually found in more than one state, and are spread across the states in which they have a presence. For instance, the nine loss-making RRBs sponsored by Central Bank of India are spread across Bihar, Madhya Pradesh, Maharastra and West Bengal. Similarly, the 12 loss-making RRBs sponsored by SBI are spread across Andhra Pradesh, Arunachal Pradesh, Bihar, Jammu & Kashmir, Jharkhand, Madhya Pradesh, Nagaland, Orissa and Uttaranchal. The case is similar with the RRBs sponsored by the Bank of Baroda and UCO. Hence there does not appear to be a strong systematic pattern from which to infer whether the peculiarities of any particular sponsoring bank, or

178

Table 6.3 Performance of RRBs across sponsoring banks and regions

Sponsoring bank	No. of RRBs	State	Loss-making
Allahabad Bank	7	Uttar Pradesh (6), Madhya Pradesh (1)	
Andhra Bank	3	Andhra Pradesh (2), Orissa (1)	
Bank of Baroda	19	Uttar Pradesh (9), Rajasthan (5), Gujarat (3),Madhya Pradesh (1), Uttaranchal (1)	Madhya Pradesh (1), Rajasthan (1), Uttar Pradesh (1)
Bank of India	16	Uttar Pradesh (3), Madhya Pradesh (4), Maharashtra (4), Jharkhand (4), Orissa (1)	Jharkhand (1)
Bank of Maharashtra	3	Maharashtra (3)	
Bank of Rajasthan	1	Rajasthan (1)	
Canara Bank	8	Uttar Pradesh (3), Karnataka (4), Kerala (1)	
Central Bank of India	23	Bihar (8), Chhattisgarh (1), Madhya Pradesh (7), Maharashtra (3), Rajasthan (1), Uttar Pradesh (2), West Bengal (1)	Bihar (6) Madhya Pradesh (1), Maharashtra (1), West Bengal (1)
Corporation Bank	1	Karnataka (1)	
Dena Bank	4	Gujarat (3), Chattisgarh (1)	
Indian Bank	4	Andhra Pradesh (2), Tamil Nadu (2)	
Indian Overseas Bank	3	Orissa (2), Tamil Nadu (1)	
Punjab National Bank	19	Uttar Pradesh (6), Punjab (3), Rajasthan (2), Bihar (4), Himachal Pradesh (1), Haryana (3)	
J&K Bank	2	Jammu & Kashmir (1)	Jammu & Kashmir (1)
Punjab & Sind Bank	1	Punjab (1)	

Sponsoring Bank			
State Bank of Bikaner and Jaipur	3	Rajasthan (3)	Rajasthan (1)
State Bank of Hyderabad	4	Andhra Pradesh (4)	
State Bank of India	30	Andhra Pradesh (5), Arunachal Pradesh (1), Assam (1), Bihar (1), Chhattisgarh (3), Himachal Pradesh (1), Jammu & Kashmir (1), Jharkhand (2), Karnataka (1), Madhya Pradesh (3), Meghalaya (1), Mizoram (1), Nagaland (1), Orissa (3), Uttar Pradesh (2), Uttaranchal (3)	Andhra Pradesh (1), Arunachal Pradesh (1), Bihar (1), Jammu & Kashmir (1), Jharkhand (2), Madhya Pradesh (1), Nagaland (1), Orissa (3), Uttaranchal (1)
State Bank of Indore	1	Madhya Pradesh (1)	
State Bank of Mysore	2	Karnataka (2)	
State Bank of Patiala	1	Punjab (1)	
State Bank of Saurashtra	3	Gujarat (3)	
Syndicate Bank	10	Andhra Pradesh (3), Haryana (1), Karnataka (4), Kerala (1), Uttar Pradesh (1)	
United Bank of India	11	West Bengal (5), Assam (4), Manipur (1), Tripura (1)	Manipur (1)
UCO Bank	11	West Bengal (3), Bihar (3), Orissa (2), Rajasthan (2), Madhya Pradesh (1)	Bihar (2), Madhya Pradesh (1), Orissa (1)
Uttar Pradesh State Co-operative (UPSC) Bank	1	Uttar Pradesh (1)	Uttar Pradesh (1)
Union Bank of India	4	Uttar Pradesh (3), Madhya Pradesh (1)	
Vijaya Bank	1	Karnataka (1)	

Note: The brackets indicate the number of RRBs sponsored by the sponsoring banks. The position was as at 31 March 2004.

Source: Statistical Tables Relating to Banks in India (various issues) and Annual Accounts of Scheduled Commercial Banks in India 1989–2001, Reserve Bank of India.

the specific state in which they operate, drives the performance of RRBs. In such a situation, we model the financial performance of the RRBs based on balance sheet information. Among other factors, we are interested in deciphering the impact of the sponsoring bank on the financial performance of the RRBs. An idea about the role of the sponsoring bank in shaping the performance of the RRBs will provide additional insight to help devise an appropriate restructuring strategy for the RRBs. Before we undertake empirical modelling of the performance of the RRBs, we review the literature on factors affecting performance of a commercial bank in general and also in the context of RRBs.

6.3   Review of the literature

RRBs, although they operate with a rural focus, are primarily scheduled commercial banks with a commercial orientation. Beginning with the seminal contribution of Haslem (1968), the literature probing the factors influencing performance of banks recognizes two broad sets of factors, internal and external. The internal determinants originate from the balance sheets and/or profit and loss accounts of the bank concerned and are often termed micro, or bank-specific, determinants of profitability. The external determinants are systemic forces that reflect the economic environment which conditions the operation and performance of financial institutions. A number of explanatory variables have been suggested in the literature for both the internal and external determinants. The typical internal determinants employed are variables such as size and capital (Haslem 1968; Short 1979; Bourke 1989; Molyneux and Thornton 1992; Akhavein *et al.* 1997; Demirguc-Kunt and Maksimovic 1998; Bikker and Hu 2002; Goddard *et al.* 2004).

Given the nature of the banking business, the need for risk management is of crucial importance for a bank's financial health. Risk management is a reflection of the quality of the assets of a bank and the availability of liquidity. During periods of uncertainty and economic slowdown, banks may prefer a more diversified portfolio to avoid adverse selection and may also raise their liquid holdings in order to reduce risk. In this context, both credit and liquidity risks assume importance. The literature provides mixed evidence on the impact of liquidity on profitability. While Molyneux and Thornton

(1992) found a negative and significant relationship between the level of liquidity and profitability Bourke (1989), in contrast, reports an opposite result. One possible reason for the conflicting findings may be the different elasticity of demand for loans in the samples used in the studies (Guru, Staunton and Balashanmugam 2004). Credit risk is found to have a negative impact on profitability (Miller and Noulas 1997). Some of the other internal determinants found in the literature are funds source management and funds use management (Haslam 1968), capital and liquidity ratios, the credit-deposit ratio and loan loss expenses (Bell and Murphy 1969; Short 1979; Kwast and Rose 1982). Expense management, a correlate of efficient management, is another very important determinant of a bank's profitability. There has been an extensive literature based on the idea that an expenses-related variable should be included in the cost part of a standard microeconomic profit function. In this context, Bourke (1989) and Molyneux and Thornton (1992) find that better-quality management and profitability go hand in hand.

As far as the external determinants of bank profitability are concerned, the literature distinguishes between control variables that describe the macroeconomic environment (inflation, interest rates and cyclical output) and variables that represent market characteristics (market concentration, industry size and ownership status). Among the external determinants which are empirically modelled are regulation (Jordan 1972; Edwards 1977), bank size and economies of scale (Short 1979; Benston, Hanweck and Humphrey 1982), competition (Phillips 1964; Tschoegl 1982), concentration (Rhoades 1977; Schuster 1984), growth in market (Short 1979), and interest rates as a proxy for capital scarcity and government ownership (Short 1979). The most frequently used macroeconomic control variables are the inflation rate, the long-term interest rate and/or the growth rate of money supply. Revell (1979) studied the impact of inflation on bank profitability for the first time. He noted that the effect of inflation on bank profitability depends on whether banks' wages and other operating expenses increase at a faster pace than inflation. Perry (1992) in a similar vein contends that the extent to which inflation affects bank profitability depends on whether inflation expectations are fully anticipated. The influence arising from the ownership status of a bank on its profitability is another much debated and frequently visited issue in the literature. The proposition that privately owned institutions are more profitable, however, has mixed empirical evidence in favour of it. For instance, while Short (1979) provides cross-country evidence of a strong negative relationship between government ownership and bank profitability, Barth *et al.* (2004) claim that government ownership of banks is indeed negatively correlated with bank efficiency. Furthermore, Bourke (1989) and Molyneux and Thornton (1992) find the ownership status is irrelevant in explaining profitability. While many of the above factors are relevant, it would be instructive to scan the literature which has focused exclusively on RRBs.

The literature on RRBs recognizes a host of reasons responsible for their poor financial health. According to the Narasimham Committee, RRBs have low earning capacity. They have not been able to earn much profit because of the policy to restrict their operations to target groups. The recovery position of RRBs is not satisfactory. At the time of their inception, RRBs were supposed to recruit employees drawn from local area with relatively lower salaries so as to reduce operating expenses. Their cost of operation, however, has been high on account of the increase in wages and salaries in line with the salary structure of the employees of commercial banks. In most cases RRBs have followed the same methods of operation and procedures as are followed by commercial banks without due consideration of the local peculiarities, and so these procedures have not found favour with the rural masses.

In many cases banks have not been located at the right place. For instance, the sponsoring banks are also running their branches in the same areas that RRBs are operating in. The issue of whether location affects performance has been addressed in some detail by Malhotra (2002). Considering 22 different parameters that impact on the functioning of RRBs for the year 2000, Malhotra asserts that geographical location of RRBs is not a limiting factor for their performance. Another potential source of influence which affects the performance of the RRBs is the role that the sponsoring banks play. In this context Malhotra (2002) finds that 'it is the specific nourishment which each RRB receives from its sponsor bank, [which] is cardinal to its performance'. In other words, the umbilical cord has an effect on the performance of RRBs. The limitation of Malhotra's study is that the financial health of the sponsoring bank was not considered directly to study the umbilical cord hypothesis.

Nitin and Thorat (2004), on a different note, provide a penetrating analysis as to how constraints in the institutional dimension[8] have seriously impaired the governance of the RRBs. They have argued that perverse institutional arrangements which gave rise to incompatible incentive structures for key stakeholders, such as political leaders, policy-makers, bank staff and clients, have acted as constraints on their performance. The lacklustre performance of the RRBs during the last two decades, according to the authors, can be largely attributed to their lack of commercial orientation. In view of the factors identified in the literature that have an impact on the performance of the RRBs, we discuss the modalities of the econometric estimation and the model specification in the next section.

6.4   Data and methodology

Net income as a percentage of total assets (*NITA*)[9] is taken to be the indicator of financial performance of the RRBs. *NITA* measures how profitably and efficiently the RRB is making use of its total assets. Deflating the net income by total assets also takes account of the variation in the absolute magnitude of the profits, which may be size-related. The performance of RRBs is postulated to depend upon two broad sets of factors which can be both internal to the RRBs as well as external to them. The internal factors are represented through the balance sheet information of the individual RRBs. RRBs are scheduled commercial banks whose source of income arises primarily from lending and investment. Balance sheet management on the part of RRBs requires a judicious mix between lending and investment. As such, loans and advances of each RRB as a percentage of total assets (*LOTA*) and investments in securities of each RRB as a percentage of total assets (*INTA*) are included as explanatory variables.

In terms of liquidity management, since banks are involved in the business of transforming short-term deposits into long-term credit, they are constantly faced with the risks associated with the maturity mismatch. In order to hedge against liquidity deficits, which can lead to insolvency problems, banks often hold liquid assets, which can be easily converted into cash. However, liquid assets are often associated with lower rates of return. Hence, high liquidity is expected to be associated with lower profitability (Molyneux and

Thornton 1992). The impact of liquidity on profitability is captured through the variable *LIQ*, which is represented through the RRBs' cash in hand as a proportion of their assets. Another internal factor that can be expected to have a significant effect on the financial health of the RRBs is their efficiency in expense management. The 'total expenses' shown in the profit and loss account of the RRBs is the sum of 'interest expenses' and 'operating expenses'. While rising operating costs (to support increasing business activities) are natural, increasing operating costs relative to non-operating expenses is a matter of concern and reflects poor expense management. To judge the impact of expense management on balance sheet health, the variable operating expenses as a percentage of total expenditure (*OE*) has been taken as another independent variable.

Apart from the internal factors, the literature recognizes the influence of the sponsoring bank on an RRB's health through what is termed the *umbilical cord hypothesis* (Malhotra 2002). According to this hypothesis, given the very close relationship[10] between the RRB and its sponsoring bank, the attitude of the sponsoring bank will have a bearing on the performance of the RRB. As it is quite complex to quantify the attitude of the sponsoring bank towards the RRB concerned, the impact of the sponsoring bank has been subsumed under a single indicator, the financial health of the sponsoring bank. This indicator is reflected through its net income as a percentage of its total assets (*NITASPON*), and has been included as one of the regressors. In order to ascertain the impact of the internal and the external factors on bank profitability, panel data regression models have been used. Equation (6.1) describes the general specification of the model. Equation (6.1) can be estimated either by least squares or through a procedure that accounts for fixed/random effects:

$$NITA_{i,t} = \eta_0 + \eta_1 LOTA_{i,t} + \eta_2 INTA_{i,t} + \eta_3 LIQ_{i,t} + \eta_4 OE_{i,t}$$

$$+ \eta_5 NITASPON_{i,t} + \varepsilon_{i,t} \qquad (6.1)$$

where η_0, η_1, η_2, η_3, η_4 and η_5 are parameters to be estimated, *NITA* is net income to assets, *LOTA* is loan as a proportion of total assets, *INTA* is investment as a proportion of total assets, *LIQ* is cash in hand as a proportion of total assets, *OE* is operating expenses as a proportion of total expenditure, *NITASPON* is net income to assets of the sponsoring bank, and $\varepsilon_{i,t}$ is the error term. The subscripts i and t refer to the year and cross-section (RRB) respectively.

In addition to the above factors, an environmental factor that may affect both the costs and revenue of the RRBs is the inflationary conditions in the economy. The impact of inflation rates on bank profitability depends on its effect on a bank's costs and revenues. The effect of inflation on bank performance depends on whether the inflation is anticipated or unanticipated (Perry 1992). If inflation is fully anticipated and interest rates are adjusted accordingly, resulting in revenues rising faster than costs, then it would have a positive impact on profitability. However, if the inflation is not anticipated and the banks are sluggish in adjusting their interest rates, then there is a possibility that bank costs may increase faster than bank revenues and hence adversely affect bank profitability. Interest rates in India were administered for a long time until the onset of financial liberalization. In the post-liberalization phase, although banks have greater freedom to price their products, manoeuvrability on the part of banks in adjusting their interest rates is rather limited on account of the preference for fixed rate deposits, administered savings, and so on. Furthermore, as all the variables in Equation (6.1) are expressed as ratios, inflation is already accounted for in the model. Hence inflation as an additional variable has been excluded from the regression model.

Another environmental factor that would affect the business of the RRBs is the economic growth taking place in their area of operation. Better economic growth improves the credit-absorptive capacity and thus has the potential to influence the balance sheet position of the RRBs. In the absence of readily available district-level data on output, we consider the growth of SDP for the state in which the RRB operates to account for the impact of overall economic activity on the financial health of the concerned RRBs. Further, It is quite possible that past year's performance has a bearing on today's performance and non-incorporation of the same in the econometric estimation would blur the impact of other variables on *NITA*. To account for the past year's performance, lagged value of *NITA* has also been considered in an extended model. The extended model is as shown in equation (6.2):

$$NITA_{i,t} = \eta_0 NITA_{it-1} + \eta_1 LOTA_{i,t} + \eta_2 INTA_{i,t} + \eta_3 LIQ_{i,t} + \eta_4 OE_{i,t}$$

$$+ \eta_5 NITASPON_{i,t} + \eta_6 SDPG_{i,t} + \varepsilon_{i,t} \qquad (6.2)$$

where ηs is the parameter to be estimated and *SDPG* is the growth of per capita SDP.

The extended model (6.2) is a dynamic panel data model. A dynamic panel model poses a number of econometric issues. The major problem that arises when a lagged dependent variable is introduced as an explanatory variable is that the error term and the lagged dependent variable are correlated, with the lagged dependent variable being correlated with the individual specific effects that are subsumed into the error term. This implies that standard estimators are biased, and as such an alternative method of estimating such models is required. The standard procedure to provide consistent estimates is to adopt an instrumental variable procedure, with different lags of the dependent variable used as instruments. Although a number of candidates are possible, the Arellano and Bover (1995) approach is adopted as this generates the most efficient estimates. While using lagged dependent variables as instruments, overall instrument validity is examined using a Sargan test of over identifying restrictions.

The study covers the period 1994–2004. The choice of end points for the period of analysis is essentially governed by two considerations. Based on the recommendations of the Narasimham Committee Report (1991), reforms were initiated in 1993 to turn around the failing RRBs. To enhance financial viability, a new set of prudential accounting norms of income recognition, asset classification, provisioning and capital adequacy were implemented. Banks were also required to make full provision for the bulk of their non-performing assets. Furthermore, they were permitted to lend to non-target group borrowers up to 60 per cent of new loans beginning in 1993–4. Permission was also granted to introduce new services, such as loans for consumer durables. Therefore, 1993–4 has been taken as the initial year for estimation when the RRBs were given the opportunity to operate in a more liberal framework. The choice of the terminal year for the empirical study is guided by the availability of balance sheet information on both RRBs as well as the sponsoring bank from the various issues of *Statistical Tables Relating to Banks in India* brought out by the Reserve Bank of India. Balance sheet information was available until 2003–4 for RRBs when the study was carried out. The study deals with all the 196 RRBs except one.[11] To get a deeper insight into the factors contributing to the financial performance of RRBs, the empirical analysis has been carried out separately for the profit- and the loss-making RRBs apart from for all the RRBs taken together. Those RRBs that earned profits consecutively for three years, 2000–1 up to 2002-3, have been categorized as profit-making RRBs, and the rest as loss-making RRBs.

6.5   Empirical results

Estimation of the extended model (6.2), which employs the dynamic panel data estimation, reveals (Table 6.4) that performance in past years had a significant[12] impact for the current year for both categories of RRBs. Advances contributed negatively to the health of the profit-making RRBs. For the loss-making RRBs, advances turn out to be positive and significant. For all RRBs taken together, advances are found to adversely affect the bottom line. As far as investments are concerned, they contributed positively and significantly to the performance of both profit- and loss-making RRBs. Although operating expenses had a negative impact on the profitability of both profit- and loss-making RRBs, it was of a higher order for the loss-making ones. The bottom line of the loss-making RRBs also seems to have been adversely affected by their liquidity position. Further, the economic conditions prevailing in their area of operations seem to

Table 6.4   Dynamic panel data (GMM) estimation results

Independent variables	Profit-making RRBs		Loss-making RRBs		All RRBs	
	Coefficient	*P*-value	Coefficient	*P*-value	Coefficient	*P*-value
NITA (−1)	0.440	0.00	0.483	0.00	0.430	0.00
NITA (−2)	0.043	0.07	0.021	0.04	0.033	0.00
LOTA	−0.041	0.01	0.097	0.00	−0.023	0.01
INTA	0.025	0.00	0.034	0.00	0.037	0.00
LIQ	0.462	0.13	−1.559	0.00	−0.419	0.09
OE	−0.117	0.00	−0.141	0.00	−0.136	0.00
NITASPON	0.362	0.00	−0.481	0.00	0.007	0.42
SDPG	0.011	0.12	0.028	0.00	0.031	0.00
P-Value of Sargan Test	0.070		0.241		0.002	

have had a positive impact on the performance of both the profit- and the loss-making RRBs.

The more interesting finding, however, relates to the umbilical cord hypothesis. For all RRBs taken together, the *NITASPON* variable is found to be positive but statistically insignificant. When we consider the results for the profitable and the loss-making RRBs separately, we find the coefficient of *NITASPON* is found to be positive for the profitable RRBs but negative for the loss-making RRBs. Had we not categorized the RRBs into these two types, the inference would have been that the umbilical cord hypothesis does not hold good. Performing separate estimates for these two kinds of RRB, however, reveals that the sponsoring bank acted as a positive force for the profitable RRBs and its impact was negative for the loss-making RRBs. The profitable RRBs are able to reap the synergy from their association with the sponsoring bank. The sponsoring bank, on the other hand, is found to act as a drag on the financial health of the loss-making RRBs. The literature (Malhotra 2002 amongst others) recognizes a host of reasons for the drag. It could be due to competition for business rather than co-operation between the RRB and the sponsoring bank, which may be co-present in a particular geographical area. Otherwise, it could simply be because of the apathetic attitude of the sponsoring bank when an RRB requires a supporting hand. Support could be in the form of advice on financial decisions, or meeting the skill requirements of the RRBs or managing its affairs.

This finding is significant in the present milieu where a number of options are being considered to restructure the RRBs. The asymmetric impact of the sponsoring bank on the functioning of the RRB needs to be factored into any restructuring scheme for the RRBs. In the absence of a systematic pattern for poorly performing RRBs, a one-size-fits-all approach to restructuring will undermine the complexities involved in the entire process. Keeping this in view, we consider the experience gained from the attempts at restructuring pursued to date to try to draw a road map for the future.

6.6   Restructuring in practice

The restructuring process begins with the sponsoring banks taking the lead in submitting an amalgamation proposal to the NABARD, which is the apex body for the RRBs. On a scrutiny of the proposals, NABARD apprises the government of India of its observations on the amalgamation proposal. The final decision with regard to amalgamation is taken by the central government. As on 31 March 2006, some 27 cases of amalgamation had been effected in 12 states. Another 13 proposals ratified by NABARD are awaiting the national government's assent. In addition, three more proposals for amalgamation, submitted by the State Bank of India in Madhya Pradesh, Jharkhand and Uttaranchal, are under scrutiny by NABARD. If the proposals for amalgamation under different stages of ratification are also considered, in all there have been 43 cases of restructuring attempted up to now. The Sardesai Committee had recommended two options for the merger of RRBs: merger between RRBs of the same sponsoring bank in the same state, and merger of RRBs sponsored by different banks in the same state. The restructuring of RRBs pursued up to the present has been designed along the lines of the first of these two options.

Amalgamation of RRBs can be conceptualized amongst three categories of RRBs. Theoretically it can be merger of two or more profit-making entities, profit- and loss-making entities, or loss-making entities. While merger amongst only profitable or only loss-making RRBs constitutes the two ends of the spectrum, the merger of the profit- and loss-making RRBs falls in between. Seen in terms of this categorization we find, in the majority of cases (19 out of 27: see Table 6.5), that it has been the merger of profitable RRBs of a particular sponsoring bank in a particular state. However, there have been instances of amalgamation of profit- and loss-making RRBs also. For example, the UCO-sponsored Begusarai Kshetriya Gramin Bank (KGB), Bhagalpur Banka KGB and Munger KGB have been amalgamated to form the new Bihar Kshetriya Gramin Bank. While Begusarai KGB made profits in 2004, the other two were incurring losses. Similarly, in Rajasthan the loss-making Marudhar KGB has been merged with the profit-making Aravali KGB, Bundi Chittorgarh KGB, Bhilwara Ajmer KGB and Dungarpur Banswara KGB to form the Baroda Rajasthan Gramin Bank. Again, in Maharashtra, Vidharbha Kshetriya Gramin Bank has been formed by merging the loss-making Akola KGB with the profit-making Buldhana Gramin Bank (GB) and Yavatmat Kshetriya GB, all sponsored by the Central Bank of India. In Bihar, under the Central Bank of India's sponsorship, Champaran KGB, Vaishali KGB, Madhubani KGB, Mithila KGB, Gopalganj KGB, Saran KGB and Siwan KGB were merged to form the Uttar Bihar Kshetriya

Table 6.5 Amalgamation of RRBs

Sl.no.	Sponsoring bank	Names of the Amalgamated RRBs	New name	State	With effect from
1	State Bank of India	Gorakhpur KGB Basti GB	Purvanchal Gramin Bank	Uttar Pradesh	12.09.2005
2	Bank of Baroda	Valsad Dangs GB Surat Bharuch GB Panchmahal Vadodara GB	Baroda Gujarat Gramin Bank	Gujarat	12.09.2005
3	Central Bank of India	Akola Kshetriya GB Buldhana GB Yavatmat Kashetriya GB	Vidharbha Kshetriya Gramin Bank	Maharashtra	12.09.2005
4	Union Bank of India	Samyut KGB Kashi GB Gomti GB	Kashi Gomti Smyut GB	Uttar Pradesh	12.09.2005
5	Punjab National Bank	Kapurthala Firozepur KGB Gurudaspur Amritsar KGB	Punjab Gamin Bank	Punjab	12.09.2005
6	Canara Bank	Tungabhadra GB Chitradurga GB Kolar GB Sahyadri GB	Pragathi Gramin Bank	Karnataka	12.09.2005
7	Syndicate Bank	Malaprabha GB Bijapur GB Netravati GB Varada GB	Karnataka Vikas Grameena Bank	Karnataka	12.09.2005
8	Dena Bank	Kutch GB Banaskantha Mehsana GB Sabarkantha Gandhinagar GB	Dena Gujarat Gramin Bank	Gujarat	12.09.2005
9	UCO Bank	Begusarai KGB Bhagalpur Banka KGB Munger KGB	Bihar KGB	Bihar	12.09.2005
10	Punjab National Bank	Vidur GB Muzaffarnagar Kshetriya GB Hindon GB	Uttar Pradesh GB	Uttar Pradesh	12.09.2005
11	Punjab National Bank	Haryana KGB Hissar Sirsa GB Ambala Kurushetra GB	Haryana GB	Haryana	12.09.2005
12	UCO Bank	Cuttack Gramya Bank Balasore Gramya Bank	Kalinga GB	Orissa	12.09.2005

13	State Bank of Saurashtra	Jamnagar Rajkot Gramin Bank Surendranagar Bhavnagar GB Junagadh Amreli GB	Saurashtra GB	Gujarat	02.01.2006
14	United Bank of India	Cachar Gramin Bank Lakhimi Gaonlia Gramin Bank Pragiyotish Gaonlia Bank Subansiri Gaonlia GB	Assam Gramin Vikash GB	Assam	02.01.2006
15	Bank of Baroda	Marudhar KGB Aravali KGB Bundi Chittorgarh KGB Bhilwara Ajmer KGB Dungarpur Banswara KGB	Baroda Rajasthan Gramin Bank	Rajasthan	12.01.2006
16	Punjab National Bank	Shekhawati GB Alwar Bharatpur Anchalik GB	Rajasthan Gramin Bank	Rajasthan	24.01.2006
17	UCO Bank	Jaipur Nagaur Anchalik GB Thar Anchalik GB	Jaipur Thar Gramin Bank	Rajasthan	27.01.2006
18	Punjab National Bank	Bhojpur Rohtas GB Magadh GB Nalanda GB Patliputra GB	Madhya Bihar Gramin Bank	Bihar	10.02.2006
19	Bank of Baroda	Raebareli KGB Sultanpur KGB Kanpur KGB Allahabad KGB Pratapgarh KGB Fatehpur KGB Faizabad KGB	Baroda Eastern Uttar Pradesh Gramin Bank	Uttar Pradesh	23.02.2006
20	Central Bank of India	Champaran KGB Vaishali KGB Madhubani KGB Mithila KGB Gopalganj KGB Saran KGB Siwan KGB	Uttar Bihar Kshetriya Gramin Bank	Bihar	01.03.2006
21	Allahabad Bank	Bhagirath GB Shravasti GB Sarayn GB	Lucknow Kshetriya Gramin Bank	Uttar Pradesh	01.03.2006
22	Allahabad Bank	Chattarasal GB Tulsi GB Vindhyavasini GB	Triveni Kshetriya Gramin Bank	Uttar Pradesh	01.03.2006

Table 6.5 (Continued)

Sl.no.	Sponsoring bank	Names of the Amalgamated RRBs	New name	State	With effect from
23	Andhra Bank	Chaitanya GB Godavari GB	Chaitanya Godavari Grameena Bank	Andhra Pradesh	01.03.2006
24	State Bank of Hyderabad	Sri Saraswathi GB Sri Sathavahana GB Sri Rama GB Golconda GB	Deccan Grameena Bank	Andhra Pradesh	24.03.2006
25	Bank of Baroda	Bareilly KGB Shahjahanpur KGB	Baroda Western Uttar Pradesh Gramin Bank	Uttar Pradesh	31.03.2006
26	Bank of India	Dewas Shajapur KGB Rajgarh Sehore KGB Nimar KGB Indore Ujain KGB	Narmada Malwa Gramin Bank	Madhya Pradesh	03.04.2006
27	State Bank of India	Kakathiya GB Manjira GB Nagarjuna GB Sangameshwara GB Sri Vishakha GB	Andhra Pradesh Grameena Vikas Bank	Andhra Pradesh	31.03.2006

Source: NABARD.

Gramin Bank. Of the merged entities, only Gopalganj KGB and Siwan KGB were earning profits in the year 2004; the rest all incurred losses. Again, ten out of the thirteen proposed amalgamations awaiting central government's ratification are amongst profitable RRBs, and only three cases are between profit- and loss-making RRBs. There have been no instances of purely loss-making RRBs merging, and none is even at the preliminary stage so far.[13]

In the present amalgamation exercise, there will be some rationalization of the branch network of the merged entities under the new dispensation. The success of the merged entity will to a great extent depend on its ability to expand business on a sustainable basis by providing better banking services. Enabling technology has greatly facilitated the scope for business growth, which the amalgamated units can adopt by taking advantage of the economies of scale, better administration and governance practices. A merger of RRBs is not only a merger of their balance sheets but also, more importantly, it is the synthesis of the different work culture, management practices and business strategies of the merged entities. In the limited sense of balance sheet strengthening, one can appreciate the merger of the profitable RRBs. The merger of profit- and loss-making RRBs, even in this limited sense, raises certain apprehensions. The merger of such RRBs operating in a contiguous area cames the possibility of bringing some rewards in terms of house keeping, better administrative control, and so on, But there is an equal possibility that the new entity becomes financially unviable, because the inefficiencies are compounded and the merged entity falls under its own dead weight. The transition phase would be relatively more difficult to tide over in such cases. Further, in the present milieu of restructuring and amalgamation, the broader question still remains unanswered as to what would be the role of the sponsoring banks *vis-à-vis* the merged entities.

Based on the recommendations of the Narasimham Committee Report (1991), reforms were initiated in 1993 to turn around the failing RRBs. To enhance financial viability, a new set of prudential accounting norms of income recognition, asset classification, provisioning and capital adequacy were implemented. RRBs were also required to make full provisioning for the bulk of their non-performing assets. Furthermore, they were permitted to lend to non-target group borrowers up to 60 per cent of new loans, beginning in 1993–4. Permission was also granted to introduce new services, such as loans for consumer durables. All these have led to a situation whereby the RRBs are placed on an equal footing with the commercial banks, but with an additional restriction on their area of operation. The restriction on their area of operation can be seen as a challenge which the RRBs must tackle by developing an appropriate business model. In the pursuit of developing an appropriate business model, the merger of RRBs with the sponsoring bank perhaps would not go against the 'spirit of setting up RRBs as local entities and for providing credit primarily to weaker sections'. In that case, the ongoing merger of individual RRBs can be seen as an intermediate step to the subsequent merger of the new entities with their sponsoring bank. The present day RRBs might be treated as the rural finance branches of the relevant sponsoring banks. In the ultimate analysis, if the present day RRBs are integrated with their mainstream sponsoring commercial bank and identified as their 'rural finance' branches, this will involve a greater stake on the part of the sponsoring bank in reaching the poor in the rural areas. The case for a vertical merger is stronger in cases where both profit- and loss-making RRBs have been merged as the sponsoring bank would be in a better position to absorb the financial burden of the loss-making RRBs.

The other option is to institutionalize certain changes in matters relating to the governance of the RRBs. First there is issue of the selection and tenure of Chairman of the RRB. At present, the sponsoring bank nominates the chairman of the RRB. Two directors on the Board of the RRB are also from the sponsoring bank. In the event that the chairman and the directors do not belong to the same level of hierarchy in the sponsoring bank, the independence of the institution of the chairman is severely constrained. Recognizing this aspect, the Sardesai Committee notes, 'The Chairmen of most of the RRBs are from sponsor banks, which limits the freedom and decision-making capacity of the RRBs.' Often the nomination of the chairman of the RRB is perceived as an unwanted assignment and is a case of mismatch between the kind of person needed and the person who actually gets nominated. As the chairman has a pivotal role to play in the RRB's functioning, the issue of nomination needs due attention. Seen from a broader perspective, there is a need to revisit the notion that the chairman be nominated by the sponsoring bank.

Is it really the case that the majority shareholder appoints the chairman in a banking concern? In practice, the Government of India holds majority shares in the nationalized banks, but the Chairman-cum-Managing Director (CMD) of the nationalized banks is selected from the banking sector through a due process of selection; the central government has allowed operational freedom to commercial banks. Selection through a due process rather than nomination perhaps would be a better way of choosing the Chairman of an RRB. The Sardesai Committee's observations in this context are pertinent: 'As the Chairmen of RRBs are from the sponsor bank, there could be several potential areas of conflicts of interest. In this context, the process of appointment may be reexamined to explore the possibility of appointing a Chairman from the open market through a transparent process.'

The institution of RRBs has been in existence for nearly 30 years since their inception, and hence there must be a pool of talent available in the RRB system itself. This pool of talent could be given an opportunity in the selection of the Chairman. Further, as has been suggested by the Sardesai Committee, the composition of the Board of the RRBs could be more broadly based by introducing professionals such as agricultural experts, bankers or management experts to strengthen the Boards of RRBs. Fixed tenure of the Chairman and other key professionals posted in RRBs, say of 3–5 years (to ensure continuity in planning and execution of various policies), was also suggested by the Sardesai Committee. As issues such as the selection of the Chairman and the introduction of professionals to the Boards of the RRBs are of crucial importance in determining the performance of the RRBs, there is a need to incorporate them in the RRB Act.

6.7 Conclusion

The RRBs, which have been in existence for around three decades on the Indian financial scene, have undergone a series of transformations over the last decade. The elements of transition were more an outcome of the forces of change that the banking system was subjected to after the onset of financial sector reforms in the early 1990s. Prudential norms for RRBs around mid-1990s are a case in point. Among other things, the single most important concern of the RRBs from the early days of their inception was their financial viability. To examine whether the problems associated with the RRBs are specific to certain sponsoring banks or to the states in which they operate, all the RRBs were categorized as either profit-making or loss-making ones. The exploratory analysis revealed that the problem of the loss-making RRBs is confined neither to some specific states nor to a group of sponsoring banks. In the absence of any strong systematic pattern to suggest that the performance of RRBs is driven by the peculiarities of any particular sponsoring bank or a specific state in which they operate, econometric estimation was employed to decipher the factors that contribute to their financial health. Based on the balance sheet information on individual RRBs for the past eleven years, econometric analysis indicated that the umbilical cord hypothesis is operational. The sponsoring bank contributes positively to the financial health of the profit-making RRBs. For the loss-making RRBs, the sponsoring bank acts as a drag on their performance.

The income from investments, coupled with synergy from the sponsoring bank's association, could mitigate the negative impact flowing from the loan portfolio for the profitable RRBs. The loss-making RRBs, on the other hand, could have done better had the sponsoring banks played a proactive role. The loss-making RRBs need focused attention from all the stakeholders in general, and from the sponsoring bank in particular, in order to transform them into profitable ventures.

The merger of the RRBs of a particular sponsoring bank within a state has been initiated to improve the financial viability of such RRBs. This merger is found both among profitable RRBs and also between profit- and loss-making RRBs. At the present juncture, it is difficult to hazard a guess as to the impact of the second type of RRB merger on their financial viability and profitability. One option could be that the sponsoring bank in the case of loss-making RRBs could be given a time frame and if, within this period, significant improvement is not made, the possibility of changing the sponsoring bank may be a worthwhile option. (This was suggested by the Sardesai Committee). As RRBs over time have graduated to shouldering the role and responsibility of their sponsoring banks, the option of merging the RRBs with their sponsoring bank may also be considered. Working as the 'rural finance' arm of the mainstream sponsoring bank, the RRBs would have additional leverage to do better in expanding the reach of banking services to the poor. Pending vertical merger, there is an urgent need to address certain key governance issues, such as the selection of the Chairman and the professionalism of the Board of the various RRBs. Resolution of these and other issues is necessary for the amalgamated RRBs to meet the test of time and emerge as financially viable entities.

Appendix 6.1   The basis for the umbilical cord hypothesis

1 Section 3 of Chapter II of RRBs Act, 1976 stipulates that only *on request* of a Sponsor Bank will the central government consider establishing an RRB.

2 Duties of the sponsoring bank have been spelled out in Section 3 (3) of the RRBs Act as:

   (a) subscribing to the share capital of RRBs;
   (b) training the personnel of RRBs;
   (c) providing such managerial and financial assistance during the first five years as mutually agreed upon.

3 Under Section 4 of RRBs Act, 1976, the RRB will have its Head Office at such place as decided by the central government in consultation with NABARD and the sponsoring bank.

4 Section 6(2) of RRBs Act stipulates that the sponsoring bank will contribute 35 per cent of the issued capital of its RRB.

5 Under Section 9(d) of RRBs Act, two directors, who are officers of the sponsoring bank, shall be nominated to the Board of RRB.

6 Under Section 11 of the Act, the sponsoring bank shall appoint the Chairman of an RRB and specify the period of appointment. The appointment, however, would not exceed a period of five years.

7 The sponsoring bank has the right to remove the Chairman at any time (Section 11(4)).

8 The sponsoring bank shall depute officers or other employees to RRBs as may be necessary or desirable (Section 17 of RRBs Act, 1976).

9 Amalgamation of RRBs under Section 23-A can be done by the central government in consultation with NABARD, the state government and the sponsoring bank.

10 Section 24-A of RRBs Act stipulates that the sponsoring bank is required to monitor the progress of RRBs and carry out inspection, internal audit and scrutiny and suggest corrective measures to be taken by the RRBs.

11 Interest rate on SLR deposits of all maturity held by RRBs with the sponsoring bank would be at 0.5 per cent over the maximum term deposit rate of the sponsoring bank.

12   The government of India and the Reserve Bank of India have further issued the directive that, 'for overall management of the RRB it is be the responsibility of the Sponsor Bank to guide the RRB in various matters on human resource management, computerization, business development, branch expansion, etc.'
13   Many RRBs have an agency arrangement with their sponsoring bank for the issue of Demand Drafts.
14   Sponsoring banks also directly help RRBs in matters of daily cash remittances, overdraft facilities, decisions on investments, etc.

7
Agricultural Growth in Indian States: The Case of Orissa

The Planning Commission of India foresees a growth rate in the range of 8 to 9 per cent during 2007–8 to 2011–12, the period of the 11th Five-Year Plan. To achieve this growth rate, one of the major challenges that has been identified is the reversal of the deceleration in agricultural[1] growth seen after 1996–7. The meagre agricultural growth of 2 per cent per annum recorded over 1997–8 to 2001–2 has further declined to 1 per cent in the subsequent three years. The deceleration of agricultural growth has been a policy concern for several reasons. First, the agriculture sector not only meets the food grain requirement of the entire economy but also helps to sustain the growth momentum of the non-agricultural sectors by contributing to the demand for their products. Second, agriculture contributes a quarter of the GDP and absorbs the maximum number of the workforce in India. As such, low agricultural growth would have an adverse impact on the living conditions of the majority of the population. Third, experience suggests that periods of substantial poverty reduction in India have come about only when agriculture has grown at a faster rate. Low agricultural growth does not augur well from the welfare perspective. The welfare implications of agricultural growth are further borne out by the fact that higher agricultural growth has an equalizing impact on the distribution of income. Thus it becomes imperative that agriculture attains a high growth rate. Recognizing its strategic importance, the Planning Commission has envisaged a 4 per cent per annum growth target for agriculture during the 11th Five-Year Plan.[2]

Reasons for the poor agricultural performance have been well documented in the literature. Falling public investment in agriculture, especially surface irrigation, poor implementation of land reforms, non-availability of timely credit, and the collapse of the agriculture extension system which provides the linkage between development of new technology in the agricultural universities and the farmers are some of the factors that have constrained agricultural growth in the post-1996–7 period. It is also widely recognized that one of the main reasons for poor agricultural performance has been the limited spread of the yield-enhancing 'green revolution' that was introduced in the late 1960s. The green revolution was essentially a technology-embedded package that needed adoption of HYV seeds, assured irrigation and use of chemical fertilizers and pesticides. Agriculture being a 'state' subject,[3] the primary initiative to adopt the HYV technology rested with the states. While certain states, such as Punjab, Haryana and Uttar Pradesh, could take advantage of the green revolution in the late 1960s, other states lagged behind in the adoption of the new technology. As assured irrigation was a pre-condition for the use of HYV seeds, states such as Punjab and Haryana were in an advantageous position to adopt the new technology as they had the benefit of canal irrigation. It has been more than 35 years since the new technology was introduced and some of the states have yet to create conditions to conducive the green revolution. The positive aspect in all this, however, is the scope to augment agricultural production by creating an enabling environment for adoption of the new technology in states where it has not been done. To drive home the point, we make an attempt to show the benefits that would have accrued by undertaking policy simulations from the adoption of the green revolution technology.

If we analyse agricultural performance at the all-India level, we do not consider the peculiarities of the place where agricultural operations take place. First, there is vast agro-climatic diversity across the states. Second, the institutional settings (land settlement systems) for agricultural operations differ across the states which affects the incentive structure for undertaking investments in agriculture. Third, agriculturally well-off states have problems which are different from those in states which are characterized by low agricultural growth. There is a substantial gap in farm mechanization and the use of agricultural input between the agriculturally better-off and the worse-off states. For instance, in the agriculturally prosperous state of Punjab, the availability of free electricity has prompted farmers to overuse water (by indiscreetly pumping ground water) leading to depletion of ground water. In contrast, many of the agriculturally trailing states are devoid of irrigation facilities. In such a situation we have tried to capture the factors responsible for influencing agricultural area and production at a level of disaggregation which will not be so aggregative as to lose sight of the local conditions and not so disaggregated, say, at the village level that we are not able to draw some broader lessons from the past behaviour of agricultural production. The unit of study for agricultural performance, as such, is chosen to be the 'state'. We consider a particular state where the adoption of the new technology has been slow as a case study. The state of Orissa has been chosen for the case study because the state government has been rather slow in creating the necessary enabling conditions for the adoption of the new technology and because there is ample scope for agricultural growth.

The importance of the agriculture sector in Orissa can be appreciated from the fact that it contributes around 26 per cent to the NSDP and provides direct and indirect employment to around 65 per cent of the total workforce of the state.[4] However, the growth of agriculture in the state has always remained below the national average. Further, Orissa's share as a proportion of all-India agricultural output has substantially gone down from 4.14 per cent in 1980–1 to 2.8 per cent in 2000–1. This worsening has often puzzled researchers as Orissa has reasonable agro-climatic diversity and its suitability for irrigation is not hugely different from that of more successful states. Orissa's vulnerability to frequent natural calamities (floods and tropical cyclones) is often offered as an explanation for the poor agricultural performance. While this is true, it is also likely that Orissa could have done better by taking advantage of the green revolution, as many agriculturally successful states did. Against this backdrop, this chapter will study the performance of the agriculture sector in Orissa over the last three decades and carry out simulations to study how agricultural area, production and yield would have evolved under alternate policy scenarios (which would have prevailed had the state created the necessary conditions for adoption of the new technology at a faster pace) and suggest policy measures for lifting agricultural growth in the state.

This chapter is schematized as follows: section 7.1 deals with the overall economic performance of Orissa. A brief overview of the agricultural operations in Orissa is discussed in section 7.2. This section also discusses the actual pattern of use of some of the important agricultural inputs in Orissa. Section 7.3 provides a brief review of the concerned literature. The empirical findings and agricultural performance under alternative policy scenarios are discussed in section 7.4. Some concluding observations are given in section 7.5.

7.1 Orissa's economic performance

Orissa, one of the major states in India, accounts for 4.7 per cent of India's land mass and 3.6 per cent of the country's population. Its share in the national output, however, is quite low and hovered around 2–2.5 per cent in the 1990s. Seen in terms of income, Orissa's per capita state income was Rs5,665 compared to the national average of Rs10,964. Amongst the major states, Bihar was the only state which had a per capita income lower than that of Orissa in 2002–3. While it ranked twelfth among the states in terms of its share in output in the 1980s, its rank went down by two in the 1990s. Further, in terms of growth of per capita net state domestic product (PNSDP), while it used to rank twelfth in the 1980s, it was ranked nineteenth in the 1990s. The growth of PNSDP has come down to 2.1 per cent in 1990s from 2.9 per cent in the 1980s. Traversing the growth of real output proxied by NSDP for Orissa over the last 33 years we find that the rate of growth of NSDP in the 1980s was double that of the 1970s. Though the 1990s witnessed a slump in growth, there has been a resurgence in the more recent period of 2001–4. Real output growth has increased to 5.8 per cent during 2001–4 from 4 per cent in the 1990s. The recent resurgence has been led by the primary and the tertiary sector (Table 7.1). Furthermore, the sectoral growth rates for Orissa (which were at comparable levels to that for the Indian economy as a whole in the 1980s) declined across all the sectors in the 1990s.

This stylized evidence suggests that save for the recent surge in growth, Orissa has failed to benefit from the nation-wide structural reforms in the 1990s. Even in the recent growth resurgence, the flip side is the negative growth of manufacturing. Orissa is saddled with a poor performance of the secondary sector, notwithstanding its strong

Table 7.1 Sectoral growth rates: Orissa (%)

Category \ Period	1971–80	1981–90	1991–2000	2001–4
Agriculture	1.07	3.08	1.27	3.46
Primary	1.20	3.04	2.93	6.60
Manufacturing	7.06	8.65	2.36	−6.09
Electricity	7.86	5.17	−1.26	7.27
Secondary	6.67	7.06	1.42	0.40
Transport	4.75	11.12	5.99	11.96
Banking	9.79	14.54	8.93	12.35
Trade	1.22	5.66	6.12	5.77
Public administration	3.91	7.55	6.03	0.94
Tertiary	3.39	6.63	6.51	6.85
NSDP	2.41	4.79	4.02	5.81

Note: Growth rates are computed from a semi log specification.

natural resource base, a declared industrial policy and its initiatives in state-level power sector reforms. Orissa has 90 per cent of India's chrome ore and nickel reserves, 70 per cent of bauxite and 24 per cent of coal reserves.

This mineral wealth notwithstanding, the contribution of the secondary sector to the SDP decreased from 17 per cent in the 1970s to 15 per cent in the 1980s. Though the lost ground might have been recovered in the 1990s, the share of the secondary sector in fact declined again to 13 per cent over 2001–4 (Figure 7.1). The share of manufacturing in NSDP also declined to 6 per cent after remaining static at 8 per cent during the 1980s and the 1990s. While primary sector on average contributed around 60 per cent to the output in the 1970s, its share declined to around 45 per cent in the 1990s, and further to 40 per cent in more recent times. The contribution of the service sector grew from 24 per cent to 38 per cent in the 1990s, and even more rapidly to 47 per cent over the recent 2001–4 period. Though the share of agriculture has come down from 50 per cent to 26 per cent, it was still the largest contributor to NSDP during 2001–4 compared to any other subsector of the economy. Further, agriculture absorbs the maximum number of the working population. Thus, its poor agricultural performance would affect future income growth and its distribution in the state. Balanced and sustainable growth requires that the different sectors of the economy should grow in

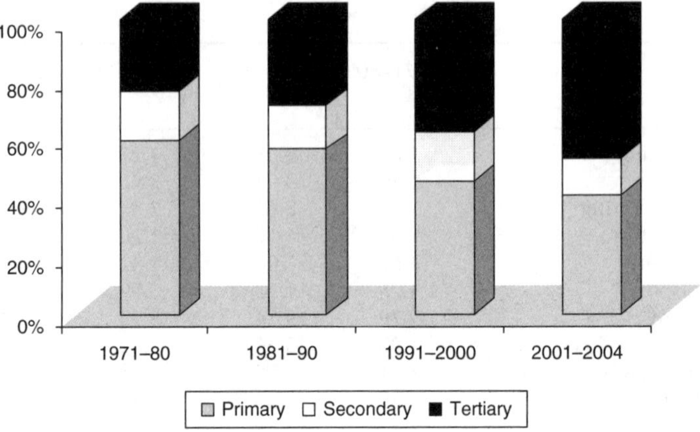

Figure 7.1   Structural shift in output

harmony. This is corroborated by the high-cross correlation among the sectors (Table 7.2).

The declining share of agriculture is a natural phenomenon in the process of development and, as such, is not a matter of concern per se. However, what is worrying is the declining growth rate of agriculture and industry in the 1990s. The service sector growth, on the other hand, is throughout on an upward curve. Though the services sector has grown at a faster pace in the last two decades, it also has the highest variability of output (Table 7.3).

While growth is important, equally desirable is the stability aspect of the growth process. Studying the variability of output across the sectors reveals the following. First, the decade of 1990s has been one of overall low variability compared to the earlier two decades. Second, while variability in the industrial and service sector outputs

Table 7.2   Sectoral cross-correlation: Orissa

Sector	Primary	Secondary	Tertiary	NSDP
Primary	1.00			
Secondary	0.73	1.00		
Tertiary	0.84	0.82	1.00	
NSDP	0.92	0.86	0.98	1.00

Table 7.3 Variability of sectoral output,[a] Orissa (%)

Sector	1970s	1980s	1990s	2001–4
Agriculture	13.0	13.0	8.5	14.0
Primary	12.3	12.5	10.3	11.4
Secondary	21.5	24.4	12.8	9.2
Tertiary	11.0	20.5	19.3	8.9
NSDP	10.8	16.0	12.5	8.5

[a] Measured in terms of coefficient of variations.

increased in the 1980s compared to the 1970s, it has come down in the 1990s. However, for agriculture, variability has remained more or less the same across the last three decades. Third, in the recent period, variability of agriculture and primary sector output has increased. Fourth, overall output variability has declined over the years. In addition, the secondary and tertiary sector output is gaining stability over the period. It is also a characteristic of the growth process in Orissa that the phases of low agricultural growth are marked by low overall growth as well. Given the comparatively low variability associated with agriculture, taking agriculture to a higher growth plane would certainly augur well for the process of development in the state. In the next section we study the structure of agricultural production over the last three decades and the behaviour of some of the major factors that influence production.

7.2 Overview of agriculture in Orissa

Agricultural operations within a geographical location are conditioned by the relevant topographical attributes. As such, a brief discussion of the topographic features of Orissa would be a good starting point.

Topographic features

Climate

The climate of the state is subtropical in nature with dry summers (maximum temperature 42°C) and a hot and humid wet season. Monsoon rains start towards the second week of June and last up to the second week of October. Average annual rainfall is 1502 mm with 73 rainy days. The winter is mild with a minimum temperature of 8°C.

Soils

The soil of Orissa differs widely from highly acidic to slightly alkaline and from light sandy to stiff. The soils are mainly acidic with degree of acidity varying widely.

Agro-climatic conditions

The state can be divided into ten agro-climatic zones with varied characteristics. Its land can be classified into three categories: low (25.6 per cent), medium (33.6 per cent) and uplands (40.8 per cent) with various types of soil including red, yellow, red loamy, alluvial, coastal B~vialilaterite and black soil, with low and medium texture.

Land use pattern

The state has a cultivated area (net sown area plus fallow) of 6.4 million hectares as against a geographical area of 15.5 million hectares, of which 2.9 million hectares are highlands, 1.9 million hectares are medium land and 1.6 million hectares are lowlands. The gross cropped area is 8.4 million hectares and the cropping intensity is 139 per cent.

While topography reflects upon the overall suitability of a place for agricultural operations, the actual production and yield will be influenced by the conduct of the monsoon and a number of other factors of production such as irrigation, use of HYV seeds, application of fertilizers etc. What follows is a discussion on the different variables that have a bearing on the agricultural performance in Orissa.

Conditioning variables for agriculture

Rainfall

In the absence of adequate irrigation facilities, it is natural that agricultural production is conditioned by the incidence of the monsoon rains. Rainfall was below normal for seven years in the 1970s, and on four occasions in the 1980s. The incidence of below-normal monsoon rains was marked for three consecutive years, from 1997–8 to 1999–2000. In all, rainfall was below normal for 5 years in the 1990s.

Orissa was hit by a super cyclone in the 14 coastal districts in October 1999. Further, in 2000–1, although rainfall was much above normal, a drought situation prevailed due to the erratic and early cessation of the monsoon. In more recent times, the state suffered a severe drought when, during 2002–3, the July rainfall fell short by 60 per cent, the lowest during the last 40 years. The growth of agricultural output indicates that, in a year when the deviation of actual rainfall from the normal is substantive (more than 10 per cent), it adversely affects the output in the next year. This pattern emerges perhaps because a poor monsoon creates uncertainty about the future and adversely affects the sowing decisions of the farmers. This is also borne out by the fact that the correlation between rainfall and the next period's output turns out to be much higher than the contemporaneous correlation between rainfall and agricultural production. This indicates that assured irrigation, by reducing uncertainty, can reduce fluctuation in output.

Irrigation

The state has 65.59 lakh hectares of cultivable land, of which 59 lakh hectares can be brought under assured irrigation through different means. Of the total cultivable land of the state only 24.69 lakh hectares were irrigated by the end of 1998–9, which is 41.85 per cent of the total irrigable area of the state. The percentage of the total area irrigated for all crops has gone up from 16.5 per cent in early 1970s to 29.5 per cent in the late 1990s. The gross irrigated area received a major setback in 2002–3 when its size nose-dived from 25 lakh hectares in 2001–2 to 17 lakh hectares, and the gross irrigated area as a pecentage of gross cropped area has fallen to 21.9 per cent in 2002–3. Out of 26.96 lakh hectares of irrigation potential created in the state by 2004–5, around 12.37 lakh hectares are irrigated through major and medium irrigation projects, 5.04 lakh hectares are through minor (flow), 3.76 lakh hectare are through minor (lift) and 5.55 lakh hectare are through other sources which include private tanks, ponds, wells, water harvesting structures and so on.[5] The state planned to provide irrigation facilities to 11.60 lakh hectares of additional agricultural land from different sources during the Ninth Plan period. The KBK districts of Koraput, Malkangiri, Rayagada, Nawarangapur, Bolangir, Sonepur, Kalahandi and Nuapada are chronically affected by drought due to low and erratic rainfall.[6]

The total irrigation potential created in these districts was 3.54 lakh hectares constituting 14.34 per cent of the total irrigation potential created in the state by the end of the Eighth Plan (1992–7). The state has a target of creating 4.65 lakh hectares of irrigation potential through major and medium irrigation schemes during the Tenth Plan (2002–7)period.

Fertilizers

Application of chemical fertilizers and organic manure plays a vital role in increasing productivity. It also protects land fertility by meeting the nutrient requirement of crops. Further, the application of fertilizer in optimum doses along with assured irrigation is a precondition for the success of HYV seeds. Total fertilizer consumption in the state, which was 300,000,000,000 tonnes in 1998–9, has increased to 355,000,000,000 tonnes in 2004–5. Consumption of chemical fertilizers in the state, which was 1.37 kg per hectares in 1964–5, has risen to 12.99 kg per hectare in 1984–5, and further to 43 kg per hectare in 2004–5. This is less than half of the per hectare average fertilizer consumption for all India (84.82 kg) and way below that for the agriculturally well developed states of Punjab (175 kg) and Haryana (153 kg). Only Madhya Pradesh and Rajasthan have lower per hectare consumption of fertilizer compared to Orissa in 2002–3. In order to boost agricultural production, the state's agriculture policy in 1996 emphasized increased use of chemical fertilizers and organic manure. The state government had envisaged increasing fertilizer consumption to 100 kg per hectare within a period of five years (i.e., by 2001–2). In contrast to the plan, actual fertilizer consumption in the state was only 39 kg in 2001–2. Notwithstanding the natural calamities (the super cyclone in 1998, drought in 1999, etc.), there is a wide divergence between policy intention and reality. The state government has again set a target to increase fertilizer consumption to 74 kg per hectare by 2006–7 (Government of Orissa 2006, p. 4/1).

Agricultural credit

There were 43 scheduled commercial banks (SCBs) operating in Orissa at the end of September 2004. These included 24 public sector banks, 10 private sector banks and 9 RRBs. The total number of branches of SCBs (excluding RRBs) in Orissa stood at 1,415 as at the end of September 2004, as against only 100 in 1969. The population group-wise distribution of these branches indicates that the rural branches accounted for 59.2 per cent of the total number of branches, as against the all-India average of 38.2 per cent. The share of semi-urban branches in Orissa was 18.9 per cent, as compared to 24.6 per cent at the all-India level. SCBs' credit to the agriculture sector (both direct and indirect finance) has increased from Rs238 crores in 1972–3 to Rs128,825 crores in 2002–3. Credit matters for agriculture as it gives access to certain key agricultural inputs, such as fertilizer, pesticides, and so on; but what matters even more is the timely availability of credit to sustain agricultural operations. The introduction of Kisan credit cards in 1998–9 was an initiative at the central government level to ensure better access to short-term crop loans for the farmers' seasonal agricultural operations. By September 2003, some 1,942,932 Kisan credit cards had been issued in Orissa with a sanctioned credit of Rs2,919 crores. The average growth of agricultural credit has been around 23 per cent per annum during the 31-year period between 1972–3 and 2002–3. From a comparative perspective, in 1999–2000, the per capita agricultural credit provided by banks was Rs1,373 for Andhra Pradesh followed by Rs1,069 for Punjab, Rs822 for Karnataka, Rs735 for Haryana, Rs399 for Rajasthan and Rs344 for Madhya Pradesh, whereas it was only Rs227 for Orissa.

Having discussed the topography the relevant inputs for agricultural operations, we now provide a synoptic view of the behaviour of area, production and yield of foodgrains during 1970–1 and 2003–4.

Behaviour of area, production and yield

Foodgrains accounted for more than 92 per cent of the total area under production in the 1970s. There was a shift in the areas under production in favour of non-foodgrains (oilseeds) in the 1980s. As such, the area under foodgrains shrank to 87 per cent in 1980s. However, the composition of area under foodgrains and non-foodgrains seems to have reverted back to the pattern observed in the 1970s. Within the foodgrain segment, while the contribution of coarse cereals and pulses to production improved in the 1980s, it decreased in the 1990s and stood at a lower level when compared to the 1970s. While the contribution of wheat in area and production followed a declining trend, that for rice shows a pattern reversal. One can say that the agricultural diversification which was seen in the 1980s seems to have dissipated in the 1990s.

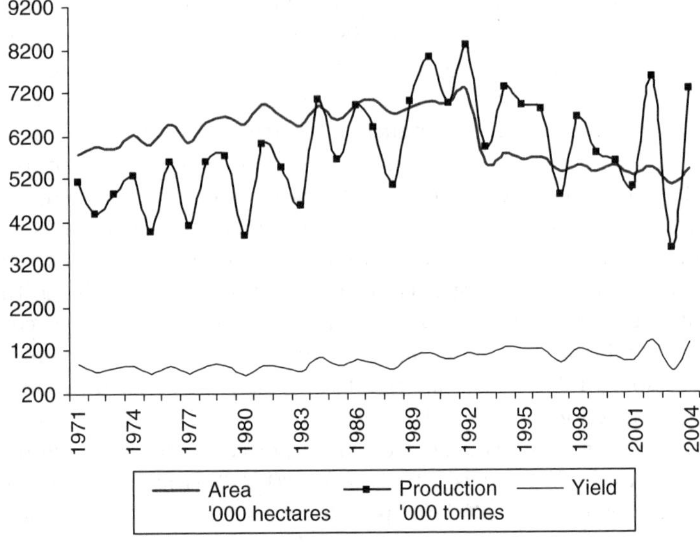

Figure 7.2   Behaviour of area, production and yield of foodgrains

The changing shares of different crops in the area under production over the last three decades reveal that the attempt to diversify in favour of non-foodgrains was most noticeable in the 1970s. Though the tempo of diversification could be maintained to some extent in the 1980s, it was reversed in the 1990s (see Figure 7.2). The area under foodgrains sharply declined from 73 lakh hectares in 1991–2 to 55 lakh hectares in one year (1992–3). While the decline in cereals was a modest 4 lakh hectares (from 51 lakh hectares to 47), the same for pulses was a steep 13 lakh hectares (from 21.42 to 8.49 lakh hectares). Agricultural production can increase broadly from two sources, either through an increase in the area under cultivation or through a rise in the yield. Given the limits as to how much more land can be brought under cultivation, a feasible option was to adopt measures to increase the yield. The technology-based HYV seeds package introduced in the late 1960s was essentially a step towards improving agricultural yield. If one examines the pattern of yield in Orissa, it seems that except for rice, the average decadal yield for wheat, coarse cereals and pulses has declined. Sugarcane and oilseeds have followed an oscillating pattern, rising in the 1980s and then falling in the 1990s as compared to the 1970s.

The phase of declining yield was associated with declining area under cultivation for that particular crop. This reflects that economies of size of operation perhaps matter in improving yield. Over a 30-year period, yield of food grains has increased from 883 kg per hectare in 1970–1 to 1,390 kg per hectare in 2001–2. The outcomes on the agricultural area, production and yield front to some extent can be explained through the behaviour of pure exogenous variables, including the conduct of the monsoons and the use of agricultural inputs over the years. What follows is a discussion about the different variables that have a bearing on agricultural performance in Orissa.

7.3   Review of the literature

Attempts to understand the sources of output change fall into two categories: (1) decomposition schemes; and (2) input–output analysis. The former seeks to measure the relative contribution of different component elements to changes in total output. Several such schemas have been proposed and applied. The relatively simple additive scheme proposed and estimated by Minhas and Vaidyanathan (1965) was to measure the relative contributions of changes in area, crop patterns and 'pure' yield to output changes. This method was subsequently extended to assess the effect of changing spatial distribution of area and yield changes of various crops (Narain, 1977; Sagar, 1980). The various studies focused on accounting for changes between two points of time rather than time series data. They were done mostly during the 1960s and 1970s and hardly any study in this tradition has been reported since, perhaps because of a growing fascination of researchers with econometric estimation of 'production functions'. Decomposition of overall growth by component elements obviously is not adequate for unravelling the determinants of the growth process, but it is an essential first step in as much as the factors influencing or shaping changes in different constituent elements are not the same. It also helps to avoid misapplication of the concept of production function when analysing output growth.

Production function defines the relation between output and inputs. Conventionally, economic theory has viewed output (usually measured by value added) as a function of primary factors, namely labour and capital (in the case of agriculture, land would be an additional primary factor). Alternative functional forms capture differences in respect of returns to scale and the degree of substitutability between inputs. Refinements take into account the fact that output is a function not only of the quantity of inputs but also of changes in the productivity per unit of inputs due to changes in the quality of particular inputs and, more importantly, changes in productivity per unit of all factors (due to economies of scale, technological changes, learning, etc.). This framework for studying agricultural performance is confronted with serious problems of data, specification and interpretation of results. A major constraint is the lack of data on primary factors. Information on land in terms of area under cultivation is available but that does not take into account variations in agro-climatic conditions. Estimates of the number of workers in agriculture are available basically from decennial censuses of population. Further, labour time spent on agriculture is estimable from sample surveys of employment and unemployment and farm management for different points of time. However, there are hardly any reliable time series estimates of total capital stock in agriculture even at the national level, not to speak of states and regions. Because of this, estimation of production functions with primary factors as inputs is not feasible and is seldom attempted.

Given the difficulties, standard practice is to use a motley collection of inputs including proportion of area irrigated, current inputs of human, animal and/or machine labour (proxies for primary factors), non-primary inputs such as improved seeds, fertilizers, manures, and pesticides, and rural infrastructure in varied combinations. Unlike the conventional production function, these specifications and the different functional forms used in estimation – linear, log linear, Cobb–Douglas and Constant Elasticity of Substitution (CES) – betray a lack of a clearly defined and coherent concept of the production process and input–output relations.

A review of the agricultural production function estimates shows that the estimated coefficients of inputs are sensitive to the choice of inputs included in estimating the production function, and also the number of inputs used in the empirical model. Further, coefficients on occasions are found to be insignificant, their values unstable and to have counterintuitive signs. Faced with the pervasive problems of multi-collinearity and simultaneity, analysts tend to drop variables with non-significant coefficients and report results for variables that give statistically significant and 'plausible' values. Beset with the above problems, it is difficult to make robust inferences from the single equation regressions, be it tests of hypotheses or judging the impact of specific inputs on productivity and measuring trends in total factor productivity. However, there has been little application of the simultaneous equations approach in any major study at the state level. This study, going beyond the single equation tradition, uses a *simultaneous framework* to study the interrelations among the various agricultural inputs and output using aggregated data at the state level.

7.4   Modelling agricultural performance

The broad indicators of agricultural performance are the area, production and yield. Given the data limitations, we confine our study to foodgrains only (which consist of cereals and pulses). The factors which govern the area, production and yield outcomes in agriculture are a complex interplay of incidence of monsoons, irrigation facilities and the availability of credit. We have tried to analyse the use of fertilizer, electricity, irrigation and rainfall in this section with the help of a structural model for the period 1970–1 to 2002–3. Here an attempt is made to model agricultural area, production and yield to draw policy inferences. While area and production have a stochastic representation, yield is expressed as an identity. Area and production can be estimated independently but there is a possibility that the disturbance terms of these equations are likely to be contemporaneously correlated. This is because some unconsidered factors that influence the disturbance term in area equation probably influence the disturbance terms in the production equations too. Ignoring this contemporaneous correlation and estimating these equations separately leads to inefficient parameter estimates. However, estimating all equations simultaneously, taking the covariance structure of the residuals into account, leads to efficient estimates. This estimation procedure is generally called Seemingly Unrelated Regression Estimation[7] (SURE: Zellner 1962). The system of equations was estimated by SURE to account for heteroscedasticity and contemporaneous correlation in the errors across equations.

The initial year was determined by the availability of agricultural statistics for India. The choice of the period for analysis has been essentially guided by two considerations. First, in the preceding years, detailed and comparable data on area, production yield and other inputs were not available. Second, the period of study takes into account the introduction of new technology (HYV seeds) and its consequent impact on agricultural production. The year 2002–3 is taken as the terminal year in view of the want of data for the subsequent years. While drawing from the various contributions in the literature, the model presented here is simple and eclectic, designed to capture the dynamics of the agricultural growth process in Orissa, and steers clear of the debate on various issues relating to the subject at an abstract level.

The empirical model

The equation for agricultural production is a supply response function dependent on the area under production, current rainfall and the previous year's rainfall, availability of irrigation facilities and fertilizer use. Inclusion of the previous year's rainfall is justified on account of the possibility that farmers' expectation about future production is built on just such a factor. This is further corroborated by the fact that correlation between agricultural output and previous year's rainfall is much higher than that for the contemporaneous correlation between the two. Below normal rainfall in a year creates uncertainty about future and perhaps prompts the farmer to scale down production activity, resulting in lower production in the next year. It could also be a reflection of the fact that while rainfall data are based on a calendar year (January to December), the agricultural season in India runs from from July to June. As such, the agricultural output for a particular year has already factored in a proportion of the previous year's rainfall when seen from the agricultural year's perspective. The level of significance of the rainfall coefficient at a higher order than the irrigation coefficient is justified by the rain dependency of agricultural yield:

$$LP_t = -3.120 + 0.913^*LA_t + 0.145^*LFERT_{t-1} + 0.302^*LIR_t$$
$$(1.534) \quad (3.789)^a \quad\quad (2.620)^b \quad\quad (1.866)^c$$

$$+ 0.650^*LRN_{t-1} + 0.112^*LRN_t \quad\quad\quad\quad (7.1)$$
$$(4.826)^a \quad\quad (0.890)$$

$$LA_t = 4.955 + 0.156{*}LIR_t - 0.092{*}LP_{t-1} + 0.521{*}LA_{t-1}$$
$$(3.597)^a \quad (1.923)^b \quad (-1.383) \quad (2.93)^a$$

$$+0.042{*}LRN_{t-1} + 0.033{*}LC_t + -0.168{*}LRP_t \tag{7.2}$$
$$(0.796) \quad (2.488)^b \quad (-2.855)^a$$

$$Y = P{*}1000/A \tag{7.3}$$

Note: figures in parenthesis indicate that the *t*-values and superscripts on the parentheses indicate the level of significance: [a]Significant at 1 per cent level, [b]Significant at 5 per cent level and [c]Significant at 10 per cent level.

  P = Foodgrain production
  A = Area under foodgrains
  Y = Yield
  F = Consumption of fertilizer
 RN = Actual rainfall as percentage of normal rainfall.
  IR = Irrigation facilities proxied by grossirrigated area as a percentage of gross cropped area
 RP = Average price of fine rice
  C = Agricultural credit from the SCBs.

The model consists of three endogenous variables, P_t, A_t, and Y_t, and eight exogenous/ predetermined variables, IR_t, LC_t, RN_t, RP_t, LF_t, RN_{t-1}, A_{t-1}, and P_{t-1}. The prefix L denotes natural logarithm of the variables.

As expected, both area and irrigation are found significantly to impact production. Fertilizer use also has a positive impact on production. The estimation of the production equation reveals that area, rainfall, irrigation and fertilizer affect production in that decreasing order. The estimation of the area equation indicates that the availability of irrigation facilities positively impacts the area under cultivation. Production in the previous year turns out to have a negative bearing on the acreage under cultivation, though the effect is not statistically very significant. A bumper crop in a particular year would prompt producers to cut down on the area under cultivation in the coming year to avoid a distress sale arising out of a glut. Credit availability has a feeble but positive impact as regards decisions concerning the area under cultivation. Unlike for the production outcome, the previous year's rainfall turns out to positively affect the area under cultivation but not in a statistically significant sense.

Model performance

All the equation estimates were reasonably robust, satisfying the usual criteria of significance and goodness of fit. Most of the signs of the coefficients were as expected. The model solution has been obtained by running a deterministic simulation in a dynamic framework using the Gauss–Seidel iterative procedure which solves equations sequentially in an iterative process until convergence is achieved. The satisfactory performance of the model is further attested to by the fact that the actual and simulated values move convergently for most of the modelled variables, and the simulations – for the most part – capture the turning points (Figure 7.3). Thus the model performs reasonably well in tracking the behaviour of the agricultural production, area under cultivation and yield during the period from 1970–1 to 2002–3.

Policy simulations

Scenario 1: Fertilizer consumption increasing at 10 per cent per year beginning with 1971

The growth of fertilizer consumption has been of the order of 7.35 per cent per year if we consider the fertilizer consumption figures in 1970–1 and 2002–3. Instead of 7.3 per cent, had fertilizer consumption grown at 10 per cent per year beginning with 1971, it would have grown to 80 kg per hectare in 2002–3. Even at this level, it could have been below the actual all-India average in 2002–3 and around half of that for Punjab (175 kg per hectare). Consequent to this shock, the model predicts a gain in production in the range of 0.1–2.6 per cent in the 1980s and 3.4–7.4 per cent in the 1990s, reaching 10 per cent in the final year (see Figure 7.4). An increase in fertlizer application influences the area indirectly through its impact on production. As fertilizer influences production positively and production affects next year's area under cultivation negatively, we find a net negative impact on the area arising out of a fertilizer shock. The model predicts a decline in area in the range of 0.1–0.4 per cent in the 1980s and 0.2–1.3 per cent in the 1990s. Yield, which is an outcome of the interplay between production and area gain, would have increased in the

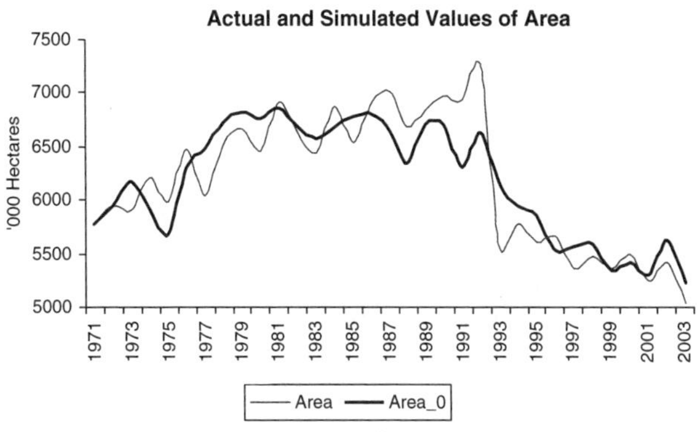

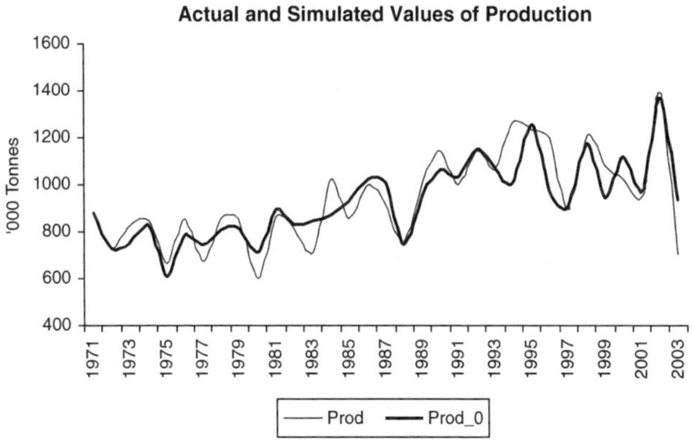

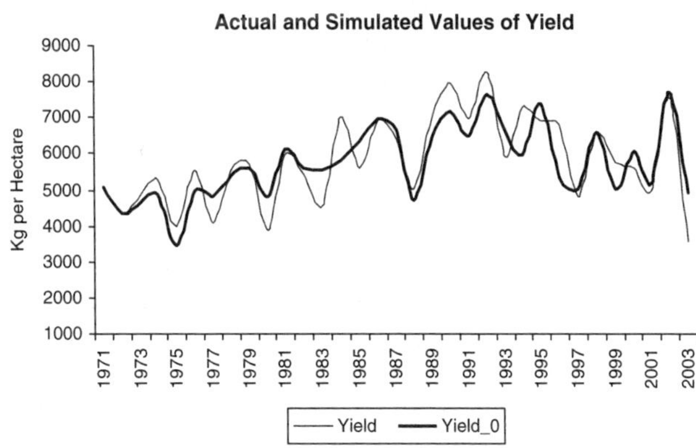

Figure 7.3   Actual and simulated values for area, production and yield

range of 0.5–3 per cent in the 1980s, 3.6–9 per cent in the 1990s and around 11 per cent towards the terminal year.

Scenario 2: an increase in irrigation capacity by 1 percentage point every year

Gross irrigated area as a percentage of gross cropped area was 16.2 per cent in 1970–1. It increased to 20 per cent in the early 1980s and to 25 per cent in the late 1980s. The irrigation capacity increased further to 29.5 per cent in 2000, but growth was not steady in the 1990s. If we take 2001–2 as the benchmark, the gross cropped area was 88 lakh hectares. Even if a 50 per cent target of this area had been set for irrigation coverage, the gross irrigated area would have been of the order of 44 lakh hectares which is well within the feasible range as regards providing irrigation facilities. Given such a scenario, we have tried to examine the impact of a gradual increase in the irrigation capacity by 1 percentage point beginning with 1971. This would have taken the gross irrigated area as a proportion of gross cropped area to 48.5 per cent in 2003. As the simulated results reveal, the gain from this increase in irrigation capacity would have been greatest for production, followed by yield and area. Gains in production would have been in the range of 0.7–13 per cent in the 1970s, and 9–21 per cent in the 1980s. In the 1990s, production[8] would have increased to the tune of 20–27 per cent in the 1990s, and the final year (2002–3) would have witnessed a production gain of around 48 per cent (see Figure 7.4). The decline in area under cultivation, which was noticed in the early 1990s, could have been largely averted had irrigation capacity increased. While the area would have been around 18 per cent more, yield would have increased by around 26 per cent in 2002–3 compared to the base line scenario.

Scenario 3: if credit growth is 10 per cent more than actual

If credit disbursed to the agriculture sector had been 10 per cent more than the actual, the impact would have been felt on agricultural area and production but of a very low order. For instance, while area would have been 0.6 per cent more than that under the base line scenario, gains in production would have been of the order of 0.5 per cent for the entire period. With the response to area being more than that for production, yield would have undergone a marginal decline consequent to the shock in credit (see Figures 7.5–7.7).

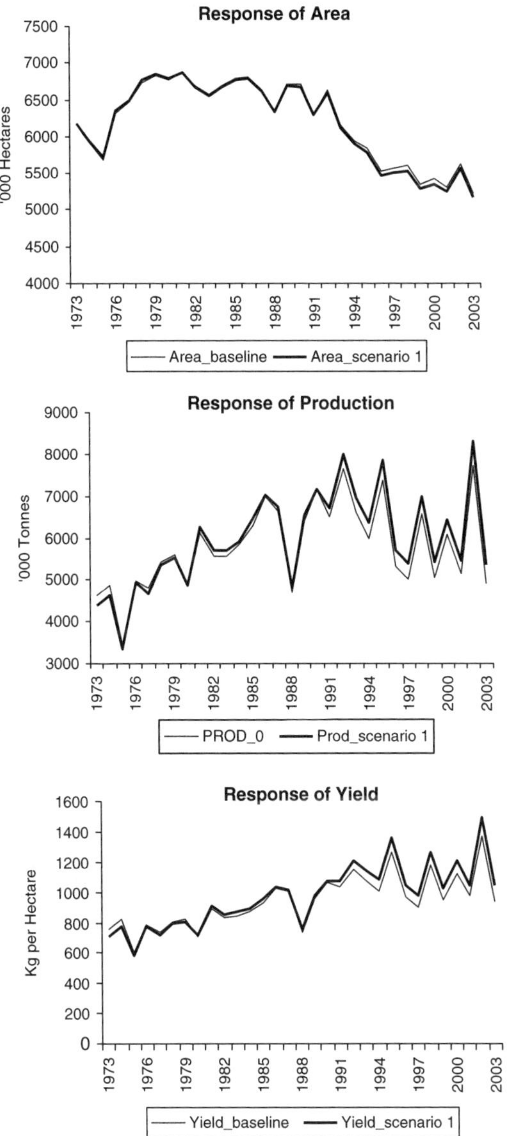

Figure 7.4   Response of area, production and yield under scenario 1

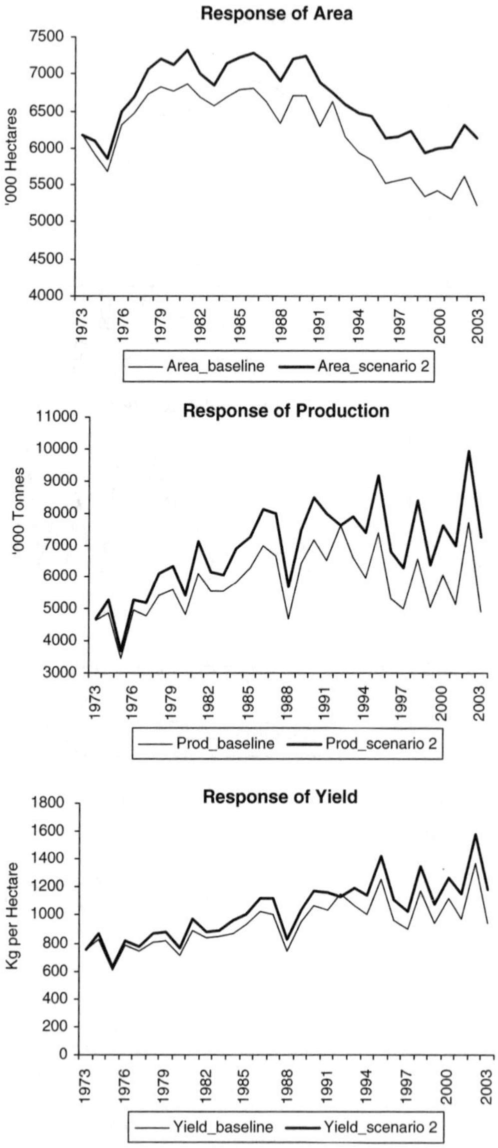

Figure 7.5   Response of area, production and yield under scenario 2

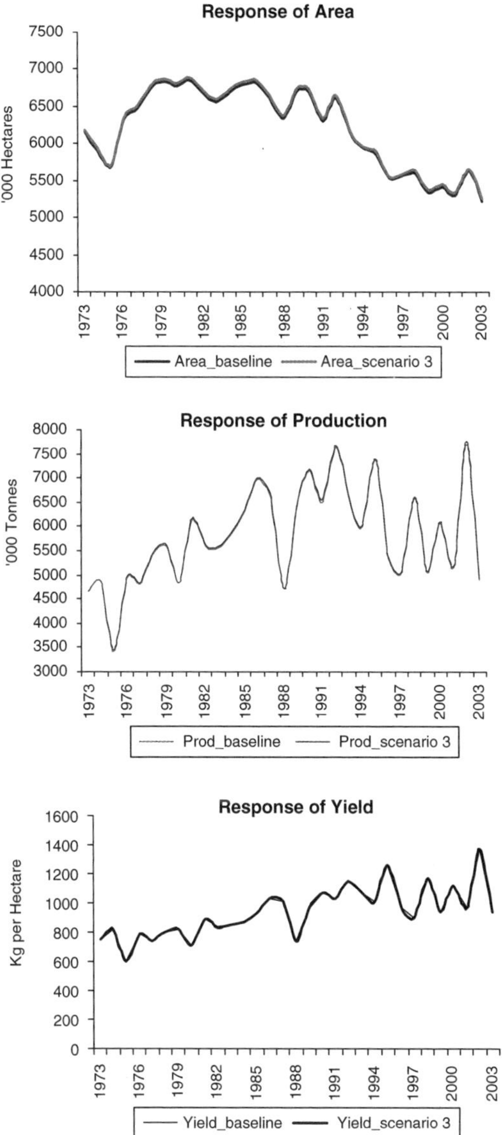

Figure 7.6　Response of area, production and yield under scenario 3

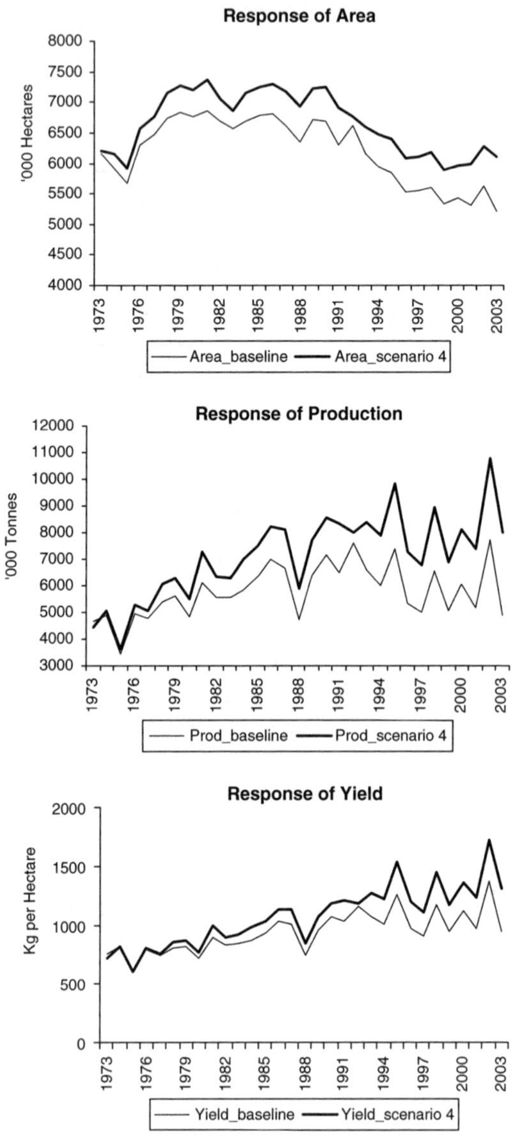

Figure 7.7   Response of area, production and yield under scenario 4

Scenario 4: combined shock

Had all the three innovations taken place simultaneously, one would have seen major gains in production and yield and the curtailment of area under cultivation contained to a great extent. In the last 10 years, area would have been higher by 9 per cent, production by 31 per cent and yield by 21 per cent compared to the base line scenario in 1993–4. The gains in area, production and yield would have been around 17 per cent, 63 per cent and 40 per cent respectively in 2002–3 compared to the base line scenario (see Figures 7.5–7.7). The combined shock had the most impressive impact on yield.

7.5 Conclusion

In this chapter we have tried to gauge the gain in production and yield that would have been possible by creating an enabling environment for the use of HYV seed technology. This was tested for the state of Orissa as a case study by giving policy shocks in a simultaneous equations framework. We found that the performance of the agriculture sector in Orissa in the post-1970 period has been far from satisfactory. While the state has reasonable agro-climatic diversity, the climate has not been particularly conducive for agricultural operations. In contrast to the national position, the agricultural sector in Orissa still has a considerable share in SDP although it is beset with considerable fluctuations. Agricultural operations have suffered from the extremities of monsoon behaviour, either from too much of rainfall or too little of it. The impact of disadvantageous climatic conditions on agricultural production and yield could have been countered by proactive action on the policy front. After decades of silence regarding policy, Orissa formulated a 'State Agricultural Policy' in 1996. The Agricultural Policy announced by the state government was a welcome step to push agricultural activity in the state to a higher trajectory. However, much more needs to be done to achieve the many goals set out in the policy.

An attempt was made to discern the impact of factors, such as availability of irrigation facilities, fertilizer consumption and agricultural credit which possibly influence area, production and yield in agriculture. The interrelations among the various agricultural inputs and output have been studied in a simultaneous framework using aggregated data at the state level. The simulations bring out the fact that the one critical area where the state needs to focus is irrigation. This is borne out by the high stimulus to production and yield consequent to a small but sustained increase in irrigation. It needs to be mentioned that increasing irrigation facilities (and, for that matter, other enabling inputs for agriculture) should not be seen as a one-time big bang measure but a sustained effort spread over a sufficiently long time horizon. This case study clearly brings out the potential gain to agricultural production and yield that can flow from the creation of an enabling environment for the adoption of the new technology. Pending institutional reforms, the spread of the green revolution to hitherto untapped regions can be an effective strategy in giving a fillip to the agricultural growth of the country.

Notes

1 Introduction

1. 'China: Planning the New Socialist Countryside', *The Economist*, 11 March, 2006.
2. As Krueger and Chinoy (2002) note, 'a series of other policy measures were enacted in rapid succession in the first two years after reforms, [which] quickly and significantly reduced the negative effects of control on domestic economic activity'.
3. In 1961 the National Integration Council held that rapid development of the economically backward regions in any state should be given priority in national and state Plans, at least to the extent that the minimum level of development was reached for all states within a stated period.
4. The Indian constitution has categorized the responsibilities for the different levels of government into three lists: a state list, a central list, and a concurrent list. Though many important subjects, such as electricity and education, are on the concurrent list, a uniformity prevailed across the states with regard to two broad factors – the dominant centre and the planning process – assuming the commanding heights of the economy.
5. A number of factors have led to the worsening fiscal situation including the implementation of the Fifth Pay Commission recommendations. The revenue deficit of the states has increased substantially with increased borrowings being undertaken to meet consumption expenditure. In a number of states, the current revenue is just sufficient to meet wages and salaries, pensions and debt service obligations, leaving little for development expenditures.
6. While many of the structural weaknesses are shared by almost all the states, such as fiscal distress or inadequacy of infrastructure, some, such as the poor law and order situation, a regressive agrarian structure and huge agricultural subsidies provided through the power sector, are specific to certain states.
7. RRB equity is held by the central government, the relevant state government and the sponsoring bank in the ratio of 50:15:35.

2 Growth performance

1. The princely states had entered into a subsidiary alliance (Lord Wellesley) with the British Crown in strategic areas such as defence, communication, etc.).
2. *India: Social Development Report* provides the details of the methodology and ranking on the individual indicators (Council for Social Development,

2006). The larger states, according to this Report's classification, corres-pond mostly to the General Category States (GCS) as per the classification used in the rest of this chapter.

3. 'How the States were Ranked: Methodology', by Bibek Debroy and Laveesh Bhandari in *India Today*, 13–19 May 2003.

4. Shankar Acharya has succinctly brought out the scope for improvement in the Ahluwalia study in 'Comment by Shankar Acharya on "State Level Performance Under Economic Reforms in India" by Montek S. Ahluwalia' in Anne O. Krueger (ed.), *Economic Policy Reforms and the Indian Economy* (Chicago: University of Chicago Press, 2002).

5. As Rao, Shand and Kalirajan (1999) observe: 'Our analysis of conver-gence takes into account the 14 major states in the Indian union. These 14 major states account for 93 per cent of population and 91.5 per cent of net domestic product in the country and are therefore representative.' They exclude the 'special category' states and the small state of Goa from their analysis because of significant differences in the structure of these economies from the rest of the states and the consequent differences in their steady state income as compared to other states.

6. The post-1980 period refers to 1980–1 until 2004–5. GDP figures for 2004–5 are provisional estimates.

7. This point can be elaborated further. The share of the GCS and the SCS, comprising 20 states, which used to be 90 per cent of all-India GDP during 1981–93, has declined to 87 per cent in the post-reform (1994–2004) period. The share of these 20 states in the all-India service sector output declined from 75 to 73 per cent in the post-reform phase compared to the pre-reform period. If we also consider the four UTs, the combined share of these 24 entities in all-India GDP was on average 93 per cent during 1981–93, and 91 per cent during 1994–2004. The combined share of them in the all-India services output was only 80 and 78 per cent respectively. This can be understood given that certain activities such as Defence or Communication belong to the service segment and are exclusively part of central government.

8. Three new states came into existence in the year 2000. The SDP figure for the 1993–4 base has been made available by the CSO for the newly created states for the period beginning 1993–4.

9. CSO, under the Ministry of Statistics and Programme Implementation, is the apex body for National Accounts Statistics in India.

3 Income Inequality

1. The controversy relates to the difference in recall period used in the 50th and 55th round of NSSO Surveys. Prior to the 55th round, NSSO surveys were based on a 30-day recall period. In the 55th round a 7-day recall period was introduced in addition to the usual 30-day recall period. This, critics apprehend, would have contaminated the survey responses and would have yielded biased results on poverty.

2. The computational details of the rank concordance index are discussed in Appendix 3.2.
3. For instance, the study by Singh, Bhandari, Chen and Khare (2002) examined convergence style regressions on a broad measure of well being, the Human Development Index, and found evidence supporting absolute (β) convergence.
4 Durlauf and Quah (1999) report that, as of 1998, over 90 different conditioning variables have appeared in the literature, despite the fact that no more than 120 countries are available for analysis of conditional convergence in the standard data sets.
5. The intercept a represents the common steady state: $a = X + [(1 - e^{-\beta T})/T]$ (ln Y_i^*), where x is the exogenous growth of technology, corresponding to steady state growth, and Y_i^* is the steady state income.
6. The specification assumes that residuals are independent and identically distributed (i.i.d.), namely that the mean of errors u_{it}, is zero, its variance is constant and that errors show no systematic correlation. However, these conditions are likely to be violated in practice. In regional growth analysis, one should also consider the possibility of spatial correlation patterns. It is very likely that neighbouring regions influence a region's growth. Fingleton (1999) suggests using a spatially autocorrelated errors model to cope with this issue. The use of country dummy variables is an alternative approximate method to absorb spatial correlation which has been used in this study.
7. While traversing from the non-linear to the linear specification, the term $(1 - e^{-\beta T})/T$ is replaced by a coefficient, b. In this case, the speed of convergence ß, however, is recoverable from the estimated coefficient b from the formula: $ß = -\ln(1 - b)/T$.
8. This point was first made by Islam (1995). It was emphasized that, by not taking into account individual specific effects, the traditional convergence analysis suffers from a downward bias of the convergence coefficient.
9. Panel data theory suggests that in the presence of fixed effects the cross-section error term $u_{i,t}$ can be decomposed into $u_{i,t} = \eta_i + \varepsilon_{i,t}$, where η_i is a fixed individual component and $\varepsilon_{i,t}$ is the remaining random error component. Hence, conventional cross-section estimates which neglect η_i can be assumed to suffer from an omitted variable bias. Region-specific unobservable factors can be modelled by employing panel data estimation techniques.
10. An alternative model in panel data estimation would be the random effects model. However, as the omitted variable effect is systematically correlated with the explanatory variable, one cannot assume random effects model.
11. This is similar to the cross-section analysis, where the intercept is defined as $a = X + [(1 - e^{-\beta T})/T](\ln Y_i^*)$; in the panel data analysis, the region-specific intercept is defined as: $\eta_i = X_i + (1 - e^{-\beta})[\log Y_i^* + X_{i(t-1)}]$. Having

substituted c for $(1 - e^{-\beta})$ and using annual data, the equation becomes $\eta_i = c\ \log y^*$ so that the steady state per capita income can be calculated according to the following relation: $\log y_i^* = (\eta_i / c)$. With the time-specific effect, λ_i, global shocks (e.g., a decline in economic activity or a technology shock), are captured. As in the traditional cross-section analysis, income growth $\log Y_t - \log Y_0$ would be negatively related to previous income if neoclassical convergence dynamics were given. Steady state income is economy-specific and is represented by the variable intercept a_i, the so-called fixed effect in the language of panel data econometrics. In this panel data model, the convergence coefficient is assumed to be identical across economies (for simplicity we take b instead of $[1 - e^{-\beta}]$).

12. Applies especially to the case where the character of the data set is 'small T, large N': that is, a standard fixed effects estimator may be subject to a rather considerable bias.
13. Application of least squares to the first differenced regression yields inconsistent estimates.
14. This instrument is correlated with the explanatory variable but not with the error term.
15. As Arellano and Bond (1991) show, the Anderson and Hsiao estimator is not necessarily an efficient estimator since it does not make use of all available moment restrictions.
16. If the lagged observation $Y_{i,t-2}$ is not correlated with the error $e_{i,t} - e_{i,t-1}$, any further lag $Y_{i,t-3}$, $Y_{i,t-4}$, etc., is also not correlated with the error term $e_{i,t} - e_{i,t-1}$, and thus is a valid instrument.
17. From the Monte Carlo Simulations.

4   State Finances

1. 'India's Fiscal Situation: Is a Crisis Ahead?' in *Economic Policy Reforms in the Indian Economy*, edited by Anne O. Kruger, Oxford; 'Fiscal Policy in India's Economic Reforms' in *India in the Era of Economic Reforms*, edited by Sachs, Varshney and Bajpai, Oxford.
2. The fiscal deficit figure for the state governments increased from 2.9 per cent in 1997–98 to 4.2 per cent in 1998–99.
3. The CIFH consists of five subindices on Resource Mobilization, Expenditure Management, Fiscal Imbalances, Management of Fiscal Liabilities and GSDP Growth, with weights in the proportion of 0.25, 0.25. 0.10, 0.20 and 0.20 respectively. Here, we focus on only two subindices, Resource Mobilization and Expenditure Management, as they are the two control variables, and Fiscal Liabilities (which is an outcome of the performance on these two counts). Details on the construction of the index can be seen from the Source.
4. Annex 2, State Finances, A Study of Budgets 2005–06 (Reserve Bank of India, 2006).

5. In India, unemployment allowance is provided under the provisions of the National Rural Employment Guarantee (NREG) Act, 2005. However, during our study period, 1991–2004 there was no such provision or Act on an all-India basis. Prior to this, the employment assurance and guarantee schemes pursued in some of the states were more to address unemployment of a structural nature rather than arising out of business cycles.
6. Banco de México's Annual Report, 2000.
7. The Hodrick–Prescott method is subject to the end point problems associated with its estimation and the choice of the parameter λ, indicating the period of business cycle. Here we have taken λ to be 100.
8. The base year for any particular state has been arrived at by considering the difference between real SDP series and the filtered real SDP series for that state. Needless to say, the base year for different states would differ.
9. Defining the cyclically adjusted budget in this way allocates the contribution of automatic stabilizers to the MFI.
10. The base year for any particular state has been arrived at by considering the difference between real SDP series and the filtered real SDP series for that state.

5 Analytics of Credit–Output Behaviour for Indian States

1. The advances to the industrial sector in total bank credit increased from 34.3 per cent at the end of 1955 to 64.3 per cent by March 1966. This was in accordance with the Plan priority for rapid industrialization during the Second (1956–61) and Third Plan (1961–6) periods.
2. The Securitization and Reconstruction of Financial Assets and Enforcement of Security Interest (SARFAESAI) Act was promulgated in 2004, which has given the banks a lot of maneouvrability to recover bad debts.
3. From 1999–2000 to 2003–4, the output gap for the Indian economy was negative though there were signs of a revival in 2003–4.
4. The State Level Bankers' Committee (SLBC) is the forum where bankers and the state government deliberate on issues relating to credit disbursal in the state. The bankers prepare the target for credit disbursal in the state in a given year in the priority and non-priority sectors through what is known as an Annual Credit Plan (ACP). The ACP, and its achievements, are discussed in the SLBC meetings.
5. The boxed item on 'Determinants of Bank Credit' in the *Report on Currency and Finance, 2003–2004*, provides a good summary of the empirical literature on the relationship between bank credit and economic growth.
6. Meghalaya is the only SCS which falls into this category whose share has marginally improved, from 0.07 per cent to 0.08 per cent.
7. The detailed tests for unit roots are given in Appendix 5.2.
8. The cointegration relationships are given in Appendix 5.3.

6   **Regional Rural Banks: Restructuring Strategies**

1. RRBs were established 'with a view to developing the rural economy by providing, for the purpose of development of agriculture, trade, commerce, industry and other productive activities in the rural areas, credit and other facilities, particularly to small and marginal farmers, agricultural labourers, artisans and small entrepreneurs, and for matters connected therewith and incidental thereto'(RRBs Act, 1976).
2. Their equity is held by central government, the state government concerned and the sponsoring bank in the proportion of 50:15:35.
3. Debate in the XV Lok Sabha on Regional Rural Bank (Amendment Bill, 2004).
4. RRBs alone have organized roughly 12 lakh self-help groups, 45 per cent of the total self-help groups in the country. RRBs have also issued over 40 lakh Kisan Credit Cards to the farmers and organized over 5,000, out of 11,000, farmers' clubs under the National Bank for Agricultural and Rural Development (NABARD) scheme.
5. Following the recommendations of the Narasimham Committee (1991), there have been gradual relaxations in their choice of clientele and area of operations.
6. Though the growth in credit when seen in isolation gives an impression of the impressive strides made by RRBs in disbursing credit, they account for a very small proportion (around 3 per cent) of the total assets of the Indian banking sector, despite their significant branch network.
7. While the CD ratio for 50 RRBs was more than 60 per cent, that for 87 banks was less than 40 per cent in March 2004.
8. Lack of a single owner and control, with no prospects for profits, diffused accountability and weakened oversight of the RRBs.
9. Net income has been defined as the excess of total income over total expenditure.
10. Specifically, the sponsoring bank contributes 35 per cent of the issued capital of an RRB, appoints its chairman, advises on decisions regarding investments, monitors its progress and suggests corrective measures to be taken by the RRB. More on the relationship between sponsoring banks and their RRBs is provided in Appendix 6.1.
11. The RRB omitted is the Kshetryia Kisan Gramin Bank due to lack of information on the sponsoring bank for the entire period of 1994–2003. This RRB is sponsored by UPSCB (Uttar Pradesh State Cooperative Bank), a co-operative bank.
12. This in a way testifies to the appropriateness of employing the extended dynamic model for estimation. Guided by statistical significance, two lags of the dependent variable have been used in the GMM estimation.
13. This refers to 31 March 2006, unless specified otherwise.

7   Agricultural Growth in Indian States: The Case of Orissa

1. 'Agriculture sector' as per the Planning Commission's terminology is 'primary sector' as per the classification used in this study.
2. *An Approach to the 11th Five-Year Plan (Towards Faster and More Inclusive Growth)*, Planning Commission, Government of India.
3. The Indian Constitution under Article 246 has categorized subjects under three broad headings: Union List, State List and Concurrent List. The subjects falling under the Union and the State List are the prime responsibilities of the centre and the states respectively. For subjects falling under the Concurrent List, both the centre and the states have joint responsibility. Agriculture falls under the state list.
4. As per 2001 Census, Annexure 21.2 (Government of Orissa 2006).
5. Information on surface and lift irrigation.

   Lift irrigation.   In regions where the topography does not permit direct flow irrigation from rivers and streams, water has to be lifted into the irrigation channels. These works are similar to diversion schemes, but in addition pumps are installed and pump houses constructed. These schemes, being costly in operation, are feasible only in areas where (i) gravity flow irrigation is not possible; (ii) there is keen demand for irrigation and cultivators are enthusiastic; (iii) water is available in the streams for at least about 200 days in a year; and (iv) cheap electric power is available. Installation of diesel-operated pump sets for lifting water makes the operation and maintenance cost of these schemes exorbitantly high. Surface flow irrigation scheme.   These schemes use rain water for irrigation purposes either by storing it or by diverting it from a stream, nala or river. Sometimes, permanent diversions are constructed for utilizing the flowing water of a stream or river. Temporary diversions are also constructed in many areas which are usually washed away during the rainy season.
6. Some regions of Orissa are more developed than others. Despite sustained efforts to develop all parts of the state, regional disparities exist. For example, the region comprising the old Kalahandi, Bolangir and Koraput districts, popularly known as 'KBK districts' and since 1992–3 reorganized into eight districts, i.e., Kalahandi, Nuapada, Bolangir, Sonepur, Koraput, Malkangiri, Nawarangapur and Rayagada, is considered one of the poorest regions in the country with about 71.97 per cent of families living below the poverty line (BPL).
7. Another reason to estimate an equation system simultaneously are cross-equation parameter restrictions. These restrictions can be tested and/or imposed only in a simultaneous estimation approach.
8. The impact of the use of the HYV seeds was not modelled directly as, without assured irrigation and application of fertilizer, using these seeds would not have been very effective in improving agricultural yield. Here we assume that availability of assured irrigation, fertilizer and credit would generate the necessary demand for the use of the HYV seeds.

Bibliography

Acharya, S. (2001), *India's Macroeconomic Management in the 1990s* (New Delhi: Indian Council for Research on International Economic Relations).

Acharya, S. (2002), 'Macroeconomic Management in the 1990s', *Economic and Political Weekly* (20–27 April), 37 (16), pp. 1,515–38.

Acharya, Shankar (2003), *Indian Economy: Some Issues and Answers* (New Delhi: Academic Foundation).

Acharya, Shankar (2006), *India's Macroeconomic Policy* (New Delhi: Oxford University Press).

Ahluwalia, Montek S. (2000), 'Economic Performance of States in Post-Reform Period', *Economic and Political Weekly*, 35(19), pp. 1,637–48.

Ahluwalia, Montek S. (2002a), 'State Level Performance under Economic Reforms in India', in Anne Krueger (ed.), *Economic Policy Reforms and the Indian Economy* (Chicago, IL: University of Chicago Press).

Ahluwalia, Montek S. (2002b). 'India's Vulnerability to External Crisis: An Assessment', in M. Ahluwalia, S.S. Tarapore and Y.V. Reddy (eds), *Macroeconomics and Monetary Policy: Issues for a Reforming Economy. Essays in Honour of C. Rangarajan* (New Delhi: Oxford University Press).

Aiyar, Shekhar (2001), 'Growth Theory and Convergence across Indian States: A Panel Study', in T. Callen, P. Reynolds and C. Towe (eds), *India at the Crossroads: Sustaining Growth and Reducing Poverty* (Washington, DC: International Monetary Fund), ch. 8.

Alesina, Alberto and Bayoumi, Tamim (1996), 'The Costs and Benefits of Fiscal Rules: Evidence from U.S. States', NBER Working Paper No. 5614. (Cambridge, MA: NBER).

Alesina, Alberto and Perotti, Roberto (1995), 'Fiscal Expansions and Adjustments in OECD Countries', *Economic Policy*, 21, pp. 205–48.

Anderson, T.W. and Hsiao, C. (1981), 'Estimation of Dynamic Models with Error Components', *Journal of the American Statistical Association*, 76, pp. 598–606.

Arellano, M. and Bond, S. (1991), 'Some Tests of Specification for Panel Data: Monte Carlo Evidence and an Application to Employment Equations', *Review of Economic Studies*, 58, pp. 277–97.

Arellano, M. and Bover, O. (1995), 'Another Look at the Instrumental Variables Estimation of Error Components Models', *Journal of Econometrics*, 68, pp. 29–51.

Auerbach, Alan J. (2002), 'Is There a Role for Discretionary Fiscal Policy?', Working Paper 9306 (Cambridge, MA: NBER). Available at http://www.nber.org/papers/w9306.

Bajpai, Nirupam and Sachs, Jeffrey D. (1996), 'Trends in Inter-State Inequalities of Income in India' (Harvard, MA: Harvard Institute for International Development), Development Discussion Paper No. 528.

Bajpai, Nirupam and Sachs, Jeffrey D. (1999), 'Progress of Policy Reform and Variations in Performance at the Sub-National Level in India', Development Discussion Paper No. 730, Harvard Institute for International Development, Harvard University.

Bajpai, Nirupam and Sachs, Jeffrey D. (2002), *Understanding Regional Economic Growth in India* (Harvard, MA: Center for International Development at Harvard University), CID Working Paper No. 88.

Balasone, F. and Franco, D. (2000), 'EMU Fiscal Rules: A New Answer to an Old Question', *Public Finance Workshop Papers*, Research Department, Banca D' Italia.

Baltagi, B.H. (1995), *Econometric Analysis of Panel Data* (West Sussex: Wiley).

Baltagi, B.H. (2001), *Econometric Analysis of Panel Data* (New York: John Wiley).

Banerjee, A. (1999), 'Panel Data Unit Root Tests and Cointegration: An Overview', *Oxford Bulletin of Economics and Statistics*, Special Issue, 61, pp. 607–29.

Barro, Robert J. (1991) 'Economic Growth in a Cross-Section of Countries', *Quarterly Journal of Economics*, 106, pp. 407–43.

Barro, Robert, J. and Sala-i-Martin, Xavier (1991), 'Convergence across States and Regions', *Brookings Papers on Economic Activity*, No. 1, pp. 107–82.

Barro, R.J. and Sala-í-Martin X. (1995) *Economic Growth* (New York: McGraw-Hill).

Barth, J.R., Caprio, G. and Levine, R. (2004), 'Bank Supervision and Regulation: What Works Best?', *Journal of Financial Intermediation*, 13(2), pp. 205–48.

Bayoumi, Tamim and Eichengreen, Barry (1995), 'Restraining Yourself: The Implications of Fiscal Rules for Economic Stabilization', IMF Staff Papers, 42(1), pp. 32–48.

Bell, Frederick W. and Murphy, Nell B. (1969), 'Impact of Market Structure on the Price of a Commercial Banking Service', *The Review of Economics and Statistics*, 51(2), pp. 210–13.

Bencivenga, V.R. and. Smith, B.D. (1991), 'Financial Intermediation and Endogenous Growth', *Review of Economic Studies*, 58, pp. 195–209.

Benston, George J., Hanweck, Gerald A. and Humphrey, David B. (1982), 'Scale Economies in Banking', *Journal of Money, Credit, and Banking*, 14(4), pp. 435–56.

Bernanke, B. and Gertler, M. (1995), 'Inside the Black Box: The Credit Channel of Monetary Policy Transmission', *Journal of Economic Perspectives*, 9(4), pp. 27–48.

Bhandari, Laveesh and Khare, Aarti (2002), *The Geography of Post 1991 Indian Economy*, (New Delhi: Indicus Analytics).

Bhat, N.S. (1997) 'Directed Credit Flows and Productivity of Commercial Bank Resources in the Indian Economy', *The Indian Economic Journal*, 44(1), pp. 101–7.

Bhattacharya, B.B and Sakthivel, S. (2004), 'Economic Reforms and Jobless Growth in India in the 1990s', Working Paper No. E/244/2004, Institute of Economic Growth. Available at http://iegindia.org/worksakthi244.pdf.

Bibek, D. and Laveesh, B. (2003), 'How the States were Ranked: Methodology', *India Today*, 13–19 May.

Bikker, J.A and Hu, H. (2002), 'Cyclical Patterns in Profits, Provisioning and Lending of Banks and Procyclicality of the New Basel Capital Requirements', *BNL Quarterly Review*, 221, pp. 143–75.

Bispham, J.A. (1987), 'Rising Public Sector Indebtedness: Some More Unpleasant Arithmetic', in Michael J. Boskin, John S. Flemming and Stefano Gorini (eds), *Private Savings and Public Debt'* (Oxford: Basil Blackwell).

Blanchard, O. (1980), 'Suggestions for a New Set of Fiscal Indicators', OECD Working Paper No. 79.

Blanchard, Olivier, Chouraqui, Jean-Claude, Hagemann, Robert P. and Sartor, Nicola (1990), 'The Sustainability of Fiscal Policy: New Answers to An Old Question', OECD Economic Studies No. 15, Autumn.

Blejer, M. and Cheasty, A. (1991), 'The Measurement of Fiscal Deficits: Analytical and Methodological Issues', *Journal of Economic Literature*, 29(4), pp. 1,644–78.

Bohn, Henning (1998), 'The Behavior of U.S. Public Debt and Deficits', *Quarterly Journal of Economics,* 113(3), pp. 949–63.

Bourke, P. (1989), 'Concentration and other Determinants of Bank Profitability in Europe, North America and Australia', *Journal of Banking and Finance*, 13, pp. 65–79.

Boyle, E.G. and McCarthy, T.G. (1997), 'Simple Measure of Convergence', *Oxford Bulletin of Economics and Statistics*, 59(2), pp. 257–64.

Buiter, W.H. (1985) 'Guide to Public Sector Debt and Deficit', *Economy Policy*, November.

Buiter, W.H. and Patel, U.R. (1992), 'Debt, Deficits, and Inflation: An Application to the Public Finances of India', *Journal of Public Economics* (March), 47(2), pp. 171–205.

Cashin, Paul and Sahay, Ratna (1996), 'Internal Migration, Center – State Grants, and Economic Growth in the States of India', *International Monetary Fund Staff Papers*, 431, pp. 123–71.

Chalk, Nigel (2002), 'Structural Balances and All That: Which Indicators to Use in Assessing Fiscal Policy', *International Monetary Fund Working Paper* WP/02/101.

Chalk, Nigel and Hemming, Richard (2000), 'Assessing Fiscal Sustainability in Theory and Practice', IMF Working Papers 00/81.

Chand, S. (1993) 'Fiscal Impulse Measures and their Fiscal Impact', in M. Blejer and A. Cheasty (eds), *How to Measure the Fiscal Deficit* (Washington, DC: IMF).

Chakraborty, P. (1999), 'Recent Trends in State Government Finances: A Comment', *Economic and Political Weekly*, 34(44), pp. 3146–8.

Chandrasekhar, C.P. (2000), 'Economic Reform and the Budget', *Economic and Political Weekly*, 1 April 2000, pp. 1,140–2.

Chelliah, Raja J. (1996), *Essays in Fiscal and Financial Sector Reforms in India*, (New Delhi: Oxford University Press).

Chidambaram, Shri P. (2006), Speech delivered at 'Advantage India' function, held during the 39th Annual Meeting of the Board of Governors, Asian Development Bank (ADB), 4th May, International Convention Center, Hyderabad.

Chouraqui, Jean-Claude, Hagemann, Robert P. and Sartor, Nicola (1990), 'Indicators of Fiscal Policy: A Re-examination', OECD Working Paper, No. 78 (April).

Cimadomo, Jacopo (2005), 'Testing Non-Linearity in Fiscal Policy: New Evidence from Real-Time Data', Preliminary Version, CEPII and ECARES (Brussels: Université Libre).

Comptroller and Auditor General of India (2005), 'State Finances – A Critical Appraisal (1990–2004)', Research Paper published by International Centre for Information Systems and Audit (*i*CISA), Office of the Comptroller and Auditor General of India.

Corsetti, Giancarlo and Roubini, Nouriel (1996), 'European versus American Perspectives on Balanced-Budget Rules', *The American Economic Review*, pp. 408–13.

Council for Social Development (2006), *India: Social Development Report* (New Delhi: Oxford University Press).

CSO (1999), 'Brochure on New Series on National Accounts Statistics (Base Year 1993–94)' (New Delhi: Central Statistical Organisation).

Dasgupta, D., Maiti, P., Mukherjee, R., Sarkar, S. and Chakrabarti, S. (2000), 'Growth and Interstate Disparities in India', *Economic and Political Weekly*, 35(27), pp. 2,413–22.

Datta, Ruddar and Sundaram, K. (2006), *Indian Economy* (New Delhi: Sultan Chand).

Demirguc-Kunt, A. and Maksimovic, V. (1998), 'Law, Finance and Firm Growth', *Journal of Finance*, 53(6), pp. 4,107–37.

Dholakia, R. (1994), 'Spatial Dimension of Acceleration of Economic Growth in India', *Economic and Political Weekly*, 21 August, XXIX(35), pp. 2,303–9.

Dickey, D.A. and Fuller, W.A. (1979), 'Distribution of the Estimators for Autoregressive Time-Series with a Unit Root', *Journal of the American Statistical Association*, 74, pp. 427–31.

Dickey, D.A. and Fuller, W.A. (1981), 'Likelihood Ratio Statistics for Autoregressive Time Series with a Unit Root', *Econometrica*, 49, pp. 1,057–72.

Domar, E. (1944), 'The Burden of Debt and National Income', *American Economic Review*, 34, pp. 798–827.

Draft Approach Paper to the Eleventh Five-Year Plan (2006), Planning Commission, Government of India.

Durlauf, Steven N. and Quah, Danny (1999), 'The New Empirics of Economic Growth', in John B. Taylor and Michael Woodford (eds), *Handbook of Macroeconomics*, Vol. 1A (Amsterdam: North Holland), pp. 231–304.

Edwards, F.R. (1977), 'Managerial Objectives in Regulated Industries: Expense-Preference Behaviour in Banking', *Journal of Political Economy*, 85, pp. 147–62.

Engle, R.F. and Granger, C.W.J. (1987), 'Cointegration and Error Correction: Representation, Estimation, and Testing', *Econometrica*, 55(2), pp. 251–76.

English, M., Grosskopf, S., Hayes, K. and Yaisawarng, S. (1993), 'Output Allocative and Technical Efficiency of Banks', *Journal of Banking & Finance*, 17(2–3), pp. 349–66.

Fase, M.M.G. (2000), 'Financial Intermediation and Long-Run Economic Growth in the Netherlands Between 1900–2000', in H. Klok, T. Van Schaik and S. Smulders (eds), *Economologues*, (Tilburg, Netherlands: Tilburg University Press), pp. 85–98.

Feldstein, Martin (2004), 'Budget Deficits and National Debt', L.K. Jha Memorial Lecture at the Reserve Bank of India in Mumbai, India, 12 January.

Fingleton, B. (1999), 'Estimates of Time to Economic Convergence: An Analysis of Regions of theEuropean Union', *International Regional Science Review*, 22, pp. 5–34.

Gali, Jordi and Perotti, Roberto (2003), 'Fiscal Policy and Monetary Integration in Europe', Working Paper No. 9773. Availble at http://www.nber.org/papers/w9773.

Galibs, V. (1977), ' Financial Development and Economic Growth in Less Developed Countries: A Theoretical Approach', *Journal of Development Studies*, 13(2), pp. 58–72.

Ghosh, B., Marjit, S. and Neogi, C. (1998), 'Economic Growth and Regional Divergence in India, 1960 to 1995', *Economic and Political Weekly*, 27 June – 3 July, XXXIII(26), pp. 1,623–30.

Goddard, J., Molyneux, P. and Wilson, J.O.S. (2004), 'The Profitability of European Banks: A Cross-Sectional and Dynamic Panel Analysis', *The Manchester School*, 72(3), pp. 363–81.

Goldsmith, R.W. (1969), *Financial Structure and Development* (New Haven, CT: Yale University Press).

Government of India (1975), 'Working Group on Rural Banks', also known as Narasimham Committee on RRBs.

Government of India (1984), *Report of the Working Group on Regional Rural Banks*, Kelkar Committee.

Government of India (1994), *Report for 1995–2000* (Tenth Finance Commission) (New Delhi: Government of India).

Government of India (1996), *Committee on Revamping of RRBs*, Basu Committee.

Government of India (1997), *Expert group on RRBs*, Thingalaya Committee.

Government of India (2000), *Report of the (E.A.S. Sarma) Committee on Fiscal Responsibility Legislation* (Department of Economic Affairs, Ministry of Finance).

Government of India (2002a), *Report of the Working Group to Suggest Amendments in the Regional Rural Banks Act, 1976*, Chalpathy Rao Committee.

Government of India (2002b), *National Human Development Report – 2001*, (Planning Commission).

Government of India (2003), *The Fiscal Responsibility and Budget Management Act* (Ministry of Finance).

Government of India (2004), *Group of CMDs of Select Public Sector Banks*, Purwar Committee.

Government of India (2005), 'India 2005', Publications Division, Ministry of Information and Broadcasting.

Government of India (2006), *Economic Survey 2005–2006*, Economic Division, Ministry of Finance.

Government of Orissa (1991), *Statistical Abstract of Orissa, 1984–85 to 1988–89*.

Government of Orissa (1996), *State Agricultural Policy, 1996*, Department of Agriculture, Government of Orissa. Available at http://orissagov.nic.in/e-magazine/orissaannualreference/ORA-2005/pdf/state_agriculture.pdf.

Government of Orissa (2002), *Economic Survey of Orissa, 2001–2002*, Planning and Co-ordination Department, Directorate of Economics and Statistics, Government of Orissa, Bhubaneswar, Orissa, India.

Government of Orissa (2005), *Economic Survey of Orissa, 2004–2005*, Planning and Co-ordination Department, Directorate of Economics and Statistics, Government of Orissa, Bhubaneswar, Orissa, India.

Government of Orissa (2006), *Economic Survey of Orissa, 2005–2006*, Planning and Co-ordination Department, Directorate of Economics and Statistics, Government of Orissa, Bhubaneswar, Orissa, India.

Granger, C.W.J. (1969), 'Investigating Causal Relations by Econometric Models and Cross-Spectral Methods', *Econometrica*, 37, pp. 424–38.

Granger, Clive W.J. (1981), 'Some Properties of Time Series Data and their Use in Econometric Models Specification', *Journal of Econometrics*, 16, pp. 121–30.

Granger, Clive W.J. (1983), 'Co-Integrated Variables and Error-Correcting Models', University of California, San Diego, Discussion Paper No. 1983-13.

Greenwood, J. and Jovanovic, B. (1990), 'Financial Development, Growth, and the Distribution of Income', *Journal of Political Economy*, 98, pp. 1076–1107.

Gregorio, J.D. and Guidotti, P.E. (1995), 'Financial Development and Economic Growth', *World Development*, 23(3), pp. 433–48.

Gupta, K.L. (1984), *Finance and Economic Growth in Developing Countries* (London: Croom Helm).

Gurley, J.G. and Shaw, E.S. (1960), *Money in a Theory of Finance* (Washington, DC: Brookings Institution).

Hadri, K. (2000), 'Testing for Stationarity in Heterogeneous Panel Data', *Econometrics Journal*, 3, pp. 148–61.

Hakkio, C.S. and Rush, M. (1991), 'Is the Budget Deficit "Too Large?" ', *Economic Inquiry*, XXIX (July), 429–45.

Hall, Viv and Rae, David (1998), 'Fiscal Expansion, Monetary Policy, Interest Rate Risk Premia, and Wage Reactions', *Economic Modelling*, 15, pp. 621–40.

Hamilton J. and Flavin, M. (1986), 'On the Limitations of Government Borrowing: A Framework for Empirical Testing', *American Economic Review*, 76, pp. 808–19.

Haque, Nadeem U. and Montiel, Peter J. (1992), 'Fiscal Policy in Pakistan since 1970', IMF Working Paper, November WP/92/97.

Haslem, John (1968), 'A Statistical Analysis of the Relative Profitability of Commercial Banks', *Journal of Finance*, 23, pp. 167–76.

Hassapis, Christis, Pittis, Nikitas and Prodromidis, Kyprianos (1999), 'Unit Roots and Granger Causality in the EMS Interest Rates: The German Dominance Hypothesis Revisited', *Journal of International Money and Finance*, 18, pp. 47–73.

Heller, Peter, Haas, Richard and Mansur, Ahsan (1986), 'A Review of The Fiscal Impulse Measure', International Monetary Fund Occasional Paper No. 44.

Hemming, Richard and Kell, Michael (2001), 'Promoting Fiscal Responsibility – Transparency, Rules and Independent Fiscal Authorities', mimeo, Fiscal Affairs Department, IMF, presented at Bank of Italy workshop on Public Finance, 1–3 February.

Hermes, Neils (1994), ' Financial Development and Economic Growth: A Survey of the Literature', *International Journal of Development Banking*, 12(1), pp. 3–22.

Horne, Jocelyn (1991), 'Indicators of Fiscal Sustainability', IMF Working Papers WP/91/5, January.

Howes, Stephen and Jha, Shikha (2001), *State Finances In India: Towards Fiscal Responsibility* (Washington, DC: World Bank).

Howes, Stephen, Lahiri, Ashok K. and Stern, Nicholas (2003), *State-level Reforms in India: Towards More Effective Government* (New Delhi: Macmillan India Ltd).

Hsiao, C. (1986), *Analysis of Panel Data* (Cambridge: Cambridge University Press).

Ikhide, I.S. (1996), 'Commercial Bank Offices and the Mobilisation of Private Savings in Selected Sub-Saharan African Countries', *The Journal of Development Studies*, 33(1), pp. 117–32.

Im, K., Pesaran, H. and Shin, Y. (1995), 'Testing for Unit Roots in Heterogeneous Panels', Manuscript, University of Cambridge.

Im, K., Pesaran, M. and Shin, Y. (1997), 'Testing for Unit Roots in Heterogeneous Panels', mimeo, Department of Applied Economics, University of Cambridge.

International Monetary Fund (2001), *Report on the Observance of Standards and Codes: India – Fiscal Transparency* (Washington, DC: IMF, Fiscal Affairs Department).

Islam, Nazrul (1995), 'Growth Empirics: A Panel Data Approach', *Quarterly Journal of Economics* (November), CX, pp. 1,127–70.

Jalan, Bimal (1996), *India's Economic Policy: Preparing for the Twenty-first Century* (New Delhi: Penguin).

Jordan, William A. (1972), 'Producer Protection, Prior Market Structure and the Effects of Government Regulation', *Journal of Law and Economics*, 15(1), pp. 151–76.

Jung, W.S. (1986), 'Financial Development and Economic Growth: International Evidence', *Economic Development and Cultural Change*, 34(2), pp. 333–46.

Kanagasabapathy, K., Pattanaik, R.K. and Jayanthi, K.A. (1997), 'Placing a Statutory Limit on Public Debt', *RBI Bulletin* (December).

Kannan, R., Pillai, S.M., Kausaliya, R. and Jaichander (2004), 'Finance Commission Awards and Fiscal Stability in States', *Economic and Political Weekly*, 31 January.

Kao, Chiwa and McCoskey, Suzanne (1998), 'A Residual-Based Test of the Null of Cointegration in Panel Data', *Econometric Reviews*, 17, pp. 57–84.

Khundrakpam, J.K. (1998), 'Sustainability of Central Government Debt', *RBI Occasional Papers*, 19(1), pp. 61–87.

King, R.G. and Levine, Ross (1993a), 'Finance and Growth: Schumpeter Might Be Right', *Quarterly Journal of Economics*, 108(3), pp. 717–38.

King, R.G. and Levine, R. (1993b), 'Financial Intermediation and Economic Development', in C. Mayer and X. Vives (eds), *Capital Markets and Financial Intermediation* (Cambridge: Cambridge University Press).

Kopits, G. (2001a), 'Fiscal policy rules for India?', *Economic and Political Weekly*, 3 March, 749–56.

Kopits, G. (2001b), 'Fiscal Rules: Useful Policy Framework or Unnecessary Ornament?', IMF Working Paper, No. 145, September.

Kopits, G. and Symansky, S. (1998), 'Fiscal Policy Rules', IMF Occasional Paper No. 162.

Krueger, Anne O. and Chinoy Sajjid (2002), 'The Indian Economy in Global Context', in Anne O. Krueger (ed.), *Economic Policy Reforms and the Indian Economy* (New Delhi, India: Oxford University Press).

Kwast, Myron L. and Rose, John T. (1982), 'Pricing, Operating Efficiency and Profitability among Large Commercial Banks', *Journal of Banking and Finance*, Vol. 6(2), pp. 233–54.

Lahiri, A. and Kannan, R. (2001), 'India's Fiscal Deficits and their Sustainability in Perspective', Paper presented at World Bank–NIPFP Seminar on Fiscal Policies for Growth.

Lerman, R. and Yitzkaki, S. (1985), 'Income Inequality Effects by Income Source: A New Approach and Applications to the United States', *The Review of Economics and Statistics*, 67(1), pp. 151–6.

Levin, Andrew and Lin, Chien-Fu (1992), 'Unit Root Tests in Panel Data: Asymptotic and Finite Sample Properties', Discussion paper No. 92–93 (San Diego, CA: Department of Economics, University of California at San Diego).

Levin, A. and Lin, C.-F. (1993a), 'Unit Root Tests in Panel Data; Asymptotic and Finite-sample Properties', University of California at San Diego Working Paper.

Levin, Andrew and Lin, Chien-Fu (1993b), 'Unit Root Tests in Panel Data: New Results', Discussion paper No. 93–56 (San Diego, CA: Department of Economics, University of California at San Diego).

Levin, A., Lin. C.-F. and C.-S. Chu (2002), 'Unit Root Tests in Panel Data: Asymptotic and Finite Sample Properties', *Journal of Econometrics*, 108, pp. 1–24.

Levine, R. (1996a), 'Financial Development and Economic Growth', The World Bank, Washington, DC, Policy Research Working Paper, 1678.

Levine, R. (1996b), 'Financial Development and Economic Growth: Views and Agenda', *Journal of Economic Literature*, 35, pp. 688–726.

Levine, R., Loayza, N. and Beck, T. (2000), 'Financial Intermediation and Growth: Causality and Causes', *Journal of Monetary Economics*, 46, pp. 31–77.

Lopez-Feldman, A. (2006) 'Decomposing Inequality and Obtaining Marginal Effects', *Stata Journal*, 6(1), 1–6.

Lucas, Robert E. (1988), 'On the Mechanics of Economic Development', *Journal of Monetary Economics*, 22(1), pp. 3–42.

Malhotra, Rakesh (2002), 'Performance of India's Regional Rural Banks (RRBs): Effect of the Umbilical Cord', available at http://www.alternativefinance.org.uk/rtf/rrbsmalhotra.rtf.

Mankiw, N. Gregory, Romer, David and Weil, David N. (1992), 'A Contribution to the Empirics of Economic Growth', *Quarterly Journal of Economics*, 107(2), pp. 407–37.

Marjit, S. and Mitra, S. (1996), 'Convergence in Regional Growth Rates: Indian Research Agenda', *Economic and Political Weekly*, (17 August), XXXI(33), pp. 2,239–42.

Masson, P.R. (1985), 'The Sustainability of Fiscal Deficit', *IMF Staff Papers* (December), 32(4).

McKinnon, Ronald I. (1973), *Money and Capital in Economic Development* (Washington, DC: Brookings Institution).

Millar, Jonathan (1997), 'The Effects of Budget Rules on Fiscal Performance and Macroeconomic Stabilization', Bank of Canada Working Paper 97-15.

Minhas, B.S. and Vaidhyanathan, A. (1965), 'Growth of Crop Output in India, 1951–54 to 1958–61, Analysis by Component Elements', *Journal of Indian Society of Agricultural Statistics*, 28(2), pp. 230–52.

Misra, Baidyanath (1983),'Deceleration of Rates of Agricultural Growth in Orissa: Trends and Explanatory Factors', *Indian Journal of Agricultural Economics*, Vol. 38(4), pp. 591–604.

Misra, Biswa Swarup (2003), 'Analytics of Credit–Output Nexus in India', RBI Occasional Papers, Vol. 24, Summer and Monsoon.

Mohan, Rakesh (2000), 'Fiscal Correction for Economic Growth: Data Analysis and Suggestions', *Economic and Political Weekly*, (10–16 June), 35(24), pp. 2,027–36.

Molyneux, P. and Thornton, J. (1992), 'Determinants of European Bank Profitability: A Note', *Journal of Banking and Finance*, 16, pp. 1173–8.

NABARD (2001), *The Expert Committee on Rural Credit* National Bank for Agriculture and Rural Development (NABARD), Mumbai, India.

NABARD (2006), *Expert Group on CD Ratio*, National Bank for Agricultural Development, Mumbai.

Nagaraj, R., Varoudakis, A. and Véganzonès, M.A. (1998), 'Long-Run Growth Trends and Convergence across Indian States', Technical Paper No. 131 OECD Development Centre, France.

Narain, Dharam (1977), 'Growth Productivity in Indian Agriculture', *Indian Journal of Agricultural Economics*, 32(1), pp. 1–44.

Nickell, S. (1981), ' Biases in Dynamic Models with Fixed Effects', *Econometrica*, 49, pp. 1,417–26.

Nitin, Bhatt and Thorat, Y.S.P. (2004), 'India's Regional Rural Banks: The Institutional Dimension of Reforms', National Bank News Review, NABARD, April–September.

Nyblom, J. and Harvey, A. (2000), 'Tests of Common Stochastic Trends', *Econometric Theory*, 16, pp. 176–99.

Nyblom, J. and Makelainen, T. (1983), 'Comparison of Tests for the Presence of Random Walk Components in a Simple Linear Model', *Journal of the American Statistical Association*, 78, pp. 856–64.

Odedokun, M.O. (1998), 'Financial Intermediation and Economic Growth in Developing Countries', *Journal of Economic Studies*, 25(3), pp. 203–24.

OECD (2002a), 'Economic Outlook, Sources and Methods', www.oecd. org/eco/out/source.htm

Olekalns, N. and Cashin, P. (2000), 'An Examination of the Sustainability of Indian Fiscal Policy', University of Melbourne Working Paper.

Osterwald-Lenum, M. (1992), 'A Note With Quantiles of the Asymptotic Distribution of the Maximum Likelihood Cointegration Rank Test Statistics', *Oxford Bulletin of Economics and Statistics*, 54, pp. 461–72.

Papola, T.S. (2005), 'Emerging Structure of Indian Economy: Implications of Growing Inter-sectoral Imbalances', Presidential Address at the 88th Annual Meet of the Indian Economic Association, Andhra University, Visakhapatnam, India.

Patrick, H.T. (1966), 'Financial Development and Economic Growth in Underdeveloped Countries', *Economic Development and Cultural Change*, 14, pp. 174–89.

Pattnaik Prabhat (2001), 'On Fiscal Deficits and Real Interest Rates', available at www.macroscan.com.

Pattnaik, R.K. (1996), 'Budget Deficit in India: Measurement, Analysis and Management', PhD thesis, IIT Delhi.

Pattnaik, R.K., Pillai, S. M. and Das, Sangeeta (2000), 'Primer on Budget Deficit in India', RBI Staff Studies.

Pedroni, P. (1995), 'Panel Cointegration: Asymptotic and Finite Sample Properties of Pooled Time Series Tests, with an Application to the PPP Hypothesis', Indiana University Working Papers in Economics 95–113.

Pedroni, P. (1997), 'Panel Cointegration: Asymptotic and Finite Sample Properties of Pooled Time Series Tests, with an Application to the PPP Hypothesis: New Results', Indiana University Working Paper, April.

Pedroni, Peter (1999), 'Critical Values for Cointegration Tests in Heterogeneous Panels with Multiple Regressors', *Oxford Bulletin of Economics and Statistics*, 61, Special Issue, pp. 653–70.

Pedroni, Peter (2001), 'Purchasing Power Parity Tests in Cointegrated Panels', *Review of Economics and Statistics*, 83, pp. 727–31.

Perotti, Roberto (1999), 'Fiscal Policy in Good Times and Bad', *Quarterly Journal of Economics*, 114(4), pp. 1,399–436.

Perry, P. (1992), 'Do Banks Gain or Lose from Inflation?', *Journal of Retail Banking*, 14(2), pp. 25–30.

Pillai, S.M., Chatterjee, S. Singh, B., Das, S. and Gupta, A. (1997), 'Fiscal Policy: Issues and Perspectives', RBI Occasional Papers, Vol. 18.

Pinto, Brian and Zahir, Farah (2004), 'India: Why Fiscal Adjustment Now', World Bank Policy Research Working Paper 3230, March.

Planning Commission of India (2002), *National Human Development Report*, http://planningcommission.nic.in/nhdrep/nhd2001.pdf.

Poterba, J.M. (1996), 'Do Budget Rules Work?', National Bureau of Economic Research, Working Paper 5550; also in Alan Auerbach (ed.), *Fiscal Policy: Lessons from Empirical Research* (Cambridge, MA: MIT Press, 1997).

Poterba, J.M. and von Hagen, J. (eds) ( ), *Fiscal Institutions and Fiscal Performance* (Chicago, IL: University of Chicago Press), pp. 59–80.

Prasad, Abha, Goyal, Rajan and Prakash, Anupam (2003), *States Debt and Debt Relief* (New Delhi: National Institute of Public Finance and Policy).

Premchand, A. (2003), 'Ethical Dimensions of Public Expenditure Management', Working Paper 03–14, Andrew Young School of Policy Studies, Georgia State University.

Price, R.W.R. and Muller, P. (1984), 'Structural Budget Indicators and the Interpretation of Fiscal Stance in OECD Economies', *OECD Economic Studies*, No. 3, Autumn.

Purfield, Catriona (2006), 'Mind the Gap – Is Economic Growth in India Leaving Some States Behind?', IMF Working Paper No. WP/06/103.

Quah, D. (1993), 'Empirical Cross-Section Dynamics in Economic Growth', *European Economic Review*, 37, pp. 426–34.

Quintos, C. (1995), 'Sustainability of the Deficit Process with Structural Shifts', *Journal of Business and Economic Statistics*, 13, pp. 409–17.

Rajaraman, I., Bhide, S. and Pattnaik, R.K. (2005), *A Study of Debt Sustainability at State Level in India*, Reserve Bank of India, Mumbai.

Rajaraman, I. and Mukhopadhyay, A. (1999), *Sustainability of Public Domestic Debt in India*, (New Delhi: NIPFP), February.

Rakshit, Mihir (2001), 'Restoring Fiscal Balance through Legislative Fiat: The Indian Experiment', *Economic and Political Weekly*, 9 June, pp. 2,053–62.

Raman, J. (1996), 'Convergence or Uneven Development: A Note on Regional Development in India', mimeo Valparaiso University, US.

Ramesh, Jairam (2002), *Kautilya Today: Jairam Ramesh on a Globalizing India*, (New Delhi: India Research Press).

Rangarajan, C. (1997), *Essays on Money and Finance* (New Delhi: UBS).

Rangarajan, C. and Srivastava, D.K. (2003), 'Dynamics of Debt Accumulation in India', *Economic and Political Weekly*, November.

Rangarjan, C., Basu, A. and Jadhav, N. (1989), 'Dynamics of Interaction between Government Deficit and Domestic Debt in India', *RBI Occasional Papers*, 10(3), pp. 163–220.

Rao, M. Govinda (2002), 'State Finances In India: A Critical Review', Working Paper No. 113, (Bangalore: Institute for Social and Economic Change).

Rao, M. Govinda (2004), 'State Level Fiscal Reforms in India', in Kaushik Basu (ed.), *India's Emerging Economy: Performance and Prospects in the 1990s and Beyond*, (New Delhi: Oxford University Press).

Rao, M. Govinda, Shand, R.T. and Kalirajan, K.P. (1999), 'Convergence of Income across Indian States: A Divergent View', *Economic and Political Weekly*, 27 March–2 April, XXXIV(13), pp. 769–78.

Rao, M. Govinda, and Singh, Nirvikar (1998), 'Fiscal Overlapping, Concurrency and Competition in Indian Federalism', CREDPR Working Paper 30b.

Rao, V.K.R.V. (1952), 'Investment, Income and the Multiplier in an Underdeveloped Economy', *Indian Economic Review* (February), 1(1), pp. 55–67.

Rao, V.K.R.V. (1964) 'Essays in Economic Development (London: Asia Publishing House).

Reddy, Y.V. (2000a), 'Fiscal and Monetary Policy Interface: Recent Developments in India', *RBI Bulletin*, November.

Reddy, Y.V, (2000b), 'Legislation on Fiscal Responsibility and the Reserve Banks' Role: some issues', Speech delivered at the Workshop on Fiscal Responsibility of Government, held at India Habitat Centre, New Delhi.

Reddy, Y.V (2000c), 'Managing Public Debt and Promoting Debt Markets in India', *RBI Bulletin*, October.

Reddy, Y.V. (2004), 'Monetary and Financial Sector Reforms in India: A Practioner's Perspective', in Kaushik Basu (ed.), *India's Emerging Economy: Performance and Prospects in the 1990s and Beyond* (New Delhi: Oxford University Press).

Reserve Bank of India (1989), *A Review of the Agricultural Credit System in India: Report of the Agricultural Credit Review Committee*, Khusro Committee.

Reserve Bank of India (1991), *Report of the Committee on the Financial System*, Reserve Bank of India, Mumbai, Narasimham Committee Report.

Reserve Bank of India (1994), *Committee on Restructuring of RRBs*, Bhandari Committee.

Reserve Bank of India (2000), *Report of the Eleventh Finance Commission, 2000–2005* (New Delhi: Ministry of Finance).

Reserve Bank of India (2001a), *Annual Report, 2000–01* (Mumbai).

Reserve Bank of India (2001b), *Report on Currency and Finance, 1999–2000* (Mumbai).

Reserve Bank of India (2001c), *Report of the Expert Committee to Review the System of Administered Interest Rates and Other Related Issues* (Chairman: Y. V. Reddy), September (New Delhi).

Reserve Bank of India (2002a), *Annual Report, 2001–02* (Mumbai).

Reserve Bank of India (2002b), *Report on Currency and Finance, 2000–01* (Mumbai).

Reserve Bank of India (2003), *State Finances: A Study of Budgets, 2002–03* (Mumbai).

Reserve Bank of India, Basic Statistical Returns of Scheduled Commercial Banks in India, various issues (Mumbai).

Reserve Bank of India (2004), *Handbook of Statistics on State Finances* (Mumbai).

Reserve Bank of India (2005), *Report of the Internal Working Group on RRBs*, Sardesai Committee.

Reserve Bank of India (2006), *State Finances: A Study of Budgets*, various issues (Mumbai).

Reserve Bank of India, *Annual Report*, various issues (Mumbai).

Reserve Bank of India, *Report on Currency and Finance*, various issues (Mumbai).

Reserve Bank of India, Statistical Tables Relating to Banks in India, various issues.

Revell, J. (1979), *Inflation and Financial Institutions* (London: Financial Times).

Rhoades, Stephen A. (1977), 'Structure and Performance Studies in Banking: A Summary and Evaluation', *Staff Economics Studies*, 92, Federal Reserve-Board, Washington, DC.

Romer, P. (1990), 'Endogenous Technical Change', *Journal of Political Economy*, 98(5), pp. 71–102.

Roubini, Nouriel and Sala-i-Martin, Xavier (1992), 'Financial Repression and Economic Growth', *Journal of Development Economics*, 39(1), pp. 5–30.

Rousseau, Peter L. and Wachtel, Paul (1998), 'Financial Intermediation and Economic Performance: Historical Evidence from Five Industrialized Countries', *Journal of Money, Credit and Banking*, 30(4), pp. 657–77.

Sachs, Jeffrey D. and Bajpai, Nirupam (1996), 'Trends in Inter-State Inequalities of Income in India', Development Discussion Paper No. 528, Harvard Institute for International Development, Harvard University.

Sachs, Jeffrey D., Bajpai, Nirupam and Ramiah, Ananthi (2002), 'Understanding Regional Economic Growth in India', CID Working Paper No. 88, Harvard University.

Sagar, Vidya (1980), 'Growth of Productivity in Indian Agriculture: A Comment', *Indian Journal of Agricultural Economics*, 35(1), pp. 129–33.

Sargent, Thomas J. (1976), 'A Classic Macroeconometric Model for the United States', *Journal of Political Economy*, 84, pp. 207–37.

Sarker, P.C. (1994), 'Regional Imbalances in Indian Economy over Plan Periods', *Economic and Political Weekly* (12 March), XXIX(2), pp. 621–33.

Seshan, A. (1987), 'The Burden of Domestic Public Debt in India', Reserve Bank of India Occasional Papers, 8(1), pp. 45–77.

Schuster, Leo (1984), 'Profitability and Market Share of Banks', *Journal of Bank Research*, Spring.

Shaffer, S. (1994), 'Bank Competition in Concentrated Markets', Federal Reserve Bank of Philadelphia Business Review, March/April, pp. 3–16.

Shand, Ric and Bhide, S. (2000), 'Sources of Economic Growth: Regional Dimensions of Reforms', *Economic and Political Weekly*, 35(42), pp. 3,747–57.

Shaw, G.S. (1973), Financial Deepening in Economic Development (Oxford: Oxford University Press).

Shenoy, B.R. (1955) 'A Note of Dissent', in *Second Five Year Plan: The Framework*, Publications Division, Ministry of Information and Broadcasting, Government of India, p. 163.

Shorrocks, A.F. (1982), 'Inequality Decomposition by Factor Components', *Econometrica*, 50, pp. 193–211.

Short, B.K. (1979), 'The Relation Between Commercial Bank Profit Rates and Banking Concentration in Canada, Western Europe and Japan', *Journal of Banking and Finance*, 3, pp. 209–19.

Singh, Nirvikar, Bhandari, L., Chen, A. and Khare, A. (2003), 'Regional Inequality in India: A Fresh Look', *Economic and Political Weekly*, 38(11), pp. 1069–73.

Singh, Nirvikar and Srinivasan, T.N. (2002), 'Indian Federalism, Economic Reform and Globalization', paper prepared for CREDPR project on Globalization and Comparative Federalism.

Skaggs, Neil T. (1999), 'Adam Smith on Growth and Credit', *Journal of Economic Studies*, 2(6), pp. 481–96.

Solow, R.M. (1956), 'A Contribution to the Theory of Economic Growth', *Quarterly Journal of Economics*, 70, pp. 65–94.

Spaventa, Luigi (1987), 'The Growth of Public Debt', *IMF Staff Paper* (December), 34(4).

Srinivasan, T.N. (2002), 'India's Fiscal Situation: Is a Crisis Ahead?', in A. Krueger (ed.) *Economic Policy Reforms and the Indian Economy* (New Delhi: Oxford University Press).

Srinivasan T.N. (2003), 'Indian Economy: Current Problems and Future Prospects', unpublished papers of T.N. Srinivasan, revised and extended text of a lecture delivered on 3 January 2003 under the auspices of the ICFAI Business School, Chennai, India, and to appear in ICFAI Journal of Applied Economics. Available at http://www.econ.yale.edu/~srinivas/

St Hill, R.L. (1992), 'Stages of Banking and Economic Development', *Savings and Development*, 16(1), pp. 65–94.

Stark, O., Taylor, J.E. and Yitzhaki, S. (1986), 'Remittances and Inequality', *The Economic Journal*, 383, pp. 722–40.

Subrahmanyam, S. (1999), 'Convergence of Income across States', *Economic and Political Weekly*, (20 November), XXXIV(46 and 47), pp. 3,327–28.

Taylor, J.B. (1995), 'The Monetary Transmission Mechanism: An Empirical Framework', *Journal of Economic Perspectives* (Fall), 9(4), pp. 11–26.

Taylor, J.B. (2000), 'Reassessing Discretionary Fiscal Policy', *Journal of Economic Perspectives*, 14(3), pp. 21–36.

Thomas, R.L. (1997), *Modern Econometrics*, (Harlow, UK: Addison Wesley).

Trivedi, Kamakshya (2002), 'Regional Convergence and Catch-up in India between 1960 and 1992', working paper, Nuffield College, University of Oxford.

Tschoegl, Adrian E. (1982), 'Concentration Among International Banks: A Note', *Journal of Banking and Finance*, 6, pp. 567–78.

Vaidyanathan, A. (2002), 'Econometric Analysis of Agricultural Growth: Reflections of a Non Econometrician', Paper presented at the 38th Annual Conference of The Indian Econometric Society.

Vithal, B.P.R. and Sastry, M.L. (2001), *Fiscal Federalism in India* (New Delhi: Oxford University Press).

World Bank (2002), *Global Development Finance* (Washington, DC: World Bank).

Wyplosz, C. (2002), 'Fiscal Discipline in EMU: Rules or Institutions?', paper prepared for 16 April meeting of the Group of Economic Analysis of the European Commission.

Zee, Howell H. (1988), 'The Sustainability and Optimality of Government Debt', IMF Staff Papers, December.

Zellner, A. (1962), 'Ancient Method of Estimating Seemingly Unrelated Regressions and Tests for Aggregation Bias', *Journal of the American Statistical Association*, pp. 348–68.

Index